Migration and Refugee Policies

Centre for Development and Enterprise,
South Africa
Institute for the Study of Economic Culture,
Boston University

Migration and Refugee Policies

An Overview

Edited by

Ann Bernstein
and
Myron Weiner

PINTER
London and New York

PINTER
A Cassell imprint
Wellington House, 125 Strand, London WC2R 0BB
370 Lexington Avenue, New York, NY 10017-6500

First published 1999
© Centre for Development and Enterprise, South Africa 1999

British Library Cataloguing in Publication Data
A catalogue record for this book is available from the British Library
ISBN 1–85567–505–6

Library of Congress Cataloging-in-Publication Data
Migration of refugee policies : an overview / edited by Ann Bernstein and Myron Weiner.
p.   cm.
Includes bibliographical references and index.
ISBN 1–85567–505–6 (hc.)
1. Emigration and immigration–Government policy.   2. Refugees–Government policy.   3. Alien labor–Government policy.
I. Bernstein, Ann.   II. Weiner, Myron.
JV6038.M54   1999
325'.1–dc21   98-36010
                                                     CIP

Typeset by BookEns Ltd, Royston, Herts.
Printed and bound in Great Britain By The Cromwell Press Ltd, Trowbridge, Wilts

Contents

Part Two: A proposed policy framework for controlling cross-border migration to South Africa

Ann Bernstein, Lawrence Schlemmer and Charles Simkins

Illustrations

Figures

Tables

Chart

Contributors

Ann Bernstein is founder and executive director of the Centre for Development and Enterprise, an independent policy think-tank based in South Africa. She previously served as an executive director of the Urban Foundation, a privately funded development and policy research organization, heading its urbanization unit and later its development strategy and policy unit. One of South Africa's leading development experts, she writes regularly for journals and newspapers on a wide range of social issues.

Gary P. Freeman is professor of government and director of the Public Policy Clinic at the University of Texas. He has been a visiting fellow at the Research School of the Social Sciences, Australian National University and the Australian Defence Force Academy. He has written extensively on comparative politics, international migration and social policy.

Robert E.B. Lucas is professor of economics at Boston University. He has been a visiting scholar at academic institutions in India, the United States and Britain, and has played a prominent role in international academic initiatives. He has undertaken projects for the World Bank, USAID and the International Labour Organisation in many developing countries, and has published scores of books and articles on migration and other social and economic issues.

Philip L. Martin is professor of agricultural economics at the University of California-Davis, chair of the University of California's comparative immigration and integration programme, and editor of *Migration News*, a monthly summary of developments in migration. He has served on several official and academic bodies studying migration in the United States. He has also helped many countries to develop practical solutions to complex and controversial migration and labour issues. He has published extensively on farm labour, labour migration, economic development and immigration issues.

Mark J. Miller is a professor of political science and international relations at the University of Delaware. He is a former US correspondent to the OECD's group of migration specialists, and assistant editor of *International Migration Review*. He has given Congressional testimony on European efforts to deter illegal migration, and recently wrote two research papers for the Commission on Immigration Reform. He has written extensively on international migration.

Lawrence Schlemmer is a director of a market research firm, and a socio-political consultant. He is former director of the Centre for Applied Social Studies at the University of Natal (Durban) and former dean of the university's faculty of social science; founder and former director of the Centre for Policy Studies and current chairperson of its board of trustees; and former vice-president of the Human Sciences Research Council, a state-funded social research co-ordinating body. He is also an elected founder member of the Academy of Science of South Africa. Professor Schlemmer has written widely on key social, political and economic issues.

Charles Simkins is Helen Suzman professor of political economy at the University of the Witwatersrand, and head of its department of economics. He has held senior teaching and research positions at several South African universities, and acted as an economic consultant to the Urban Foundation. He has written extensively on political, economic and demographic issues.

Astri Suhrke is a senior fellow at the Chr. Michelsen Institute in Bergen, Norway, and resident associate of the Carnegie Endowment for International Peace in Washington DC. She has held senior research and teaching positions at several universities in Australia and the United States. She has been a consultant to the United States Department of State, The World Bank, the Ford Foundation, the Norwegian international development agency NORAD, and the United Nations High Commissioner for Refugees (UNHCR). She has given expert testimony to the US Congress on refugee policy, and to a UNHCR conference on strategies to reduce outmigration. She has written extensively on refugee movements, migration and related issues.

Myron Weiner is Ford International professor of political science at the Massachusetts Institute of Technology (MIT) and a former director of

MIT's Centre for International Studies, and chairs the external research advisory committee of the UNHCR. He has taught or held research appointments at Princeton University, the University of Chicago, Harvard University, Delhi University, Hebrew University, the University of Paris and Balliol College at Oxford. He is a member of the American Academy of Arts and Sciences, and chairs its joint German–American project on migration and refugee policies. A world authority on migration and refugee movements, he has written extensively on these and related issues.

Aristide R. Zolberg is university-in-exile professor at the graduate faculty of the New School for Social Research in New York, director of the International Centre for Migration, Ethnicity, and Citizenship, and co-chair of the MacArthur Program on Global Change and Liberalism. He serves on the editorial and advisory boards of numerous academic publications and institutions, as well as Human Rights Watch/Africa and the Fondation Médecins sans Frontières. He is a member of the Council on Foreign Relations and the Group of Lisbon. He has written extensively on comparative politics and historical sociology, ethnic conflict, and immigration and refugee issues.

Preface

In 1991 Ann Bernstein spent three months in Boston as a visiting fellow at Professor Peter Berger's Institute for the Study of Economic Culture. One of the most important and long-lasting associations formed at that time was with Professor Myron Weiner of MIT. Since then, much knowledge and numerous contacts have generously flowed across the Atlantic from Boston to Johannesburg. This book is the product of that collaboration, stemming from the period before South Africa's democratic elections in 1994 when it became apparent that issues surrounding migration would present the country's new government with some of its toughest challenges.

Until then, the debate on migration in South Africa had been dominated by questions surrounding internal migration – particularly the apartheid government's policy of influx control, designed to control the access of black South Africans to the country's urban areas. In the early 1980s, Bernstein and others at the Urban Foundation had been heavily involved in a large-scale research and then public policy campaign to persuade first business leaders and then the government of the day to remove the discriminatory, onerous, costly, and ultimately ineffective pass laws from the country's statute books. This occurred after considerable pressure had been applied, not least by millions of South Africans 'voting with their feet' in defying these laws. In the process, the Urban Foundation and its staff and consultants garnered considerable knowledge and understanding of the internal migration process.

When, in the early 1990s, the first steps were taken towards democratization, it became clear that issues of international migration would soon become both prominent and controversial – and that the country lacked the expertise to deal with them. It was in this context that this project was initiated.

We want to acknowledge the assistance provided by members of the MIT Inter-University Committee on International Migration – William Alonso (Harvard University), John Harris (Boston University) and Reed Ueda (Tufts University) – and, at MIT, Nazli Choucri, Karen Jacobsen, Liz Leeds, Melissa Nobles, Jerome Rothenberg and Sharon Russell. Excellent logistical support was provided by the MIT Center for International Studies, with staff assistance from Robert Davine, Cathy Scholtz and especially Lois Malone, who served as project co-ordinator at MIT. We are particularly grateful to the six authors of the chapters on international experiences of migration and refugee policies. Their papers were initially presented and discussed at a workshop at MIT in 1995, and subsequently revised. Each of the authors drew on a vast array of both empirical and theoretical material to write balanced, non-technical accounts of the experiences and policy choices confronting governments of migrant and refugee receiving countries. The lessons learnt from these studies were brought to bear on the South African debate in the study prepared by CDE, which constitutes the second part of this volume.

We also want to acknowledge the assistance of a number of people who participated in discussions on the draft proposals (business leaders, members of the CDE board, NGO leaders, and concerned citizens). Our thanks to Professor Douglas Irvine, senior associate at CDE, who helped to draft an important section of the report; Judi Hudson, a CDE research co-ordinator who helped collate and edit the international papers; Jenny Marshall, CDE researcher, who helped Ann Bernstein at a crucial stage; and Riaan de Villiers, publishing consultant to CDE, who helped to structure the final manuscript. And, finally, our thanks to Elisabeth Bradley, chair of the CDE board, who supported the initiative throughout and encouraged CDE, if the research warranted it, to take a bold position on the policy issues, however controversial this might be.

Ann Bernstein
Myron Weiner
February 1998

Introduction

The opening of national markets to trade, foreign investment and technology and the expansion of global communications have had two important consequences for international migration. The first is that more employers want to recruit manpower outside their national boundaries. A construction firm in Berlin prefers to hire skilled, hard-working Polish workers rather than employ unionized German workers on higher pay and benefits. An agricultural grower in Texas wants low-wage labourers from Mexico, while Microsoft wants foreign students who have completed their studies in computer sciences at Cal Tech or MIT. A Tokyo restaurant owner wants entertainers from Thailand. The dean of a South African university would like to recruit from universities in Ghana and Nigeria in an effort to Africanize his faculty. In short, many employers would like to see as free a global market in labour as there is now in trade, investment and technology.

The second consequence is that an increasing number of individuals in medium- and low-income countries would like to improve their lives and the lives of their families by finding a job in a high income country. Many Mexicans know they can increase their income tenfold in Texas or California. Ghanaians and Nigerians know they can do better in South Africa. So do Albanians and North Africans who would like to move to Italy, Turks who would like to move to Germany, Algerians who would rather be in France, and South-east Asians who would like to find jobs in Japan. Individuals know how to cross international boundaries for employment. They can apply for a visa and work permit. They can get a tourist visa, then illegally enter the labour market. They can walk (or swim) across an unpatrolled border or enter illegally by ship. They can fly to a country, apply for asylum and, while the case is pending, look for a job. Migrants share the vision of free-market capitalists that there be a global market for labour.

No government in the world shares this vision, nor do the majority of nationals in any country. Many countries do, however, see benefits from limited migration. The admission of individuals with high levels of education and technical skills can enhance a country's productivity and increase its competitiveness. Migrant entrepreneurs may generate new economic activities. Low-skilled, low-wage workers may fill a demand for jobs that local people do not want at the prevailing wage. Most countries permit their migrant citizens and long-term resident immigrants to bring in family members and most countries recognize that they have an obligation to admit refugees. The citizens of countries founded by migrants – the United States, Canada, Australia, Israel – are particularly predisposed towards migrants.

On the other hand, many governments and their citizens are concerned that migrants, skilled or unskilled, may take jobs away from local people, and add to the costs of state supported social services. There is a concern that migrants from other cultures can be a source of social disharmony, crime, drug traffic and terrorism. Many green environmentalists advocating low or zero population growth would restrict migration. As the capacity of states declines under the forces of globalization, some governments see as among their few remaining functions to protect their citizens from the onslaught of low-wage migrant workers, to ensure that their citizens have first claims over migrants upon employment and on public goods, and to preserve (or create!) a sense of national identity.

Therefore, in one country after another, migration and refugee questions have become a matter of political controversy. In Europe and in the United States voters have supported candidates opposed to migration. Under public pressure European governments halted the employment of guest workers and tightened the rules for the entry of asylum claimants. In the United States there are legislative efforts to halt illegal migration, reduce the number of migrants, and restrict access to government benefits. Even labour exporting countries want to restrict entry. Mexico, for example, closed its southern borders to migrants and asylum seekers from Central America. The governments of Poland, Hungary and the Czech Republic restrict access on their eastern borders. And in South Africa, the post-apartheid government has attempted to halt the inflow of illegal migrants, and there is a debate over whether employers should be permitted to recruit managers, engineers, teachers and doctors from other parts of Africa.

In 1994, Ann Bernstein, then director of the Development Strategy and Policy Unit (DSPU) of the Urban Foundation, a colleague, Dr Tim Hart, and Professor Myron Weiner, director of MIT's Inter-University

Committee on International Migration, discussed undertaking a project that would address the migration and refugee issues confronting South Africa's new democratic government. Clearly, many of the old apartheid migration policies were no longer relevant, but it was less clear what should replace them. Within months after the formation of the Government of National Unity, the question of how migration policies should be changed became part of the political debate.

The emerging debate centred on five issues. First was the question of illegal migration: what steps should the new government take to halt the growing influx of illegal immigrants from Zimbabwe, Mozambique, Swaziland and Zaire, and from as far away as Nigeria, Ethiopia and Sierra Leone? Second was the question of whether the hiring of skilled people from other parts of Africa would reduce the opportunities for South Africa's black population? Would 'Africanization' become a substitute for 'indigenization'? Third was the issue of whether foreign guest workers from Lesotho, Mozambique and Swaziland in the mining industry should be replaced by indigenous workers in an effort to expand employment opportunities for South Africans. The fourth issue was whether South Africa could reduce the pressure of migration from its neighbours by promoting economic development in the region. Would an expansion of trade, aid and investment reduce the gap in wages and employment that induce Africans to seek jobs in South Africa? Fifth was the issue of South Africa's policies with respect to the protection of refugees. What responsibilities did South Africa have for assisting countries that were flooded with refugees, hosting refugees within its own borders, and addressing the political issues within countries that induce people to flee?

Although there was a specific South African context to each of these questions, it was apparent that South Africa was by no means alone in wrestling with these issues. Indeed, in one form or another the issues facing South Africa were also germane to many other countries. Stated more generally, these were (1) control over illegal migration; (2) guest worker policies; (3) skill migration policies; (4) policies towards countries of migrant origin; and (5) refugee policies. Many countries had devised policies to address these issues, with varying degrees of success, and scholarly studies of their consequences were beginning to emerge.

As a result, the leading participants in the project agreed that it should not focus solely on South Africa but should also comprise a thorough study of what Bernstein described as 'the international experience' of migration policies. Accordingly, the project leaders asked a number of leading scholars of international migration to prepare studies of migration and refugee policies, describing alternative strategies adopted by governments and assessing their efficacy. The MIT Centre for International Studies under Professor Weiner assumed responsibility for organizing the project, and the Urban Foundation provided financial support. Five studies were commissioned, and the authors, along with invitees from the Inter-University Committee of Migration, participated in a workshop held at MIT in February 1995. The research papers were completed in 1996.

In early 1995 the Urban Foundation was wound down, but the migration project remained very much alive. It became one of the first major projects of the Centre for Development and Enterprise, successor to the Urban Foundation's Development Strategy and Policy Unit (DSPU), and was directed by Ann Bernstein. CDE was established after South Africa's transition to democracy to undertake policy research on critical national issues. Funded by South African business, it operates as a totally independent national policy think-tank.

Meanwhile, in South Africa the issue of migration was becoming increasingly important. Inflows of illegal migrants intensified, adding to pressure on urban areas at a time when crime rates increased sharply as well. As the presence of these immigrants became more visible, perceptions grew among certain sectors of the public that the new entrants were responsible for much of the crime, and were also taking jobs away from South Africans. Tensions mounted: in one instance, a large group of South Africans tried to drive all foreigners out of a township north of Johannesburg. The public debate intensified, with some arguing in favour of strict action against illegal entrants, and others arguing that xenophobic responses would not resolve the situation.

The government responded by announcing harsher measures against illegal influx, but also stepped up its efforts to formulate a more lasting solution to the set of problems surrounding migration. In late 1996 the South African minister of home affairs, Dr Mangosuthu Buthelezi, appointed a task group to consider policy options on migration and formulate a new policy framework.

Against this background, CDE intensified its own work on the South African component of the study. A research team – comprising Bernstein; Professor Lawrence Schlemmer, senior consultant to CDE and one of the country's leading sociologists; and Professor Charles Simkins, Helen Suzman professor of political economy at the University of the Witwatersrand – was formed to study all the relevant data and other important factors. Eventually, it was decided to evolve detailed policy proposals which could help the government to formulate its new policy framework. This aspect of the study was concluded in mid-1997.

In June 1997, CDE published a summary of the results of the international study, as well as the results of its local research and its policy proposals, as two volumes in its ongoing series of CDE Research Reports. The government's draft Green Paper on international migration was released shortly afterwards.

The results of the entire project have been drawn together in this volume. Part one reflects the findings of the international comparative study of policies on migration and refugees. It begins with a contribution by Weiner in which he recapitulates the major themes dealt with in the five research papers and at the workshop held at MIT, and considers their implications for efforts to reform national refugee and migration policies. The five commissioned studies follow.

Part two reflects the results of CDE's research into the South African situation, and presents its policy proposals. It begins with an introduction, setting out the broad considerations that shaped the research team's approach to the issue of migration. Next, key issues arising from South Africa's migration policies are isolated, and the South African government's current approach to migration outlined. Then, the research team formulates some preliminary frameworks: lessons from international policy experience are summarized; different views on how policy-makers should deal with migration are listed; eleven analytical points of departure are formulated; and the implications of CDE's analysis, values and orientation analysed. Next, the policy proposals are made.

These involve a two-tier approach, distinguishing between skilled and unskilled migration. With respect to skilled migration, CDE advocates that skilled people – including entrepreneurs – from anywhere in the world should be allowed to move to South Africa. CDE argues that the focus on illegal, generally unskilled, migrants has drawn attention away from the real crisis issue: the enormous and growing shortage of managerial and other skills, which undermine prospects for sustained economic growth.

By contrast, unskilled migrants should be accepted from the Southern African Development Community (SADC) countries only, and, in order to remain in South Africa, they must demonstrate that they are able to become self-supporting, tax-paying, law-abiding residents.

Unskilled migrants from SADC countries would have six months to prove that they can find or make work to support themselves; they would also be required to provide an address in South Africa. Following this period, those who have succeeded in finding or making work would have to serve a further two-year probationary period. Following this, migrants would be rewarded with permanent work, and residence rights, and access to more than minimal health services. Citizenship would be accessible after a further three-year period of successful work and law-abiding residence.

These measures are designed to stimulate economic growth and strengthen the South African economy by enlarging the pool of skilled people and entrepreneurs, and by promoting a more efficient labour market. They accommodate regional pressures for migration, while limiting the claims on public resources until immigrants have demonstrated their capacity to contribute to the country.

In conclusion, an executive summary of the government's draft Green Paper is reproduced, followed by a response drafted by CDE and submitted to the Department of Home Affairs in June 1997.

The South African study is presented as an exercise in applying the lessons offered by international experience to a specific country with substantial and intractable problems surrounding migration; as a result, the authors hope it will be relevant to a wider audience than those with a particular interest in South Africa.

Part One

Migration and refugee policies: the international experience

Migration and refugee policies: an overview

Myron Weiner

In this chapter, I introduce the major themes of the five commissioned research papers on international migration and refugee policies as well as the discussions at the workshop on the project held at MIT in February 1995, and consider the implications for efforts to reform national refugee and migration policies.

Many of the questions concerning migration and refugee policies involve moral judgements ('how do we weigh the needs of our own citizens against those in other societies?'), national self-images ('what kind of society do we want to be?') and questions of foreign policy ('can we and should we seek to change conditions in other societies that impel people to leave?'). There is enormous variability in the responses of governments to these questions, based on their previous histories with migration, geographic position, administrative and financial capabilities, political institutions, and their 'national' values. What 'works' for a country surrounded by an ocean may not work for a country with a large land border. What a country regards as a successful policy at one time – a guest worker programme, for example, to meet existing demands for unskilled labour – may be looked upon years later as mistaken and costly. A policy to recruit highly skilled people to strengthen the country's competitive capacity may have consequences not foreseen or intended by policy makers. The financial aid that one government provides another to promote economic growth may in time reduce pressures for emigration, but aid may also be diverted by a predatory regime into private bank accounts. As we turn to each of the policy questions we will note that hard choices have to be made in the face of considerable uncertainty as countries search for policies that meet their national interests and are compatible with the values of their citizens.

Migration controls

Control over entry is the subject of the chapter by Mark Miller. Countries vary greatly in their capacity to control who can enter and remain within their borders. Most governments succeed in exercising some control, but are rarely able to prevent illegal migration completely. Miller notes, moreover, that there is a global pattern towards increasing permeability. People may enter a country legally as tourists, businessmen or students and then overstay their visas. Others may enter surreptitiously across inadequately patrolled borders. And still others arrive at airports seeking asylum, then slip out of the control of officials into an underground labour market.

Governments have sought to exercise control through a variety of means: interdicting illegal crossings at borders, requiring visas for entry, asking foreigners to register when they change their residence, insisting that both citizens and foreigners carry identification documents, limiting employment to those authorized to work, imposing penalties on employers who hire illegal migrants, denying illegal migrants access to most public welfare services, detaining illegal entrants or asylum-seekers upon arrival, and swiftly repatriating those who are in the country illegally. For the most part, governments regard border controls as preferable to internal controls, principally because the former intrude less upon the lives of their own citizens. A country surrounded by sea and located a considerable distance from sources of migrants is clearly in a better position to control its borders than one with a large land border touching on a country with a lower standard of living. Australia and the United Kingdom have had an easier task of controlling their borders than Germany or the United States. Entry is, nevertheless, a subject of concern for all these countries. In recent years, many governments have sought to strengthen control at the land borders by increasing the number of border personnel and by developing new technologies for the detection and apprehension of illegal entrants. Australia requires visas of all tourists (except those from New Zealand), and records exits as well as entries as part of its control strategy, thereby enabling the government to track which country's citizens overstay their visas. Australia's consular officers abroad are thus in a better position to tighten visa controls. Border controls, however, can conflict with a country's other goals, such as easing border trade, facilitating tourism, and moving its own citizens quickly through border and airport checks. It is also costly to patrol long land borders.

The more effective border controls are, the less the need for internal controls. Most internal controls depend upon the use of identity cards or an identity number by all residents of the country, including citizens, which enable hospitals, employers and government agencies to determine eligibility for services and/or jobs. As in the case of border controls, governments differ in their ability to implement internal controls effectively. For example, some governments are better able than others to prevent employers from hiring illegal workers. The government must be prepared to provide an adequate number of labour inspectors; identity documents must be reliable and not easy to forge so that employers can determine whether someone is in fact authorized to work; and financial penalties on employers must be sufficiently high and the probability of being caught sufficiently great that employers will be reluctant to hire low-wage illegal workers. Moreover, employer sanctions and inspections may not work well when there is a large, unregulated, informal labour market. In the United States, employer sanctions have been poorly implemented because of the easy availability of forged identity documents and the absence of a reliable verification system. European governments generally exercise more effective internal controls than does the United States government, but there are also great variations within Europe. In Sweden, the universal identity card reportedly works well in deterring employers from hiring illegal migrants; in France, the police conduct spot checks of individuals in the Metro to identify illegal aliens and fines are regularly imposed upon employers for hiring illegal aliens; but in Italy and Spain, governmental controls are weak and the number of illegal migrants correspondingly higher than in other parts of Europe.

There are politically strong forces in most industrial countries that oppose effective control over illegal immigration. Farmers in need of seasonal workers, owners of restaurants and small businesses, and housewives want a source of cheap labour; human rights activists are opposed to the use of identity cards and express concern that employer sanctions may lead employers to discriminate against 'foreign-looking' legal residents; and ethnic groups lobby against migration restrictions.

Among Third World countries, the capacity of governments to control borders or to enforce internal checks is generally minimal, and the informal sector is so large that it is virtually impossible to use employer sanctions. Nonetheless, even among Third World countries there are increasingly greater efforts to control entry. The governments of both India and Pakistan have recently issued voter identification cards to prevent illegal migrants from voting. For a brief period, moreover, India sought to build a barbed wire fence to prevent unauthorized Bangladeshis from crossing the border, but after protests from Bangladesh it was removed.

The United States, France, Venezuela, Italy and Spain have granted amnesty to illegal migrants, partly in recognition of the fact that mass deportation is politically unacceptable, and partly to ensure that employers provide illegal migrants with adequate wages and working conditions. The decision to grant amnesty is usually controversial, since it may induce others to enter or remain illegally in anticipation of a future amnesty. 'Over the long run', concludes Miller, 'recourse to legalization may undermine migration control policies and erode the perceived legitimacy of immigrant settlement and incorporation so important to their long-term integration.'

Several governments, mostly those of low-income, developing countries, have massively deported illegal migrants. When the price of oil dropped in 1983, the government of Nigeria deported tens of thousands of illegal migrants from Ghana and other parts of west Africa; the governments of the Persian Gulf have periodically rounded up illegal workers who have overstayed their guest worker permits; and when Pakistan's civil war ended in 1972 (following India's armed intervention), India forcibly repatriated to Bangladesh an estimated ten million refugees who had crossed into India during the conflict. For domestic and foreign policy reasons, as well as for moral considerations, industrial countries have been reluctant to engage in any large-scale coercive repatriation and deportation. As Miller notes, a massive deportation of illegal migrants from Mexico would disrupt US–Mexican relations and alienate the Mexican–American and Hispanic populations in the United States.

Faced with a persistent uncontrollable influx, a number of governments have approached officials in sending countries to ask for their assistance in controlling exit. Germany, for example, has established joint border patrols with the Czech Republic, Poland and Hungary and has agreements with these countries that third-country nationals will not be permitted to cross their borders to seek asylum in Germany. In return for their co-operation, these countries receive financial assistance and technical help from the German government. Similarly, in 1994 the United States persuaded the Cuban government to prevent people from leaving for Florida in return for a US promise to allow twenty thousand Cubans to enter legally through normal procedures. The United States has also attempted to persuade the Mexican government to permit exit only through designated border locations, but thus far no agreement has been reached. The Mexican government, however, does deport thousands of illegal migrants annually who enter its southern borders from Central America, many of whom intend to cross over to the United States. The member states of the European Union are urging the governments of Italy and Spain to take forceful measures to halt illegal migration from Africa and North Africa. In the future we are likely to see more instances of governments pressing their neighbours to control exit – usually in return for financial assistance. It is also likely that governments of industrial countries will resort increasingly to deportations – perhaps not mass deportations, but forced and orderly departures of individuals who are rejected asylum-seekers or who are found to be illegal residents.

Three major themes emerge from Miller's paper. The first is that governments must assure their own populations that control policies are in place, even though there may be a considerable amount of leakage. Unless citizens are reassured that borders are controlled, xenophobic attacks against foreigners are likely to increase, since the smooth integration of legal migrants depends upon public assessment that their number is finite.

A second major theme is that controls at the borders – land borders, along the coast, and at airports – are preferable to internal controls. Increasingly, governments are also pressuring other governments to control borders: good neighbours, it is argued, do not permit their own citizens or those of other countries to violate their borders freely. The weaker the border controls and the greater number of visa overstayers, the more it is necessary to have some form of identification system – a politically costly, but sometimes unavoidable, measure if the number of illegal migrants is to be contained.

The third major theme is that, in the last decade, the norm has shifted as to what is acceptable for a democratic society with respect to the expulsion of illegal migrants. It is now increasingly acceptable for democratic governments to interdict and forcibly return ships carrying illegal migrants as well as to deport screened-out asylum-seekers and individuals who have entered illegally or overstayed their visas. An orderly, rational approach with appropriate administrative and legal reviews is acceptable; what remains unacceptable is an episodic crackdown, a round-them-up-and-ship-them-out approach that offends human decency.

Guest worker policies

Some governments believe that their country needs labourers, but they do not want permanent immigrants and are reluctant to permit the free employment of illegal migrants. An alternative policy, therefore, is to admit foreign guest workers for a limited duration. Philip Martin, in his review of these programmes, summarizes the major consequences of these policies in a series of aphorisms: there is, he says, nothing more permanent than temporary workers; guest worker programmes are easier to start than to stop, and one of the best ways to ensure continuous, as distinct from short-term, labour migration from a country or region is to recruit guest workers!

Governments, he notes, import guest workers for a variety of reasons: to deal with macro economy-wide labour shortages or shortages in particular industries, occupations and areas; to manage labour migration better when the flows, e.g. bi-national or commuter labour flows, seem inevitable; to provide work-and-learn opportunities for foreign workers, including foreign students and industrial trainees, who can then use their newly acquired skills when they return home; and finally, to promote socio-economic integration, as in the European Union.

For the countries of origin, the benefits of guest worker policies in theory are the three 'Rs' of recruitment, remittances and return. Under a 'successful' guest worker programme workers obtain employment, their families and home governments benefit from remittances, and return workers bring back skills and invest in the home economy. However, the benefits of many guest worker programmes have not been realized by countries of origin. Although most guest workers do return home initially, over time many remain in their host countries and even summon their families to join them — especially when governments threaten to halt recruitment. Employers may even encourage their good workers to stay on and may help them bring their families. In some instances, guest workers marry locally; in such cases remittances to the home country eventually decline. Furthermore, while remittances do make a significant contribution to the balance of payments of the home country, the use of remittances by migrant families, and of savings by the returning migrants, are invariably limited by the government's macro economic policies.

Many governments have made it easy for guest workers to remain. In Western Europe, governments permitted employers to renew contracts, and as the contracts were renewed the workers acquired additional rights — at first, to bring their families and, in time, to remain. In the United States, young people who attend universities on student visas are permitted to join the labour force temporarily to improve their skills, but employers can help them obtain work permits and immigrant status, so that student status is often in fact a probationary immigration system. Indeed, some governments regard the recruitment of foreign students for higher education as a good mechanism for bringing highly skilled workers into the economy.

The main costs of foreign worker programmes, according to Martin, are distortion and dependence. Distortion refers to the fact that economies and labour markets are usually flexible and can adjust to labour shortages: when low-wage foreign workers are available, employers are unlikely to invest in updating their technologies to deal with their labour needs. Moreover, they are likely to make investment decisions on the assumption that foreign workers will continue to be available. In the United States, notes Martin, farmers planted orange trees in areas where there were no people, no housing and no prospect of getting any local workforce to pick the crop. Once investment decisions are made on the assumption that guest workers will be available, it becomes hard to change policy. In the short term, guest worker programmes look like an attractive way to deal with what appears to be a short-term problem. Most of the costs come later.

Guest worker programmes also create dependence. As employers depend upon a supply of low-wage foreign workers, the jobs themselves come to be perceived by the native population as work fit only for foreigners, and it is increasingly difficult to find local people willing to take jobs that have become regarded as dirty and demeaning. The labour market grows dependent upon guest workers, and the alternatives – higher wages, a greater use of labour saving technology, more employment for groups hitherto unemployed, and shifting of manufacturing to other countries, etc. – no longer seem either necessary or possible. These costs of guest worker programmes are not easily measured, since how the economy might have responded had employers not been permitted to bring in foreign workers is a matter of speculation. Moreover, it is not easy to measure the social costs associated with integrating a foreign population, nor to estimate how many local workers would have been employed in the absence of a guest worker programme.

One of the striking findings in Martin's study is that, notwithstanding the long-term costs associated with guest worker programmes, a number of middle-income developing countries have turned towards the use of immigrant workers. Malaysia, Thailand, Poland, Korea and Greece – all once labour exporting countries – have begun to import unskilled labour. In each of these countries, the government does not regard the use of foreign labour as a permanent solution to tight labour markets nor, indeed, have these governments – with the exception of Malaysia, which Martin examines in some detail – put in place formal guest worker programmes. In practice, however, each of these countries has permitted foreign workers to enter with the expectation that they will only be 'temporary' workers.

Governments have sought to put in place a number of policies that would ensure the return of guest workers to their countries of origin and minimize the distortions due to their presence. A forced saving scheme is one credible device for compelling workers to return home. Governments can deposit part of guest workers' wages in interest-bearing accounts that become available only when they return home following the end of the work contract. It has also been suggested that employers contribute to a payroll tax for employment of foreign workers – money that can be deposited into pension and social security programmes, workmen's compensation schemes, and other social welfare programmes – partly to reduce the incentives to hire foreign workers over local ones, but also to cover the long-term costs associated with guest worker programmes. Even if the net gain for the employer is not eliminated, this tax could equal the social costs engendered by the programme. Government can also closely monitor the labour market to ensure that illegal migrants are not substituted for legal guest workers. But most important, argues Martin, governments need to consider the alternatives before they are persuaded by employers with labour shortages to initiate a guest worker programme. Once initiated, programmes are difficult to terminate; indeed, the abrupt termination of programmes often results in 'anticipatory settlement' because guest workers realize that they will not be able to return if they leave. And when programmes are terminated, the level of illegal migration may increase since employers have become dependent upon low-wage workers and the workers themselves have created networks to find jobs and housing.

Skilled migration policies

Traditional countries of migration – the United States, Australia, Canada, many of the countries of Latin America, and South Africa – have often considered race and national origin a legitimate factor in determining who could immigrate. Australia, for example, first restricted immigration to residents of the United Kingdom, and then admitted only other white Europeans. Similarly, from the end of the nineteenth until middle of the twentieth century, the United States excluded Asians. Today, the widely accepted international norm is that it is morally unacceptable to exclude individuals in this fashion – although in practice many countries do give preference to individuals whose ancestors originated in the country or who are culturally similar to the native population. The moral line between negative and positive discrimination is clearly thin.

Criteria for admission that are universally regarded as legitimate are family unification and the skills of the potential migrant. Family unification is justified on the grounds that the family constitutes a natural unit which should not be arbitrarily separated by international boundaries; families legally residing within a country thus have a moral claim to bring in their parents, their children and, in some instances, other relatives. The skills criterion is justified on the grounds that countries have a reasonable interest in admitting those who best meet the needs of their economy. The assumptions underlying the acceptability of skilled migration policies are that governments can assess what kind of manpower the economy needs, and that skills can be assessed in some objective fashion.

Gary Freeman reviews the experience of several immigrant-receiving countries that have established policies to facilitate the migration of skilled labour. Skills, he notes, can be ascertained in any one of several ways: the education level or the occupational experience of the migrant, the financial capacity of the migrant to invest in economic activities that would employ local people, and the migrant's fluency in the local language. Some skill-related characteristics are observable, but others, including entrepreneurial talent, ambition, creativity, work ethic and cultural adaptability – what scholars call 'cultural capital' – are not. Australia gives preference, using a point system, to individuals with a successful business background and capital to invest, to those whose education, age, skills and other characteristics indicate a high capacity to contribute to the Australian economy, and to those with outstanding creative or sports talents. Like Australia, Canada also has a point system based largely on the labour market skills of the candidate, including education, fluency in English or French, and business and investment experience. In both Canada and Australia, immediate family members who also qualify under the skill categories are given first preference for admission. The United States places less emphasis on skills than do Australia and Canada and greater emphasis on family unification. In 1990, however, a new immigration act increased the number of employment-based visas available to professionals with advanced degrees and to individuals with business skills or investment capabilities.

In all three countries, universities indirectly play an important role in the choice of new migrants. In the United States, for example, students with advanced degrees and high levels of professional skills are often able to find employers who then assist them in obtaining the coveted 'Green Card' which entitles its holder to remain in the United States and, subsequently, to seek citizenship. Universities provide potential immigrants with employer connections and employers may, in effect, nominate individuals for admission.

Although migrants' skills are often regarded as central to migration policy, skill is only one of several criteria for determining who will be granted immigration status and competing criteria affect the outcome of skilled migration programmes. In all three countries, family reunion is a high priority. As the number of family members admitted each year increases, the number who can be admitted under skill criteria correspondingly declines. On average, moreover, family members tend to have a lower level of skills than the migrants with whom they are being united. The skill balance can be restored, according to Freeman, either by reducing the number admitted under family reunion (by excluding brothers and sisters or adult children), or by increasing the annual quota so that more skilled migrants can be admitted.

Skilled migration is further complicated, as Freeman points out, by the fact that there is disagreement over the appropriate method for choosing skilled migrants in all the traditional countries of immigration. Should governments seek well-educated, highly skilled people without regard for present labour force requirements? The consequence for Australia of this policy is that many of the skilled migrants – especially engineers – have been unable to find employment, either because there has been a decline in the demand for certain skill categories or because there is a poor fit between the pre-migration experience and qualifications of migrants and the experiences and qualifications sought by host country employers. Indeed, unless they are selected to fill specific positions, skilled migrants can be disadvantaged by the fact that their overseas qualifications may not be recognized, they may lack adequate language and cultural skills, and they may suffer from discrimination. Alternatively, recruitment could be tied to occupations where there are known shortages and even to specific job openings. In short, how closely should migration policy be linked to existing labour force needs and some form of labour certification? How does a government decide what skills are or will be needed?

The most contentious debate over skill migration, however, centres around the question of whether immigrants take more jobs than they create. Do migrants contribute to the improvement in employment and earnings of the native population as well as their own? Business migration programmes to attract investors and capital are generally regarded as a failure in both Canada and Australia, since much of the investment has gone into real estate rather than into the creation of employment. When migrants do create small businesses, they often prefer to hire migrants from their own ethnic communities rather than employ locals. However, economists argue that an increase in human capital will result in a rise in productivity, which in turn generates more employment; therefore, displacement should not be a chief concern of migration policy. If migrants are skilled and young, in time they will make a contribution to the economy that will provide benefits to the entire country. Skilled people drive the economy and therefore provide employment for the less skilled; if firms need engineers and managers they should be free to recruit outside the country when locally skilled people are not available. Firms in Third World economies must compete, not only against one another, but also against firms in the First World, and, therefore, must have the kinds of highly skilled people that enable them to compete globally. Malaysia, for example, imports people with skills, even though at the same time some of its own educated citizens seek employment abroad.

Critics of skill migration programmes are less sanguine. They are concerned that local graduates of high schools and colleges will be resentful if good jobs are taken by immigrants. The political consequences could be alarming. Moreover, if skilled migrants are not available, governments are more likely to move energetically to upgrade their educational system to produce the engineers, doctors, nurses and managers that employers seek. If skilled migrants are needed to drive the economy at a time when locally skilled people are in short supply, then firms should be permitted to recruit older qualified migrants from abroad who can temporarily fill the gap until the education system can expand the country's human resources. Migration policies should not jeopardize the position of the next generation of young people whose parents lacked the skills to move into the higher levels of the economy.

Trade, investment and development assistance

Can countries of destination influence conditions in countries of origin so that fewer people will emigrate in search of jobs and higher wages? Robert Lucas provides us with an economic analysis of three major policy instruments — trade, foreign investment and development assistance — aimed at stimulating the economies of sending countries in an effort to reduce the socio-economic incentives for exit.

In theory, the most promising instrument is the expansion of trade. From the point of view of reducing migration, trade has two benefits: it stimulates employment in the country of origin, and it also reduces the demand for low-wage labour in the country of destination. Destination countries can give preferential access to goods produced in the country of origin, selectively lower trade barriers, and lower or end protection against labour intensive imports. The effect of such policies can be to expand production and investment in the country of origin, provide more employment and, for the country of destination, eliminate many low-wage jobs that attract migrants. That is the theory. In reality, however, trade policy is a complex tool. In the short term, a reduction in trade barriers can result in the closing down of protected industries in the country of origin and increasing unemployment. The removal of trade barriers between the United States and Mexico, for example, is expected to result in a loss of employment in Mexico's agricultural sector, especially in corn production, since corn is more cheaply and efficiently produced in the United States. Moreover, the development spurred by freer trade can often increase, rather than reduce, incentives to emigrate. Higher incomes make emigration financially easier and lead to raising expectations. Development induces migration from rural to urban areas, and thus sets in motion a process of step migration. Although development provides more jobs, in some sectors of the economy labour opportunities may deteriorate. Lastly, with greater development comes an increase in communication and information about opportunities elsewhere. It is unclear which of these factors is most influential in inducing emigration. Lucas is inclined to believe that the most decisive variable is the loss of employment in some sectors of the economy, but there is evidence that the other variables are also significant determinants of migration. And it is undisputed that the short-term effect of eliminating trade barriers and increasing development is more, rather than less, migration: Korea, Taiwan, Hong Kong, Turkey, Greece and Puerto Rico generated large numbers of migrants as their economies expanded under the impetus of trade. In time, however, as development continues, emigration declines. Lucas provides evidence to suggest that emigration declines, not when employment and wages between countries of origin and countries of destination are the same, but when a specified level of GDP per capita is reached. This 'migration transition' appears to take place when GDP per capita for countries of origin moves into the $2000 to $3000 range.

The movement of international capital to low-wage regions can hasten development but, at present, investment in very poor countries remains low. One important reason is that there is a higher rate of return on investment in higher-income economies. Moreover, many governments of low-wage economies have been hostile to foreign investment or have failed to take appropriate measures to make investment attractive. Local labour laws are often a disincentive; infrastructures, such as power and transportation, are unsatisfactory; and in the absence of mass primary education, human resources remain neglected. Governments are often unstable or corrupt. Lucas emphasizes that there is often little that can be done by countries of destination to promote direct foreign investment, since the obstacles to such investment can generally be addressed only by the country of origin.

Similarly, development assistance aimed at improving employment, wages and productivity which might, in the long run, reduce emigration can be undermined by the policies of the country of origin. Many Third World governments are dominated by rapacious elites more concerned with their own prosperity than that of their country. Much development aid has gone into projects that do little to expand employment, and food aid has often brought down the price of agricultural goods and hurt job creation in the agricultural sector. However, aid may be effective in creating infrastructures and for relief of poverty – though neither are likely to do much to stem migration. More importantly, development assistance can be an instrument for inducing governments to adopt labour absorption investment strategies and to promote economic liberalization. In other words, aid, either bilateral or through multilateral international institutions, can serve as leverage for changing the policy framework of the sending country.

Where aid can be effective is in enabling refugees to return home once strife and violence has ended. Aid is principally needed for two reasons: to provide refugees with transportation and supplies to go home and to help in the task of reconstruction. Assistance can range from mine-clearing operations to measures to restore transportation and irrigation facilities so that returning refugees can resume agricultural production. Refugees may need seeds, agricultural implements and financial assistance to enable them to plant crops, as well as supplies of food and clothing to get them through until the harvest.

Refugee policies

Refugees are a world-wide phenomenon, but Africa has the largest number of refugees and internally displaced persons. In their study Astri Suhrke and Aristide Zolberg note that different regions of Africa have developed a variety of refugee flows. In southern Africa, for example, violent decolonization, the presence of white settlers and external intervention by outside powers (including South Africa's apartheid regime) exacerbated ethnic and regional cleavages. The major flows in the region have been from Angola, Mozambique and, to some extent, from Zaire. In the Horn of Africa, secessionist movements and irredentist claims – all part of a process of competitive state formation – led to large-scale violence and refugee flows in Ethiopia, Eritrea, Somalia and Sudan. External intervention related to the Cold War played a role, particularly through the flow of stocks of weapons. Elsewhere in sub-Saharan Africa, weak predatory states, characterized by contending elites concerned with their own gain, led to the misallocation of resources, exploitation, repression and in some instances the domination of an ethnic group. Chad, Uganda, the Central African Republic, Liberia, Sierra Leone, Rwanda and Burundi have all experienced violent implosions which produced massive refugee flows. These flows, in addition to the suffering imposed on the refugees themselves, have placed a heavy burden on the countries that receive them.

In 1995, there were 5.2 million refugees in Africa, and an even larger number of displaced persons (10.2 million), originating in 22 countries and dispersed among 36 countries. Governments in Africa, and elsewhere, have responded with a number of strategies intended to limit the number of refugees that are produced as well as to reduce the number entering their countries: by providing temporary protection in lieu of outright refugee status, by facilitating the return of the refugees when conditions have improved, and, in a few instances, by intervening in the country of origin in order to eliminate the causes of the refugee flows.

Suhrke and Zolberg trace the development of the international refugee regime and the Organisation of African Unity's (OAU) more generous regional refugee regime. Would-be migrants often seek entrance into developed countries by claiming asylum; in the north this has raised issues regarding the criteria and procedures for choosing those who seek protection and screening out those who do not qualify. By contrast, in Africa, Asia and Latin America the major issues have been how to obtain adequate financial assistance for the care and maintenance of people in refugee camps, and then how to arrange for their return when the conflicts that led to their flight end. The burden refugees place on a country's land, environment and economic resources is particularly great for developing countries. Suhrke and Zolberg note that the United Nations High Commissioner for Refugees has attempted to develop a 'comprehensive' refugee policy and to get at the 'root causes' of refugee flows, but, in practice, governments and international agencies have largely responded to refugee flows in an *ad hoc* case-by-case fashion. The United States and the governments of Western Europe have tightened up their asylum processes and limited access either through interdiction or by creating 'safe havens' in third countries. The states of Western Europe have also signed a variety of regional agreements intended to harmonize their asylum procedures, to create buffers in Central Europe to reduce the flows into

Germany and to establish procedures for continuous inter-governmental consultations. Developed countries have made clear their unwillingness to resettle significant numbers of refugees from the South. As such, the expectation is that there will be relatively few intercontinental asylum-seekers and that refugees will stay in the South, in return for which the North will provide financial assistance.

The Western European governments have had little success in changing conditions in the Balkans or in the former Soviet Union that have generated refugee flows, including those from Bosnia, Croatia, Slovenia, Serbia, Chechnya, Azerbaijan, Armenia and Tajikistan. International interventions have largely been for the purpose of providing humanitarian assistance or peacekeeping operations when the contending sides have agreed to an international presence.

There is a growing world-wide consensus that external intervention to deal with political and economic crises within states that generate refugee flows can be legitimate, but only if there is authorization by the United Nations or by regional bodies. United States intervention in Haiti, French intervention in Rwanda, and multinational armed interventions in Iraq, Somalia, the former Yugoslavia, Cambodia and elsewhere have been carried out with United Nations approval. Bilateral negotiations for preventing or accommodating refugee flows or arranging the return of refugees have also become more pronounced, such as those between the United States and Cuba, Germany and Poland, Bangladesh and Burma, and India and Bangladesh. After years of hesitation, NATO militarily intervened against Serbia, forced a cease fire and agreement among the contending parties, and then sent in troops to separate the armed forces. There have been similar efforts at regional intervention by West African governments in the civil conflict in Liberia. Regional peacekeeping operations by countries within Africa are particularly promising, but they are likely to need financial and sometimes logistical support from developed countries.

Lessons for migration reform

In a concluding session of the workshop, the participants were asked to consider the implications of their findings for reforming migration and refugee policies. There were more questions than easy answers. They made three points.

The first is that in every country migration intersects with a variety of domestic policy questions – especially those involving employment, inter-ethnic relations and welfare policies. It follows from this that governments must weigh conflicting objectives in addressing refugee and migration issues and should recognize that there are often trade-offs among difficult choices.

Faced with a large number of asylum requests, for example, governments must choose among difficult and politically controversial options for the treatment of asylees while their reviews are pending: permit them to enter the labour force, prevent their unauthorized employment through a national system of labour market controls, or place them in detention centres. Another difficult choice is the question of the extent to which legal migrants, illegal migrants, asylum-seekers and refugees are granted access to government-financed social services. The greater the access and the higher the costs, the more citizens and policy makers are likely to want to limit the number of migrants and refugees, but a denial of some benefits (education for the children of illegal migrants, for example, or health care) has broader social costs. In the debate over whether employers should be permitted to recruit skilled people (e.g. physicians, computer technicians, chemical engineers) from abroad, governments will have to decide whether they should instead allocate more resources for the education and training of their own citizens, though the financial costs may be higher, and the benefits less certain and less immediate. In determining whether family-sponsored migration should include siblings as well as spouses and minor children of permanent residents, policy makers must decide whether they can increase the overall level of immigration or, if not, whether the other categories for admission (e.g. refugees and employment based immigration) should be reduced.

The second point that emerged from the workshop is the need for policy makers to become better informed as to the attitudes of their own citizens towards migration. It is striking to note how ill-informed policy makers in many countries have been about the views of their own citizens and how much the views of elites and the public diverge. A 1995 public opinion survey in the United States, for example, reported that 72 per cent of the American public answered 'yes' to the question of whether large numbers of immigrants and refugees coming into the United States represented a critical threat to US vital interests in the next ten years, but only 31 per cent of a sample of US leaders shared this concern – a disparity which helps to explain the 1994 revolt of California voters on the issue of providing social services to illegal migrants. Similarly, in India, the central government paid little heed to public concerns over the illegal influx from Bangladesh to Assam until protests (and violence) resulted in the defeat of the state government by a newly formed anti-migrant party. In Germany, France and Great Britain non-mainstream, anti-migrant political parties captured substantial public support before government leaders demon-strated that they were taking steps to gain control over the borders and to establish more acceptable migration and refugee policies. A government that is not informed about the views of its citizens on these issues is likely to become overly responsive to special interests or to its own ideological preferences. This is not to suggest that policy makers must simply follow public moods which are likely to be anti-migrant during a period of unemployment, and pro-migrant during a time of labour shortages. Policy makers have an educational role, but to perform that role satisfactorily they must be better informed, not dismissive of public attitudes and even visceral anxieties.

A third point made at the workshop was the need to put in place a policy-making process that can generate coherence in policy. In most countries migration and refugee policies are not the responsibility of any single government department. In the United States, for example, migration and refugee issues are handled by the Departments of Justice, Labour, State and (indirectly) Commerce. Congress writes the legislation that determines how many migrants should be admitted and the criteria for admission, but provides no funds to municipal or state governments to cover additional welfare, education and medical costs – with the result that some state and local governments attempt to overturn federal policies requiring the provision of these services to immigrants. While fragmentation of decision making is particularly pronounced in the United States, fragmentation is typical of migration and refugee policy making in most countries since the issues intersect with the concerns of so many ministries, including education, labour, commerce and industry, and external affairs. Few countries (Canada and Australia are notable exceptions) have a single ministry or department with responsibility for co-ordinating migration and refugee policies. In the absence of a co-ordinating mechanism for setting migration and refugee policies, special interests – employers in most countries, and ethnic minorities in some – exercise a major influence.

In the past, moreover, when migration has moved to the top of the political agenda in response to an immediate crisis or an awareness of growing public anxieties, national leaders have often responded in an *ad hoc* fashion. Governments have hastily attempted to seal their borders, interdict ships at sea, expel guest workers, and prevent individuals from seeking asylum – all in an effort to reassure the public. A few governments have sought to develop more humane, coherent and consistent policies through the establishment of an immigration and refugee commission, made up of government and party officials and representatives of the business community, trade unions, ethnic groups and academia, or by turning responsibility over to a lead department. Australia revised its White Australia policy (which excluded non-European immigrants) under the influence of the Department of Foreign Affairs rather than the Department of Immigration. The FitzGerald Commission subsequently played a major role in shaping Australia's migration and refugee policies. In the United States, the Select Commission on Immigration and Refugee Policy, which included members of the US Congress and Senate as well as the executive branch, formulated the policy of employer sanctions to deter illegal immigrants and provided amnesty to those who had resided in the

United States for an extended period. Similar national commissions have designed long-term immigration and refugee policies in Canada and in several European countries. One other reason for having a lead agency or commission take the initiative in designing policies is that there is a greater likelihood that the process will generate the kind of data that are essential for addressing these issues. Whether a special commission is the best mechanism or a lead ministry should be given primary responsibility for reforming policy may be less important than the broader questions of how a policy process can be created that is informed by research, that considers public opinion but is not wholly guided by it, and that takes into account a country's diverse interests and objectives.

Migration and refugee issues are likely to become more important in the future. So long as there are large disparities in income and in employment opportunities between countries and so long as some countries are torn by civil conflict, violence, and deny human rights, then large numbers of people will seek opportunities and safety outside their own country. The more successful some countries are in achieving and maintaining high economic growth, democratic rights, generous social services, and stable government, the more likely they will become a magnet for illegal migrants and refugees. The more attractive a country becomes to others, the more necessary it is to address migration and refugee issues. But as one participant put it, 'no matter how complex or difficult it seems to manage immigration, it is better than being so unattractive that one does not have to worry about it'. Or as one wit put it, 'migration is the sincerest form of flattery'.

1

The prevention of unauthorized migration

Mark J. Miller

The regulation of international migration is not inherently morally objectionable. The maintenance of public order is the first obligation of every government, and effective immigration regulation is important to the achievement of a host of valued goals and objectives. Prevention of unauthorized migration is thus a customary prerogative of sovereign states and reflects the basic rights of states and their citizens to determine who should be admitted into the country as residents and future citizens. This chapter examines the variety of policy instruments adopted by governments to control entry and to limit the number of illegal migrants. We will consider four types of policies: those intended to control entry at borders; the use of internal controls to detect the presence of illegal migrants and restrict their access to employment and public goods; the repatriation and expulsion of illegal migrants; and finally, policies to legalize migrants' status.

Border and port-of-entry control

Charles Tilly once likened the process of state formation to a protection racket (Tilly 1985). Viable states emerged where rulers were able to ensure protection and security for a population. Since time immemorial, rulers and governments have sought to exercise control over ingress to and egress from their jurisdictions. The current migratory epoch, which is demarcated by the predominance of migration for employment purposes, dates from the last quarter of the nineteenth century when the emerging industrial states of the North Atlantic began to regulate international migration.

Unauthorized migration is a by-product of governmental regulation of international migration, which usually involves placing both quantitative and qualitative limitations on alien entry and stay.

Prevention of unauthorized entry at the border has long figured in regulation of international migration. The earliest steps towards regulation required aliens to carry identification and register with authorities. In the United States, for instance, early qualitative restrictions barred entry to criminals, the insane, prostitutes, bearers of infectious diseases and the like. Inspections were required at ports of entry, and undesirables were turned away. In Imperial Germany, seasonal foreign workers in agriculture could pass border inspection but would violate the terms of their entry and face deportation if they took employment in other sectors.

In the United States, literacy requirements were imposed by 1917, and policing of the US–Mexican border became militarized. In the 1930s, after wartime recruitment of temporary Mexican workers, sizeable repatriations of Mexican citizens considered unlawful entrants or burdensome as a group were organized by local and state governments. Agents of the federal government disclaimed a role in this, partially for diplomatic purposes.

In interwar France, a process for admission of foreign workers was established by a series of bilateral agreements. But most foreign workers arrived 'spontaneously' outside the system set up by employers with the co-operation of the French government. By the 1930s, repatriations of Polish workers were organized by the French government as unemployment and opposition to immigrants mounted. In 1938, the government increased the frontier police 'by 1,500 men to better control the entry of illegal immigrants' (Cross 1983: 211). The efficacy of border control even back then hinged on the personnel and monetary resources committed to it.

Since World War II, border control has been affected by a number of developments. The independence of formerly colonized areas, progress towards regional integration, the transportation and communications revolutions and the evolution of what can be termed border control technology. Clearly, geography dramatically affects border control capacity, as does the nature of the economy and polity. The island continent of Australia, for instance, simply does not confront as extensive a problem of illegal entry as do states like France and Germany with their long land and sea borders and location at the heart of Europe (Birrell 1994). The United Kingdom's insularity and peripheral location likewise make it much less likely to be affected by illegal entry than most of its continental neighbours.

Some states have created highly effective border controls, but usually this flows from a perception of acute threat from unauthorized entry. Many of the former communist states of central and eastern Europe constitute well-known examples. A number of west European states have of late used their armies to cope with migration emergencies. In most instances, however, perceptions of threat to national scrutiny from incomplete or ineffective border control are not as acute. More typically, concern over unauthorized entry is mitigated by perceived benefits arising from tourism and minimally impeded movement of people for economic, educational and other purposes. World-wide tourism has grown enormously and is often a critical economic concern. Globalization of the economy has increased economic interdependence which, in turn, often involves greater business and employment-related entry and stay by aliens. However, it is interesting to note that in the most advanced case of regional economic integration, movement of labour has not been as extensive as one might have expected, given the freedom of labour provisions of the Treaty of Rome. Creation of regional labour mobility rights, as in the European Union, can partially ease border control obligations but is usually only politically feasible in contexts characterized by underlying socio-economic similitude. This is why Turkey was rebuffed in its effort to accede to full membership in the European Union and one of the reasons why labour mobility did not figure in the US–Mexico discussions leading to the North American Free Trade Agreement (NAFTA).

Virtually everywhere, growing economic interdependence and tourism together with advances in communications and transportation have rendered states increasingly permeable to unauthorized entry. The borders of many African states are unpoliced, and, in some instances, legal notions of citizenship in one state or another are fuzzy. Some African states cannot afford censuses and elementary identity documents, and vital statistics for administrative purposes are lacking. Movements across national boundaries within transnational ethnic groups are common and occur without regard to boundaries drawn at the Berlin Conference of 1885. National governments have little or no capacity to regulate border entry anyway. They often lack the financial resources and administrative wherewithal to do so (Ricca 1990: 16–25, 96–100).

States, then, exhibit extremely variable capacities for effective border control (Freeman 1994). All states are permeable, but border controls can and do deter unauthorized migration. A host of variables determine how effective border controls are. The principal ones include the sheer extent and terrain of frontiers, as well as the number of ports of entry and their degree of vulnerability, the personnel and financial resources available for surveillance and the quality of their utilization, which is affected by use of technology.

The costs of border control are commonly viewed as burdensome, even in a relatively rich country like the United States. Border control at the US–Mexican border has been porous, in part because of insufficient funding of the Immigration and Naturalisation Service (INS). Some contend that the US government tacitly tolerates unauthorized alien entry as it benefits certain politically influential economic sectors. Others contend that the possibility of unauthorized entry to the United States promotes regional stability (and therefore US strategic interests) by providing a safety valve for unemployment and underemployment in Central America and a return flow of wage remittances (Stanley 1993).

The United States has not secured Mexico's co-operation in border enforcement. Indeed, recent bolstering of US border controls at several points on the Mexican frontier has had adverse repercussions upon US–Mexican relations. Other states have been more successful in securing bilateral co-operation on border control than has the United States. Germany has linked foreign assistance and other trade and foreign policy questions to Czech and Polish co-operation on prevention of unauthorized alien entry. Joint policing of the Czech–German border has begun, which should help deter unauthorized entry. European states are co-operating at the regional level to lessen unauthorized entry. For instance, information on alien smuggling rings is now being shared. Organized criminal smuggling of aliens is proliferating world-wide and frequently involves extreme hardship, even death, for the aliens involved.

Regional integration has only partially reduced the need for border controls in the European context. The border-control-free internal market envisaged by the Single European Act is not yet operational. Ricca has documented and lamented the sorry history of African regional schemes in this regard (Ricca 1990: 108–21). Boudahrain's analysis of Arab regional arrangements and their inefficacy is similarly damning (Boudahrain 1985).

Technological advances have had mixed effects upon border control. Technology to scan passports and travel documents has facilitated controls, but document fraud has become more sophisticated, as has alien smuggling. One recent innovation by European governments has been to support information campaigns in areas sending large numbers of unauthorized aliens, warning potential aliens against the dangers of illegal immigration.

A growing number of industrial democracies have adopted laws levying fines upon airlines held responsible for transporting improperly documented aliens. Areas have been created at airports to prevent such aliens from applying for asylum. These steps have been criticized for violation of the *non-refoulement* provision of the Geneva Convention regarding refugees. In reality, moreover, relatively few fines have been levied against airlines in Western Europe and, when fines have been assessed, they have, in many instances, been reduced or voided under appeal.

Visa policies

Many states require aliens to obtain a visa, an official authorization of admission often for a designated time period and purpose which usually is affixed to a passport. This requirement forces aliens to secure authorization to enter a country prior to travel to that country. Usually a visa is obtained at an embassy of the destination country.

Visa requirements make international travel more difficult and costly. They enable governments to discourage travel by individuals thought likely to violate immigration and other laws. Where administered well, as in Australia, they enable authorities to track alien entries and departures. Quite credible estimates of illegal migration in Australia are made from visa-generated data on entries and departures.

Imposition of visa requirements upon states and regions has had perceptible effects on 'unwanted' alien populations. A classic case was the decline in asylum applications by Turks in the Federal Republic of Germany in the early 1980s after the imposition of a visa requirement. The dip in asylum applications, however, was short-lived. The imposition of visa requirements upon Bosnians and citizens of other successor states to the former Yugoslav federal state has been a factor preventing mass exodus of refugees and displaced persons estimated to number over four million by June 1994. Only about fifteen per cent of the people dislocated by conflict and ethnic cleansing have been able to reach safe haven in Western Europe, and visa requirements have contributed significantly to this outcome.

Globally, only an estimated two per cent of the world's population has recently moved across international borders. It seems reasonable to suppose that many more would move if there were no barriers to doing so. For instance, young Algerians, many of whom face poor prospects for employment and upward mobility, have expressed a widespread desire to emigrate. The difficulties faced by Algerians seeking visas for travel to Western Europe undoubtedly discourage many from doing so.

Critics of visa requirements contend that the requirements themselves are an important cause of illegal entry and residency. They argue that the French government's tightening up of visa requirements for visiting family members resident in France manufactures illegal immigration. In this optic, too restrictive visa requirements themselves become a determinant of illegality. A number of scholars doubt that governmental regulations can alter transnational migration processes. The key to successful policy in this optic is recognition and acceptance of migratory realities as given (Cornelius *et al.* 1994).

Most would now concur that violation of immigration laws after legal entry is the prevalent form of illegal migration in Western democracies. Some countries keep statistics which reveal quite divergent proclivities for overstay by country of origin. Greeks, for instance, are notorious for overstay in the United States. Governments like that of the United States respond by instructing its consular officials to be more stringent. Perhaps the most difficult job in US government today is that of the young foreign service officer assigned to consular work at a US Embassy. He or she faces interminable lines of applicants and must make difficult decisions affecting the lives of the applicants and others under less-than-ideal conditions. In some instances, the anger provoked by the difficulty in obtaining a visa to the United States has adversely affected sensitive diplomatic relations and, increasingly, has provoked physical attacks on consular personnel.

Visa requirements can adversely affect tourism and increase business costs. They also demand administrative infrastructure. Computer-assisted technology, however, makes such policies feasible and perhaps desirable even for some lesser developed countries.

France imposed generalized visa requirements in the mid-1980s after a series of violent incidents perpetrated by mainly non-resident aliens. Security considerations have also figured in the emerging European visa policy. But immigration control is the major reason behind the increased visa requirements of most Western European states over the past several decades. Former colonial powers have gradually transformed visa-free travel zones like the Franco-African Community (Picard 1979) or the Commonwealth and, now, visa requirements are the rule rather than the exception between OECD states and the rest of the world.

Interior controls, expulsion, deportation and repatriation

The aforementioned trends have rendered modern states permeable to unauthorized entry and stay. Even a state like Israel, with quite effective militarized border and port-of-entry controls and extensive screening at entry and exit, is thought to have a significant illegally resident population. Most democratic governments distinguish border and port-of-entry control from immigration law enforcement in interior settings. The distinction frequently is manifest in the development of separate administrations and corps of enforcement personnel. Different rules and procedures often obtain. Unauthorized aliens apprehended at a border or port of entry generally do not have the same legal recourse to prevent return to their country of origin as illegal migrants who can document years of residence and employment. It is not unusual for illegally resident aliens to have close family ties with citizens or legally resident aliens, so these circumstances typically are treated differently than apprehension at a border, both legally and administratively.

One of the most striking, but unheralded, aspects of US discussions of immigration law and policy in recent times is the absence of advocacy of measures similar to Operation Wetback in 1954, which led to the apprehension and return to Mexico of one million Mexican citizens. This military-style enforcement action was focused in the south-west and resulted in a subsequent sharp decrease in apprehensions of illegal entrants concomitant with a large increase in legal entry by Mexican temporary foreign workers. Previously, there had been large-scale returns of Mexicans in the 1930s. These decentralized campaigns had both voluntary and coercive aspects (Kiser and Kiser 1979: 33–66). Such measures were viewed as unacceptably draconian and unworkable by the late 1970s and appear not to have been given any consideration at all by the Select Commission on Immigration and Refugee Policy. The repatriation drives of the 1930s had badly frayed US–Mexican relations and had resulted in hardship for US citizens and legally resident aliens of Mexican origin. Some US citizens were deported and families were split.

It seems important to speculate on why large-scale coercive repatriation and deportation campaigns are not on the agenda in industrial democracies, since they are quite commonplace elsewhere. In the United States, such a campaign has been unthinkable in the context of US–Mexican relations. Moreover, it would be too disruptive of society and politically divisive. It might irreparably alienate the rapidly growing Mexican–American and Hispanic–American populations, which constitute a non-negligible political force. Moreover, US citizens are not required to carry identity documents. In Western Europe, where citizens of many countries are required to have an identity document or number, memories of the population deportations of World War II remain vivid. Although comparison of deportation of illegal immigrants to deportations of Jews, Gypsies and other populations trivializes the Holocaust, Western European states shy away from measures reminiscent of police states. This is particularly true for Germany, where such concerns have even limited enforcement of employer sanctions.

Episodically, France permits area controls to verify identities. Although French citizens are not required to carry identity cards, most do. All aliens are required to possess documents authorizing their presence. Generally, such controls are employed in the Parisian metro, at perceived trouble spots and gathering points like the Beaubourg Museum and, occasionally, in immigrant neighbourhoods. Their efficacy in preventing illegal residency is dubious, but they are reassuring to a large element of the French population. Identity controls were discontinued for a while under socialist rule out of fear that they discriminated against French citizens of North African background. Previously, such controls had been much more prevalent. Their extensive use in the latter stages of the Algerian war, in a civil war-like situation in Metropolitan France, led to little-known abuses in the early 1960s (Einaudi 1991).

Outside of the industrial democracies, mass alien repatriation and deportation campaigns have been recurrent but little studied. Ricca, who terms such campaigns the worst solution to illegal migration, has analysed their currency in sub-Saharan Africa (Ricca 1990: 100–7). The best known of these occurred in Nigeria in 1983 and 1985, when a change in government and recession linked to declining oil revenues led to reinterpretation of the legal status of alien residents and employees from nearby lands. Governmental announcements of intent to expel illegally resident populations and to close borders led to panic-stricken flight and mass repatriation involving millions. As in the United States in the 1930s, the Nigerian campaigns involved an element of coercion and deportation, but most aliens seem to have left voluntarily. However, whereas Mexico helped organize transportation of its citizens from the United States in the 1930s (much as the Polish government co-operated with the French return policy of the 1930s) homelands nearby Nigeria appear only to have opened their borders to permit re-entry. Ghana was the principal recipient of the mass returns and received considerable international assistance to lodge returnees temporarily, return them to their areas of origin and find them employment. Two years after the first mass expulsions, some 450,000 returnees had agricultural work (Ricca 1990: 160–6).

Mass expulsions also have been commonplace in the Arab region (Castles and Miller 1993). Migrant populations which are tolerated and considered legally resident one day sometimes find themselves considered illegal and branded as undesirable the next. The legality of alien residency and employment is often a matter of interpretation, even whim. Egyptian workers in Libya have frequently paid the price for deterioration of their government's relations with its western neighbour. The large Palestinian population of Lebanon has been subject to attacks by extremist groups which consider Palestinians illegal aliens and a threat to Lebanese sovereignty. The massacres in Palestinian refugee camps in 1982 sought to trigger mass panic and flight.

The Iraq–Kuwait crisis of 1990 and its sequels witnessed the mass expulsion and displacement of millions of aliens, most of whom were legally admitted or employed but whose status was jeopardized by the conflict (Shami 1994). Weiner has analysed comparable events in South Asia, conclusively demonstrating their importance in regional and bilateral relations and conflict (Weiner 1993). Balkan and Eastern European history is replete with mass expulsions and ethnic cleansing of minority populations whose presence is regarded as illegitimate, threatening or inconvenient (The New Europe 1992).

Mass expulsions of aliens almost invariably violate international norms espoused by the International Labour Organisation and the branches of the United Nations concerned with human rights. While states do have a right to return illegal migrants, long-term, legally admitted alien residents and citizens have a different status in international law and in democratic settings. The international community took action against Iraq to stop the mass flight of Iraqi citizens of Kurdish background into Turkey. Mass expulsions in Africa and the Arab region also frequently violate international norms and regional agreements and have adverse and disruptive effects far beyond the lives of those expelled, but generally the international community has acquiesced to such acts.

Western European states have grudgingly accepted that long-term resident aliens cannot be repatriated against their will. Government-organized voluntary repatriation drives featuring cash and other financial incentives for return have yielded meagre results, as indicated by the French data in Tables 1 and 2. These policies were not open to illegal residents and differed in fundamental ways from the forced expulsion of Palestinians from Kuwait and of Yemenis from Saudi Arabia in the early 1990s.

The steep rise in asylum applications in industrial democracies has fostered largely novel problems and issues germane to consideration of governmental capacity to remove aliens. European states were caught off

Table 1   Results of financially assisted return policy in France, 1984–92

Year	Industry-national immigration office agreements	Dossiers submitted	Individuals repatriating	Employees repatriating
1984–8	3 520	32 889	68 866	30 032
1989	109	562	1 194	669
1990	60	265	421	235
1991	75	195	285	173
1992	82	215	260	164
Total	3 846	34 126	71 026	31 273

Source: Lebon 1994: 24

Table 2   Nationality of beneficiaries of financial assistance for repatriation from France, 1984–92

Nationality	Workers	Spouse[1]	Children[1]	Total
Algerians	12 645	2 693	9 063	24 401
Moroccans	4 001	1 014	3 017	8 032
Tunisians	1 749	828	2 395	4 972
Africans	1 376	193	470	2 039
Spaniards[2]	456	311	467	1 234
Portuguese[2]	5 748	3 841	6 566	16 155
Turks	3 944	1 738	5 067	10 749
Yugoslavs	1 196	727	1 219	3 142
Others	158	41	103	302
Total	31 273	11 386	28 367	71 026

[1] Residency in France and returning home with a worker
[2] Until September 1986

Source: Lebon 1994: 109

guard by the sudden influx of asylum-seekers. Administrative services were overwhelmed. In many cases, adjudication dragged on and on.

By the early 1990s, only a small fraction of applicants were determined to be bona fide refugees entitled to the grant of asylum. A larger fraction were found to be not entitled to asylum but could not be returned home without risk — so-called grey area cases. But most applicants were determined not to be entitled to any protection whatsoever and became subject to deportation if they did not voluntarily return home.

In the early 1990s, it was estimated that less than a quarter of denied asylum applicants had been removed from the country in which they had applied for asylum. Insufficient personnel and administrative services meant that many such aliens were simply released. In France, for instance, authorities could detain an alien for roughly a week. But if the alien could not be returned home during that period, special judicial permission to detain the alien further was required. Sometimes deportable aliens were released for humanitarian reasons. In other instances, aliens destroyed their identification documents and the presumed homeland government refused to co-operate with the deportation. And in still further instances, deportation was frustrated by an inability to secure seats on an airliner. Deportation is often very expensive. It requires detention facilities, personnel and the co-operation of authorities elsewhere.

Recently, though, a number of west European states have made deportation more credible. One innovation involved the offer of financial incentives for voluntary return home. A fraction of denied asylum-seekers, as seen in Tables 3 and 4, now opt for these packages in Germany and France, rather than face deportation. Bilateral return agreements with homelands, usually involving financial assistance, have elicited greater co-operation in repatriation. German–Romanian co-operation has facilitated the return of large contingents of gypsies.

Staffs and budgets of administrative and enforcement services have been bolstered so that adjudication now is more timely. This helps prevent aliens from gaining residency for humanitarian reasons. In most west European states, asylum-seekers are no longer voluntarily granted employment permits.

Table 3   Results of the policy to aid repatriation by aliens invited to leave France

Year	Invitations to leave reported	Requests for information	Applications	Aliens departing
Sept–Dec 1991	6 173	1 561	610	355
1992	12 631	4 410	1 338	1 212
Total	18 804	5 971	1 948	1 567

Source: Lebon 1994: 25

Table 4   Results of German policy encouraging voluntary departure of asylum-seekers

Year	Asylum applicants (new entries)	Persons transported under the REAG programme	Percentage of all new asylum-seekers transported (%)
1979	51 493	137	0.3
1980	107 818	2 316	2.1
1981	49 391	4 291	8.7
1982	37 423	6 962	18.6
1983	19 737	7 598	39.0
1984	35 278	6 383	18.1
1985	73 832	5 404	7.3
1986	99 650	9 495	9.5
1987	57 379	9 473	16.5
1988	103 076	9 269	9.0
1989	121 318	10 910	9.0
1990	193 063	10 418	5.4
1991	256 112	10 605	4.1
1992	438 191	13 856	3.2

Source: Federal Ministry of the Interior 1993: 80

In France and Germany, recent administrative and legal reforms have contributed to a dramatic decline in asylum applications which will reduce the population of denied asylum-seekers requiring removal. While Europe's asylum crisis is not over, a variety of steps, some legitimately open to ethical reservations, have helped reduce it. This may help explain the dramatic fall off in voting for the Republikäners in the 1994 German elections and for the apparent cresting of the National Front's electoral appeal witnessed in 1993 legislative election in France.

The United States similarly has experienced a large increase in asylum applications in the 1990s. Inadequate detention facilities, insufficient personnel and a variety of other deficiencies have meant that many aliens, even violent criminals, slated for deportation have been routinely released. In 1994, new regulations were implemented regarding asylum-seekers which clearly were inspired by Western European reform measures. Asylum-seekers would not be granted employment authorization for six months. Manifestly unfounded claims would be distinguished from claims deserving more detailed adjudication. Resources would be allocated to increase administrative and enforcement personnel, with the goal being prompt adjudication of cases within six months. Additional detention facilities would be built.

Moral, ethical and legal concerns have shaped governmental capacities to detect and remove aliens beyond border and port-of-entry controls. In democratic settings, the difficulty and expense of removing aliens has contributed to the appeal of legalization and employer sanctions policies. In many lesser-developed nations, scant attention has been paid to human rights and legal considerations and mass expulsions frequently result. Intimidation, violence and widespread disruption of lives and economies are not uncommon outcomes.

Recent developments such as the ability of the German government to repatriate thousands of Vietnamese and the US repatriation of Cuban and Haitian boat people suggest that, in the frequently difficult trade-off between ethical concerns and the credibility of immigration control policies, the pendulum is swinging to the latter. Moreover, this may ultimately serve ethical ends by restoring credibility in broader migration policies.

Employer sanctions

Laws penalizing employers for illegal employment of aliens were on the books in Germany and had been contemplated in France by the interwar period. The concept was primarily championed by organized labour, socialist and communist parties. The labour movement has an abiding interest in regulation of international migration. Punishment for infraction of regulations concerning seasonal agricultural employment of aliens in Imperial Germany was deportation of the alien workers. Yet, employers were at least equally culpable. Employer sanctions remedy this discrepancy.

In North America, the concept was advocated by the Mexican government during the Bracero policy period, 1942 to 1964. The Mexican government saw penalties for illegal alien employment as a way to prevent employers from hiring Mexicans outside the legal framework of the US– Mexican bilateral agreement concerning temporary employment of Mexicans. Employer sanctions were to have been enacted in 1952, but they were eliminated at the last minute. Instead, the Texas Proviso to the 1952 law was interpreted as prohibiting punishment of employers for illicit employment of aliens. This situation prevailed until 1986.

In Western Europe and in other industrial democracies, enactment of reinforcement or laws punishing illegal employment of aliens coincided with an upsurge in concern over illegal migration in the 1970s. Typically, these laws have been refined and penalties made more extensive and severe since then. Chart 1 (at the end of the chapter) summarizes the evolution of French measures from 1976 to 1993. More recently, Japan and the United States have joined the ranks of industrial democracies punishing illegal alien employment. Several non-OECD countries have also adopted such laws. Such laws are now commonplace. Australia and the United Kingdom constitute special cases. In Australia, illegal employment of aliens violates terms of the awards which result from collective bargaining between employer and labour-organizations and which regulate employment. In the United Kingdom, employers can be punished for harbouring aliens, which can include employing them. Neither country, however, has laws specifically prohibiting and penalizing illegal employment of aliens.

Over the past decade, enforcement of employer sanctions has been increasingly scrutinized by scholars and policy makers. Reports on enforcement of employer sanctions and other laws designed to deter illegal migration are now regularly made by a number of governments, including, most importantly, France, Germany and the United States. There are quite divergent assessments made of the efficacy of such laws. Politically, enforcement of employer sanctions was most controversial in the United States. Although most Americans support the concept, opponents of the imposition of employer sanctions ranged from employers to civil libertarians. Many Hispanic organizations feared that enactment of employer sanctions would increase discrimination in employment against Hispanics. As a whole, Hispanics were roughly split on the issue.

The controversies that have raged in the United States over the wisdom of employer sanctions have only been faintly echoed elsewhere. Generally, the concern is that employer sanctions are insufficiently enforced and therefore constitute only a weak deterrent to illegal alien employment. Most critics of the status quo seem to want more enforcement of employer sanctions. Nevertheless, some critics regard employer sanctions as a failure, as derisory, or as more important for their symbolism and their legitimization of control policies than for their dissuasive effects upon illegal migration.

Problems and issues in enforcement of employer sanctions are numerous. As in the realm of border and port-of-entry control, allocation of personnel and budgetary resources obviously affects enforcement. In Western Europe, since roughly 1970, the prevailing trend has been slow, incremental expansion of personnel and budgetary resources for enforcement of measures against illegal migration. In Germany and, more recently, France, the effort against illegal alien employment has been assumed within a broader effort to deter and punish all forms of illegal employment (Marie 1994). In this optic, illegal alien employment constitutes only one aspect of a broader problem of delinquency which principally involves citizens, not aliens.

Several countries publish statistics on enforcement of various legal provisions punishing illegal alien employment. Interpretation of these figures is difficult since one never knows, for instance, whether an increase in violations reflects an increase in illegal alien employment and, therefore, a weakening or absent deterrent effect, or whether the upswing suggests more vigorous enforcement and a complementary gain in deterrence. Do decreases in detected infractions reflect gains in deterrence or a weakening of commitment by enforcement services to prevention of illegal alien employment? As long as questions like these persist, assessments of the efficacy of employer sanctions will vary. There is no incontrovertible way of measuring the deterrent effects of employer sanctions.

The French data on imposition of an administrative fine for the illegal employment of aliens (see Table 5) need to be interpreted with care. Many of these fines are never paid. However, these statistics do not include data on complementary punishments, such as fines levied for non-payment of payroll taxes. The results of a recent French study of punishment for illegal employment presented in Table 6 reveal that employers are, in fact, punished for illegal alien employment. Indeed, they are punished more severely than comparable offenders. Many of these punished are themselves aliens.

As for other effects of such laws, an agency of the US government did conclude that employer sanctions had exacerbated employment discrimination against minorities. This finding, however, has been hotly disputed, and many dismiss it as politically motivated. The finding set in motion a process that could have led to the repeal of employer sanctions, but other remedies were found in measures designed to prevent and punish such discrimination. Allegations of discrimination heard in the US apparently are *sui generis*. Discrimination has not been a major concern elsewhere, although there was some discussion of it in the British context.

Enforcement of laws prohibiting illegal alien employment is usually a responsibility of several services, most notably labour inspectors, immigration agents and various police corps. Co-ordination of enforcement has been a major obstacle but progress has been made on this front in

Table 5 Evolution of citations for the illegal employment of aliens in France communicated to the Office for International Migrants (OMI), and notifications of the special fine

Year	Citations	Notifications
1977/8	1 899	1 899
1979	2 151	2 151
1980	1 313	1 313
1981	1 844	1 844
1982	684	684
1983	1 143	1 143
1984	1 268	1 268
1985	1 316	1 316
1986	1 188	1 188
1987	1 547	1 547
1988	1 702	1 702
1989	1 773	1 773
1990	1 508	607
1991	3 250	1 220
1992	2 356	2 498

Source: *L'Office des Migrations Internationales, numéro spécial d'actualités migrations* (1992), p. 78. Between 1977 and 1989, OMI statistics were only kept for notifications.

Table 6 Sentencing for routine violations of French laws prohibiting illegal employment in 1988–9, by nationality

Nature of conviction (Nationality of convicted)	Total	Convictions — Imprisonment			Convictions — Fines		
		Total	Confirmed	Av. Term (mths)	Total	Confirmed	Av. Levy (in francs)
Doing illegal work	2346	544	122	4.0	1710	1417	3900
(French)	1769	369	71	3.5	1331	1086	3913
(EC)	131	31	8	–	94	82	3961
(non-EC)	363	133	41	4.9	216	189	3867
(N. African)	199	63	19	4.6	127	113	4180
(Turkish)	32	–	–	–	24	20	3675
Recourse to illegal work	993	153	20	3.2	808	708	4000
(French)	819	121	15	3.0	669	584	4030
(EC)	41	6	1	–	35	33	3557
(non-EC)	90	21	3	–	66	55	4213
(N. African)	58	12	2	–	44	37	4054
(Turkish)	15	–	–	–	10	6	5333
Regulations concerning alien employees	1329	346	74	4.3	954	886	5000
(French)	713	117	20	4.6	572	526	4878
(EC)	99	9	1	–	89	83	5031
(non-EC)	462	207	51	4.3	252	241	5333
(N. African)	220	77	20	3.1	143	137	5025
(Turkish)	78	47	17	5.7	30	30	4493

Source: adapted from *Infostat Justice*, No. 29, September 1992, p. 5

both Western Europe and the United States. Enforcement agents frequently have multiple priorities, and enforcement of laws prohibiting illegal alien employment is not necessarily one of them. Labour inspectors, in particular, may feel that punishment of employers for illegal alien employment detracts from their primary function of protecting employee rights and safeguarding their welfare.

An inter-agency task force was created in France in 1976 to co-ordinate and encourage enforcement of a panoply of laws designed to deter illegal migration. Much of its educational effort has focused on enforcement agents. It proposes new laws and regulations to enhance enforcement. It also has sought to sensitize judges to the social harm caused by illegal employment of aliens. Its patient work has borne fruit. French courts – particularly in the Paris area – now tend to take prosecution and punishment of employers hiring illegal aliens more seriously. Repeat or egregious offenders can be jailed. Administrative fines are automatically levied but can be appealed. Criminal proceedings can result in additional fines and other punishments. Since illegal alien employment is often accompanied by other infractions of labour laws, complementary fines and punishment (e.g. for non-payment of social security taxes) are not unusual.

There are reasons to believe that enforcement of laws prohibiting illegal alien employment has become more effective in Western Europe over the past fifteen years. However, in many respects, it remains insufficient. More enforcement agents with large budgets for field and factory inspections would increase deterrence. Revisions of laws have made it more difficult for employers to elude detection and prosecution.

Concurrently, prospects for effective enforcement are clouded by a number of discouraging trends. Declining unionization means more and more places of employment do not have a union presence, which often made illegal employment of aliens more difficult. This does not imply that illegal alien employment is necessarily adverse to union interests, since some illegal aliens do join unions and are protected by them.

More importantly, employment in medium- and large-scale firms is declining, while employment in small firms is expanding (Marie 1994). This evolution is ominous because small enterprises are most likely to hire aliens illegally who lack employment authorization. And, these same small firms are the most difficult for labour inspectors and other enforcement agencies to monitor. Trends in the construction industry, in particular, with growing utilization of sub-contractors, often make enforcement of employer sanctions quite complex undertakings.

Global trends towards economic liberalization and reductions in economic rigidities do not bode well for the enforcement of employer sanctions. To paraphrase remarks by a head of the French inter-agency task force, it is difficult to ask for authorization to hire more labour inspectors specialized in detection and punishment of illegal alien employment in a period of down-sizing government.

Nevertheless, it is likely that most industrial democracies will continue to enhance incrementally their capability to detect and punish employers who illegally hire aliens since there are few responsible alternatives to such a course of action. And, political measures to do something concrete about illegal migration are likely to grow. Enforcement of employer sanctions, for all its difficulties and shortcomings, is far preferable to mass roundups and expulsions or measures like Proposition 187 in California, which seeks to deter illegal migration by blocking immigrant access to governmental services.

In the United States, document fraud has hurt effective enforcement of the 1986 law. The Commission on Immigration Reform has recommended that the US government institute a secure employment verification document. This measure, along with increased enforcement, personnel and resources, would greatly increase the deterrent effects of the 1986 law.

Legalization

Legalization policy enables aliens without required residency and/or employment authorization to acquire legal status. Such policies vary greatly in their eligibility requirements, administration and results. Most legalizations have occurred in OECD states, but as seen in Table 7, a number of Asian, South American and African countries have enacted them as well. There also have been informal legalizations. For instance, Germany formally eschews legalization policy, but it has discretely permitted small numbers of irregular-status aliens to accede to legal status from time to time. In Switzerland, another country which eschews legalization, a certain number of aliens, mainly denied asylum-seekers, are deemed cases of unusual administrative rigor and allowed to accede to legal status.

Calculated assessment of the administrative feasibility and/or likely results of legalization policy appear less central than other motivations to understanding why governments choose or choose not to adopt legalization policy. Western European legalization policies were often linked to other policies designed to foster the integration of legally admitted foreign populations. Legalization policies also sometimes arise from an acknowledgement that past governmental policies, particularly the absence of explicit laws forbidding and punishing illegal alien employment, tacitly served to encourage unauthorized migration. This factor influenced advocacy of legalization policy in the United States in combination with the aforementioned reluctance to pursue a mass deportation or expulsion policy. In many industrial democracies, legalization policies have preceded the imposition or reinforcement of other policies to deter illegal migration — particularly employer sanctions. Legalization is the carrot, followed by the stick of employer sanctions.

Table 7 Legalization policies and results, 1980–92

Country	Year	Aliens legalized
Canada	1980	11 000
Venezuela	1980–1	351 000
France	1981–2	124 101
Argentina	1984	142 330
Gabon	1985	110 000
Italy	1987–8	105 176
Spain	1985–6	43 815
United States	1987–8	3 000 000
Spain	1991	108 848
France	1992	10 000
Republic of Korea	1992	61 000
Malaysia	1992	320 000
Taiwan	1991–2	22 549

Source: Adapted from Stalker 1994: 152; Meissner *et al.* 1986; and other sources

The Venezuelan legalization policy of 1980–81 was preceded by the announcement of a planned crackdown on remaining illegal immigrants who shunned the legalization opportunity. Nonetheless, the total of 351,000 legalized fell well below expectations. Estimates of Venezuela's illegal alien residents, as elsewhere, varied wildly – from the government's estimate of 1.2 million to 3.5 million out of a population of 13.5 million. When the crackdown did come, it netted only 6,000 persons (Meissner *et al.* 1986: 12). Venezuelan specialists gave seven possible explanations for the shortfall of legalizations relative to the estimated size of the illegal population. They cited a problem of securing the trust of the immigrants, the reluctance of those with other legal problems to step forward, the restriction cut-off dates for eligibility, the reluctance of many employers to co-operate, an excessive focus upon urban residents to the detriment of illegal residents in rural areas, the obligation for legalized aliens to remain in Venezuela for one year after legalization and the reluctance of temporary immigrants to sever ties with their homelands (Meissner *et al.* 1986: 11–12).

Eligibility requirements have varied markedly. Some legalizations, like that in France in 1980 and a supplemental Spanish programme in 1991, were restricted to specific nationalities (Turks and Moroccans, respec-tively). The 1980 French programme was also industry-specific, for garment industry workers only. Typically, there is a cut-off date for eligibility to apply which requires aliens to document that they were in the country prior to that date. Otherwise, the legalization opportunity would be open-ended and permit any and all aliens to qualify for the grant of legal status. Germany has formally eschewed legalization policy precisely because authorities fear it would attract additional illegal migrants. The cut-off date is intended to prevent that. One of the principal difficulties of the major US legalization programme authorized by the Immigration Reform and Control Act (IRCA) of 1986 was its 1 January 1982 cut-off date for eligibility, although the legalization programme did not begin until May 1987. Hence, illegal resident aliens who had arrived after 1 January 1982 were not eligible for legalization unless they could qualify in one of the smaller legalization programmes authorized by IRCA. A less gaping disjuncture arose in the French legalization of 1981/2.

Policies also vary in terms of the criteria used to establish proof of residency and/or employment. Under French legalization policies, applicants in some cases needed to prove that they were employed in order to qualify. To encourage employers' co-operation in 1981, participating employers were forgiven past legal infractions. Nonetheless, many employers would not co-operate, so some potential applicants found it difficult to document their claims. In other instances, employers appeared to have provided false documentation, sometimes for a fee. Critics of the 1982 legalization in France claim that it encouraged fraud and failed to legalize much of the target population. Governmental authorities claimed success. The legalization policy was prolonged beyond the legalization period originally foreseen, and additional categories of aliens, particularly seasonal workers in agriculture, eventually were permitted to legalize. Recent legalizations in Spain and Italy were also prolonged beyond original cut-off dates, and there was advocacy of a similar course of action in the United States.

In the major US programme authorized by IRCA, employment was not an eligibility requirement; only residency was. However, in a second programme, which had many different rules, documentation of employment in agriculture was required. Questionable implementation of the second programme resulted in widespread fraud.

In addition, in the United States substantial fees were required from applicants. This may have discouraged some applications. Situations in which some family members qualified for legalization, and others did not, also caused concern. Eventually, a family fairness policy evolved which protected such ineligible family members from deportation.

The efficacy of legalization policies in South America was thought to have been greatly affected by public and community relations efforts prior to the onset of the legalization periods. Two of the difficulties faced by governments are mistrust of their intentions and eligible illegal immigrants not knowing about the legalization opportunity and how to take advantage of it. The semi-formal legalization in Gabon sheds some light on the general problem faced by governments. In 1985, all aliens were invited to register with authorities by going to designated points around the country. The act of registration entitled aliens to a document which, in effect, legalized their status and gave them certain rights. About half of the 110,000 aliens who registered were in irregular legal status. The Gabonese government threatened to expel aliens who did not register. However, since aliens were asked about their authorization to be in Gabon on the registry form, it was thought that many did not register for fear of admitting their illegality (Ricca 1990: 24).

To help overcome this distrust and fear, the Argentine government undertook a publicity and public relations campaign and tried to work through the Roman Catholic church and various cultural and labour organizations to reassure migrants. The French in 1981/2 and the United States in 1986/7 tried to emulate this, but opinions vary as to their success. Over three-quarters of the three million successful legalization applicants in the United States were Mexicans. It is possible, indeed probable, that large numbers of eligible illegal migrants did not apply despite governmental efforts to reassure migrants and their representatives. Evaluations of the efficacy or success of the French legalization of 1981/2 have hinged on contrasting perceptions of the degree to which legalization reduced resident illegal populations. There is no scholarly consensus on this and no way of knowing whether the claims of the government or those of its critics are more accurate.

Administrative organization and implementation of legalization policies also constitutes a key variable. In some French legalization policies, employers were able to legalize their employees. In the Spanish programme of 1992, the Moroccan Embassy and consulates received applications which were then transmitted to Spanish authorities. The administrative structures and procedures involved in the 1981/2 French legalization were hailed by some as exemplary.

The procedure was initiated by the alien or by organizations acting on his or her behalf. The major French trade unions and pro-immigrant associations were empowered to aid aliens to prepare applications. The application itself was costless. The government hoped to offset part of the costs by payment of a fee by employers to the National Immigration Office when their illegal employees had legalized (particularly since the French government has long levied a fee on employers who legally hire foreign workers).

Applicants were required to provide information about their manner of entry, employment history and details about their personal lives. All this information was declared confidential and could not be used against the applicant. Applications could be submitted to local mayors' offices, police stations or prefectures. They were then forwarded to departmental labour and employment ministry offices for processing. Administration was decentralized at the department level — the principal sub-unit in French public administration — but was co-ordinated and monitored by a group of administrators who attempted to ensure consistent implementation of the legalization policy nation-wide. There is disagreement over whether they succeeded in doing so. Applications then were reviewed at the departmental level. About 80 per cent of applications were approved without further review. Those denied were sent to review panels where 31 per cent were approved. Finally, there were further appeal opportunities.

The major legalization programme and the special programme for agricultural workers authorized by IRCA in the United States were administered differently. In the major programme, the Immigration and Naturalisation Service established a network of 107 regional legalization centres. Applications could be made by entities – such as Roman Catholic churches designated as Qualified Designated Entities (QDE) – which were approved to pre-screen and counsel applicants. Most applications (over 80 per cent), however, were made directly to the legalization centres by the individual alien concerned. The use or non-utilization of a QDE had financial implications and may have affected the overall effectiveness of the legalization. As it was, financial constraints caused some of the legalization centres to close and others to pare their staffs.

One key difference between the major legalization programme and the one for agricultural workers was the ability of applicants to the latter to apply at the US–Mexico border. Applicants immediately received temporary authorization for employment in the United States. Not unsurprisingly, fraudulent applications were rampant, and rates of denial were considerably higher than in the major programme, where only about 2 per cent of applicants were denied.

Do legalization policies attract additional illegal immigration, as German authorities fear? There is reason to think that the French programme of 1981/2 did. There are credible reports of additional inflows despite governments' efforts to prevent them. While legalization policies enable aliens to accede to legal status and thereby improve their lives, they do not eliminate factors within and without societies which foster illegal migration and illegal alien employment. In France and the United States, illegal alien residency and employment is probably as extensive today as it was prior to the legalization policies of the 1980s. By any objective measure, the US legalization programme for agricultural workers was a fiasco (Martin 1994b) which will likely preclude serious consideration of legalization as an option in the future.

One major benefit of legalization policies in France and the United States was the additional insight such programmes provided into the sociology of migration. To the extent that legalization policies did not succeed in legalizing illegal alien populations, however, so too might the profiles and data derived from interviewing only part of the illegal population be skewed.

What, if any, effect legalization policies have on immigration debates and politics in general is unclear. One suspects that the French legalization policy of 1981/2 contributed to an anti-immigrant backlash manifest in the electoral successes of the National Front by 1983. Legalization policies may also serve to weaken the credibility of governmental immigration policies, but there is no compelling evidence of this. While the French government allowed tens of thousands of denied asylum-seekers to apply for legalization in 1992 (one in a long series of 'exceptional measures'), there would appear to be little support for a repetition of such policies in either France or the United States. The dramatic political changes in Italy in 1994 make it unlikely that legalization policy will be renewed there as well. However, French historical experience may be particularly instructive. Legalization constituted the major mode of legal admission to residency in France from 1945 to 1970. Thereafter, all legalizations have been termed 'exceptional'. Yet they recur. They do so because they offer a humanitarian solution to problems at little short-term cost. Over the long run, however, recourse to legalization may undermine migration control policies and erode the perceived legitimacy of immigrant settlement and incorporation which is so important to the long-term integration of immigrants into their host societies.

Reflections on the past and the future

From what international relations specialists term a realist perspective, utopian visions of the transcendence of sovereign states are illusory and a prescription for trouble. Even in the region with the most advanced socio-economic political integration, states remain the authoritative decision makers and the locus of democratic legitimacy. The European Union has recently received the authorization to fashion a European migration policy, but this will be accomplished gradually through inter-governmental consultation and co-operation in which the lowest common denominator is likely to prevail. European Union member states (particularly the United Kingdom) have jealously guarded their prerogatives in immigration regulation. And, it should be obvious that progress towards regional economic and political integration in the European context has not diminished immigration control concerns and problems.

For better or worse, the sovereign state system will endure over the fathomable future, but processes of globalization and regional integration aimed at fashioning a progressively more interdependent, transnational world will endure as well. This situation seems fated to make prevention of illegal migration an even more salient concern for many states in the future. As in the past, states endowed with higher standards of living, employment-generating economies, living space, natural resources and political stability will be affected the most, as will states experiencing demographic decline. However, all states are concerned about regulation of international migration. Indeed, in many respects, less endowed states and societies are the most at risk because governments lack the resources to regulate migration.

The imperative of immigration regulation might be likened to a Sisyphean fate. It is a foregone conclusion that whatever the steps taken to prevent illegal migration, they will fall short of totally and demonstrably achieving their objectives. There will always be critics pointing to gaps between stated policies and attainment of those objectives. It is important to take such criticism constructively and to learn from it. The genesis and implementation of effective policies – particularly in democratic settings – is sometimes decades in the making. International migration has not been a priority concern until recently. While migration-related problems and issues abound, and it is regrettable that this was not a top agenda issue in the past, it also is important that governments do not overreact and act unduly harshly or rashly. Many of the mass deportations and expulsions witnessed around the world seem to arise in situations which fester due to governmental neglect and then are 'remedied' in a draconian way. Such measures can foster international conflict.

The trend towards linkage of migration control to national security considerations, perceptible in industrial democracies since the 1980s, is likely to continue. Although the risk of war remains high in many areas, as prospects for conventional warfare decline due to the end of the Cold War, states rich and poor will increasingly view international migration as germane to national security. And well they should. International migration affects public order, and cohesion of societies and the legitimacy of governments. Mobilization of opposition to immigrants or the disenfranchisement and alienation of immigrants can adversely affect political stability. Migrants are often terribly vulnerable to crimes and violence. Violence against them and perceived harsh treatment can adversely affect bilateral and regional relations.

Border and port-of-entry control, visa policies, interior controls and deportation capabilities, legalization and employer sanctions comprise the core of modern migration control policies. States fashion their policies out of these specific instrumentalities and the resources they commit to them, but they must then complement their migration policies with linkages to policy making in related areas which bear on migration.

As the late Reinhard Bendix reminded us, governments will be influenced by demonstration effects and can usefully learn from experiences and mistakes elsewhere. Such cross-national learning is much in evidence in the immigration control area. But ultimately, each state will fashion an original response to the challenge of migration control in the late twentieth century, and this is how it should be (Bendix 1978).

However, decisions made in this area have major implications for other states and societies, making bilateral and regional consultations on international migration control measures a wise prescription. This is how sovereign states constructively adapt to the constraints and exigencies of globalization and an increasingly interdependent world. How skillfully this is done will probably greatly affect future prospects for regional and global order.

Chart 1 Principal steps in the evolution of French policy to curb illegal alien employment and the underground economy

Date	Measure
11 July 1972	Illegal employment made an indictable offence. Initial ordinances promulgated concerning temporary work, trafficking of labour and manpower leasing.
July 1974	Non-seasonal alien worker recruitment suspended.
31 December 1975	Civil law regulating subcontracting in public and private markets adopted.
1974–76	Laws which provide for the hiring of labour inspectors specializing in control of foreign labour in 23 'priority' departments adopted.
10 July 1976	A 'special contribution' civil fine payable to the National Immigration Office for illegal employment of alien workers instituted.
10 August 1976	Interministry Mission to Combat Manpower Trafficking created.
1980–83	Four governmental studies of illegal work and the under ground economy completed.
17–29 October 1981	New laws make illegal employment of aliens a more serious offence – a misdemeanor subject to police courts, and fines are increased.
2 February 1982	New ordinances reinforce regulation of manpower leasing.
31 August 1983	Cabinet reinforces policy against illegal alien migration and employment by:
	● the creation of 55 new positions for labour inspectors specializing in control of foreign labour;
	● the creation of department-level interagency committees to combat illegal alien migration and employment in 23 'priority' departments;
	● the creation of a branch office of the Interministry Liaison Mission to Combat Manpower Trafficking in Marseilles;
	● augmentation of the 'special contribution' civil fine from 500 to 2000 times the minimum hourly wage (30,200 francs as of 1 January 1990).
25 July 1985	Illegal work made a misdemeanour.
16 January 1986	Laws pertaining to illegal alien migration and employment extended to overseas departments.
14 March 1986	Decree replaces department-level interagency committees created 31 August 1983, with similar committees with a broader mandate to combat illegal work (the underground economy) in addition to illegal alien migration and employment.
27 January 1987	Law redefines illegal employment infraction. The definition of illegal work is simplified and its applicability broadened.
21 July 1988	Amnesty law expressly excludes those punished for illegal work, illegal alien employment and manpower trafficking and leasing.
13 January 1989	Law again redefines the definition of an illegal employment infraction.
16 January 1989	Interministerial decree extends the competency of the Interministry Liaison Mission to the underground economy.

Date	Measure
10 July 1989	New labour law measures adopted which: • newly incriminate illegal alien employment through intermediaries; • redefine and more severely punish violation of the prohibition against reimbursement of fees paid to the International Migrations Office for foreign worker recruitment.
2 January 1990	Labour law amendment enables officers of the Judiciary police, after court authorization, to enter workplaces on the presumption of illegal employment or illegal alien employment.
12 July 1990	Law modifies labour code articles pertaining to subcontracting and leasing of labour. Fines for infractions from 8,000 to 40,000 FF. Unions authorized to act on behalf of the workers involved.
25 July 1990	Decree redefines the role of department-level commissions.
3 January 1991	Law extends authority to bring charges for illegal work infractions to social security and other enforcement agents.
18–22 April 1991	Government makes grant of employment authorization to Poles contingent on no adverse labour market effect.
26 September 1991	Asylum-seekers no longer automatically authorized to work (as of 1 October 1991).
1 October 1991	Decree facilitates abrogation of short-term visas for aliens who work without authorization.
3–4 October 1991	Government acts to facilitate recovery of social security payments due in illegal work cases.
30 October 1991	Decree reinforces the role of judicial authorities within departmental commissions and associates more fully socio-professional representatives in department-level campaigns against illegal work.
31 December 1991	Major new law overhauls and brings together legislation concerning illegal employment.
24 January 1992	Prime minister authorizes departmental officials to sign partnership agreements with unions and employer organizations to reduce illegal employment.
31 December 1992	Experimental requirement obligating employers to declare their employment intentions prior to actual employment of an employee made a general requirement for all employers.
29 March 1993	Decree authorizes social security organisms to use a national identification system to verify whether employers have complied with the obligation to declare all employees prior to the start of employment.

Sources: Hue 1990: 4–7; Marie n.d.

2

Guest worker policies: an international survey

Philip L. Martin

Guest or foreign worker programmes aim to add workers to the labour force without adding permanent residents to the population. This chapter emphasizes programmes initiated by labour-importing countries during or after World War II in response to employer requests for foreign workers to curb labour shortages. It focuses on two distinct types of programmes: US programmes that aimed to deal with labour shortages in agriculture by importing non-immigrant workers, and German programmes that sought to curb economy-wide or macro labour shortages with probationary immigrant workers.

Rationale for importing workers

There are four major reasons for countries to initiate programmes to import foreign workers:

(1) To alleviate labour shortages — either macro economy-wide shortages or shortages in particular industries, occupations, and areas.
(2) To better manage inevitable migration, as occurs after binational labour markets are created, or to deal with commuters in border areas.
(3) To provide work-and-learn opportunities, especially for foreign youth, so that the country of immigration both gains access to another country's workers and can claim to be accelerating the development of their countries of origin.
(4) To promote socio-economic integration, as in the European Union.

Table 8   Common rationales for guest worker programmes

Rationale	Typical origin	Examples
Labour shortages	Macro or economy-wide or sectoral – agriculture, mining construction, private households	Macro: European guest worker programmes Micro: US H-2 and Bracero programmes
Manage inevitable migration	Deal with micro illegal immigration problems	US Bracero programme after Operation Wetback in 1954; German seasonal worker programme, Malaysian worker programme
Recognize that borders can divide 'natural' labour markets		Most European countries have border commuters, as do the US and Mexico and the US and Canada. There is also weekly and seasonal commuting
Provide training and development assistance	Manufacturing, nannies	Japanese training system; US nanny programme

Most foreign worker programmes begin as efforts to relieve economy-wide labour shortages *or* labour shortages in particular industries and occupations (see Table 8). In some cases, after bilateral or multilateral labour markets are created, the rationale for foreign worker programmes is expanded to admit otherwise unauthorized workers through legal channels and thereby improve immigration management.

Most industrial nations also have programmes under which young foreigners, in particular, are able to engage in work and study which, upon their return, accelerates economic development in the country of origin. Such programmes expanded significantly over the past decade, and are the primary rationale for Japan and Korea to import foreign workers. Lastly, as in the case of the European Union, labour migration is seen as a factor that could help bind member countries closer together and therefore is sometimes part of efforts to promote political integration.

Labour shortage rationale – macro

During the nineteenth century, countries in North and South America and Australia welcomed immigrants in order to meet general labour shortages. However, in Western Europe in the 1950s most countries were not countries of immigration, so when employers complained of labour shortages, foreign worker programmes were initiated to alleviate what were essentially economy-wide or macro labour shortages.

Although it is true that most guest workers were employed in a handful of industries – manufacturing, mining and construction – and in a few occupations, such as operative and labourer, these industries and occupations in Europe in the 1960s employed at least half the labour force. Micro labour shortage programmes such as the various US programmes to obtain alien farmworkers were meant for an industry and occupation that employed less than 10 per cent of the labour force.

Germany provides a classic example of using guest workers to remedy macro labour shortages. In the early 1960s, when there were five to ten registered job vacancies for each registered jobless worker, four reasons were advanced to justify importing foreign workers (Martin 1998).

(1) The German labour force was shrinking in the early 1960s for demographic and related reasons, such as a delayed baby boom, the spread of education, and better pensions that prompted earlier retirements.

(2) There was a reluctance to risk what was still perceived to be a fragile post-war economic recovery on industrial policies that would have avoided the need for foreign workers, such as the government encouraging firms to pay higher wages or mechanize at home, or lowering trade barriers and promoting investment abroad.

(3) Europe was unifying anyway, and Germany had agreed that Italians and other EC nationals would have freedom of movement rights after 1968. With Italians soon able to enter as they wished, Germany thought it was simply unilaterally regulating the rate at which EC workers would in any event soon arrive.[1]

(4) The early 1960s provided Western Europe with a peculiar international economic environment. Germany had an undervalued currency in a world of fixed exchange rates, so that local and foreign capital was invested there to produce goods for export markets.[2] Germans reinvested their savings inside the country, and American multinationals poured so many dollars into Europe that a French writer warned of *The American Challenge* to Europe's identity.

There was relatively little discussion in the 1950s and 1960s of alternatives to importing foreign workers. The absence of such discussion was later criticized by those who argued that the need to mechanize and encourage labour-intensive industries to move abroad was inevitable, and that it would have been cheaper and better in the long run to start the adjustment process sooner (Schiller *et al.* 1976). In one shorthand expression, it was said that Germany by the 1980s had Turks to integrate, while Japan had robots on its assembly lines.

Labour shortage rationale – micro

In contrast to foreign worker programmes for economy-wide labour shortages, US non-immigrant programmes aim to remedy labour shortages in particular industries and occupations. In the United States, one industry, agriculture, and occupation, farm worker, have consistently taken the lead in requests for temporary foreign workers.

The US agriculture case demonstrates how efforts to use non immigrant programmes to remedy seemingly isolated labour shortages can produce distortion and dependence that affect the wider economy and society. US agriculture since World War II has never employed more than 5 per cent of the labour force as hired wage and salary workers; today US agriculture employs just 2.5 million wage and salary workers at some time during a typical year – about 1 per cent of the US labour force. But over half of the foreign-born Hispanics in the US labour force have had at least one US farm job, and about one-fourth of the total 6 million immigrants who entered the US labour force during the 1980s had at least one farm job, illustrating how using foreign workers to remedy labour shortages in a revolving-door labour market can lead to unanticipated immigration.[3]

Braceros

Foreign workers have typically been admitted for seasonal farm worker jobs in the United States by making exceptions to general immigration policies. The first exception came near the end of World War I, when the United States, which was attempting to limit European immigration with literacy tests and head taxes, exempted Western Hemisphere nationals who were coming to the country to perform seasonal farm work. There was opposition to making this immigration exception but, with 'Food to Win the War' as a motto, California farmers in May 1917 persuaded the US Department of Labour to suspend the head tax and the literacy test, and farmers were permitted to recruit Mexican farmworkers to work in the United States for up to one year. These Mexican workers had contracts requiring them to remain in the employ of the farmer who recruited them or face deportation (Fuller 1942: 19853).[4]

The need for workers who will accommodate themselves to seasonality is as old as agriculture. American agriculture dealt with seasonality in three distinct ways. In most of the United States, diversified family farms relied on large families to help during busy periods; during lull periods, farm families had more leisure time. In the South, plantations were so big that even large families could not handle peak season labour needs and, since warmer weather made the working season longer, slavery was economical. In the West, large farms turned to workers without other job options – usually immigrants excluded from urban jobs by language, ethnicity, and/

or legal restrictions. In this manner, succeeding waves of immigrants – Chinese, Japanese, Filipino, and Mexican – were available for seasonal farm work when they were needed. Farms, railroads and mines soon made business decisions under the assumption that immigrant workers would be available when they were needed – and paid the minimum wage for that time. This helps explain why US employers for decades resisted restrictions on Mexican immigration.[5]

California farmers took the lead in developing arguments for importing foreign farmworkers. They asserted that Americans and European immigrants could not be relied upon to be seasonal farmworkers because farmers 'cannot employ them profitably ... more than 3 or 4 months in the year – a condition of things entirely unsuited to the demands of the European labourer' (Fuller 1942: 19813). Asian and Mexican immigrants fill the bill, the argument went, because 'crouching and bending (farm) operations must be performed in climatic conditions in which only the Orientals and the Mexicans are adapted' (Fuller 1942: 19868).

These assertions obscured the underlying economic justification for immigrant workers: seasonal workers who were paid only when they were needed were cheaper than year-round hired hands. A California farm spokesman in 1872 observed that hiring Chinese immigrants who housed themselves and then 'melted away' when they were not needed made them 'more efficient ... than Negro labour in the South [because] if [Chinese labour] is only employed when actually needed, and is, therefore, less expensive' than slavery (Fuller 1942: 19809).[6] Also, the subsidy implicit in paying seasonal workers only when they were employed raised land prices, giving farmers an incentive to preserve access to immigrant workers and thereby maintain their wealth and/or the value of their investment.

Development patterns in Mexico contributed to the willingness of Mexicans to emigrate seasonally to the US. The seven central states of Mexico – Nuevo Leon, Tamaulipas, Zacatecas, San Luis Potosí, Guanajuato, Jalisco and Michoacán – contributed over half of all migrants to the United States for most of the twentieth century (Cross and Sandos 1981: xvi). During the Mexican Revolution (1913–20), these states became the battleground between the central government in Mexico City and revolutionaries from Mexican states near the US border, and the fighting led most haciendas to reduce their employment. As a result, many Mexicans left. Between 1910 and 1930, by one estimate, 20 per cent left the region, including 1.5 million, or 10 per cent of Mexico's entire population, who migrated to the United States (Cross and Sandos 1981: 9–10).

Despite the binational labour market created during the 1920s, the economic depression and US deportations of Mexicans during the 1930s practically stopped Mexican immigration. However, during World War II, farmers saw another chance to obtain Mexican workers on their terms, and a series of so-called Bracero programmes institutionalized the dependence of farmers on one to two million Mexican workers, many of whom returned year after year, as well as the dependence of many rural Mexicans on the US labour market.

Like many other foreign worker programmes, the Bracero programme was smallest in size during the period of most acute 'labour shortage'. During World War II, admissions peaked at 62,000 in 1944, less than 2 per cent of the nation's four million hired workers. The US government sent unmistakable signals about farm work by admitting Braceros, by permitting interned Japanese to 'volunteer' to do farm work for wages, by sending German prisoners of war to the western states to be farmworkers, and by making federal, state and county prisoners available as farmworkers.

Disputes with Mexico over the treatment of Braceros led to several years of private farmer recruitment in the late 1940s. This suited both Mexican workers and US farmers.[7] The programme quickly changed from one in which Mexican workers were recruited, screened and provided with work contracts in the interior of Mexico to one in which Mexican workers arrived in the United States, found jobs, and then had their status legalized in what came to be termed, even in official US government publications, 'drying out the wetbacks' (President's Commission 1951).[8]

Foreign workers from Mexico were controversial. A President's Commission on Migratory Labour was established in 1951 to determine whether US agriculture needed Mexican immigrants, and it recommended that 'no special measures be adopted to increase the number of alien contract workers beyond the number admitted in 1950', which was 67,500 (President's Commission 1951: 178). However, farmers argued that Braceros were needed to produce food for the Korean War emergency.

In 1951, Congress listened to farmers and enacted PL–78, the Mexican Farm Labour Program, which sowed the seeds for contemporary Mexico-to-US migration by permitting US agriculture to expand and create a demand–pull for Mexican workers. As US workers with the option of seeking non-farm jobs learned that they did not face Bracero competition in non-farm labour markets, they abandoned the farm labour market, and the Bracero share of the workforce harvesting citrus, tomatoes and lettuce soon passed 50 per cent. Farm wages as a percentage of manufacturing wages fell in California during the 1950s, when Braceros set the tone of the farm labour market.

Some argued that the Bracero programme would make it easier to control illegal immigration. However, there was considerable illegal immigration alongside legal Bracero entries. Between 1942 and 1964, there were 4.6 million Braceros admitted and 4.9 million illegal Mexicans apprehended in the United States. Apprehensions peaked during

'Operation Wetback' in 1954, a successful government effort to encourage Mexican workers and US farmers to use the Bracero programme.

The Mexican government was concerned during the late 1940s about its nationals going north illegally and 'The Mexican government, press, and citizen [sic] ... contended that the wetback exodus could be stopped only when [US] employers were penalized for hiring them' (Craig 1971: 75); i.e., Mexico requested that the United States adopt employer sanctions to discourage illegal emigration, since the Mexican constitution prohibits exit from the country except at authorized points.

By the early 1960s, Braceros were essential to harvest only a few crops. As cotton and other geographically dispersed crops were mechanized, the Bracero programme became a non-immigrant programme for a handful of farmers, and political support in the US for its continuation weakened.

The end of the Bracero programme in 1964 provides one of the few examples of how an industry adjusts to the *absence* of immigrant workers. Braceros made up 80 per cent of the harvest workers in California's tomato processing industry in the early 1960s, and growers argued that 'the use of Braceros is absolutely essential to the survival of the tomato industry' (California Senate 1961: 105). What happened when they nonetheless disappeared? The termination of the Bracero programme accelerated the mechanization of the harvest in a manner that quadrupled production to 10 million tons between 1960 and 1990. Cheaper tomatoes permitted the price of ketchup and similar products to drop, helping to fuel the expansion of the fast food industry.

Managing inevitable migration

Foreign worker programmes are sometimes justified as a way to better manage inevitable migration. For example, the 1954 'Operation Wetback' removed illegal Mexican workers and made it easier for US farmers to employ Mexican workers legally. As a result, the number of Mexicans admitted legally as temporary farmworkers or Braceros almost doubled, from 201,000 in 1953 to 399,000 in 1955, and the number of illegal aliens apprehended fell from 886,000 in 1953 to 254,000 in 1955 (Martin 1993: 63).

In 1989, Germany similarly recognized 'inevitable immigration' by creating seasonal worker programmes through which Eastern Europeans could work for up to 90 days on German farms and in German hotels and restaurants. About 170,000 seasonal workers were employed in such programmes in 1993, the equivalent of over 40,000 full-time employees.

Border commuters make up a second type of 'inevitable migration' that acknowledges that natural economic zones and labour markets cross national borders. In Western Europe, there are thousands of persons who live in one nation and commute every work day to a job in another. There are significant two-way commuter flows across the US–Canadian and US–Mexican borders. Many US and Asian managers of maquiladoras in Mexican border areas, for example, live in the United States. In Asia, more than 50,000 Malaysians commute daily to jobs in Singapore. In addition to cross-border commuter workers, there are also commuting shoppers and even commuting students. In many cases, workers commute to nearby nations on a weekly or seasonal basis. Workers commute weekly from the West Bank to Israel, for example, and in northern Malaysia, Thais commute seasonally to harvest rice.

Training for development

Japan and Korea are distinctive in that their rationale for having legal foreign workers is the training of workers, ostensibly to accelerate economic growth in the developing nations from which they come. Since 1954, for example, the Japanese government has had a programme under which young Asians could enter the country to receive training that was expected to accelerate their country's development. There were 40,000 trainees employed in Japan in 1994, 40 per cent of them from China. Most of these trainees – 83 per cent – were employed in manufacturing, usually by small- and medium-sized firms, and most were very well educated by the standards of their countries of origin.

Many Japanese advocate expanding the trainee system to permit up to 500,000 foreigners to enter Japan. To most outside observers, this would mean that Japan is opening itself to foreign workers, and calling them trainees. Trainees get paid $400 to $800 monthly, or one-quarter to one-half as much as similar Japanese workers. The quality and content of the training is left up to each firm, so there is room for abuse in both training and housing that employers are required to provide trainees. There is supposed to be a one-year limit on how long trainees can stay in Japan, although employers are pushing for a two-year limit in order to recoup some of the costs of the training.

On 1 June 1994, South Korea stepped up efforts to detect and deport illegal alien workers, and launched a programme under which the Korean Federation for Small Business could import up to 20,000 foreign trainees for 4200 small businesses. The foreign trainees are to be housed, fed, and paid $260 a month.

Germany has a trainee programme that permits foreigners between the ages of 18 and 40 to work and learn with German employers, and young Germans to make similar arrangements with East European employers. There are about 7000 foreign trainees in Germany, and they are 'hired' regardless of the availability of local workers in the German labour market.

The United States has several programmes through which foreigners can enter and work while they are acquiring experience that will enrich their lives and accelerate development at home; it admitted 253,000 foreign students in 1993, plus 4400 vocational students and 3100 industrial trainees. In addition, there were 198,000 'exchange visitors' admitted in 1993. Although the exchange visitors' programme is meant to be personally enriching, many exchange visitors are young women admitted to care for children in American families.

Regional labour agreements

The fourth major rationale for cross-border labour migration is to promote economic and political integration. The European Economic Community was founded in 1957 on the principle of freedom of movement, and since then the Nordic countries have permitted labour migration among member nations (Widgren 1994: 23).

Within the EEC, however, there was normally a lag between a country joining the community and its nationals having freedom of movement rights. For example, Italians had to wait ten years, until July 1968, for full freedom of movement rights, while Greece, Portugal and Spain had to wait seven years before their nationals had the right to migrate, for example, to France or Germany and compete for jobs on an equal basis with natives.

Freedom of movement has a peculiar meaning within the European Union. Articles 48 through 51 of the Treaty of Rome give EU nationals the right to seek jobs in other member states on an equal basis with natives. The first implementing regulation, No. 15/61 on 16 August 1961 authorized intra-EU migrants to be hired if no local worker was available within three weeks after the vacancy was registered by the employer with the local Employment Service (Böhning 1972: 10). This regulation also called for the eventual establishment of an EU-wide employment service so that unemployed workers in one country could learn of job vacancies in other countries.

A second regulation, 38/64 on 25 March 1964, was applicable to all migrant workers – permanent, seasonal, and frontier. Article 1 of Regulation 38/64 gave intra-EU migrants the right to fill vacancies registered with the employment service without giving local workers hiring priority after three weeks. Regulation 38/64 also gave EC-member states fifteen days to fill job vacancies in other EC countries before those countries could recruit workers in non-EC member states.

Freedom of movement within the EU is today governed by Regulation 1612/68, originally adopted in November 1968 and means that, for example, an Italian worker can enter France and search for a job for up to three months without restriction.[9] If the worker finds regular employment in France within three months, dependent family members (spouse, children and dependent parents) have the right to join him regardless of their nationality and to take their place in the institutions of the host country, which means, *inter alia*, that the children of an intra-EU migrant have the right to attend the host country's schools. Local authorities must issue any necessary work and residence permits valid for at least five years. European Union workers who believe they suffered discrimination in hiring because of national origin may bring suits in the EU Court in Luxembourg. The standard remedy for such discrimination is a cease-and-desist order which instructs the offending employer or public employment service to consider or to serve all EU nationals on an equal basis.

Despite freedom of movement guarantees, it was widely recognized that barriers to migration for employment remained. The Single European Act of 1985 was adopted to implement the four economic freedoms more fully — the free movement of services, goods, capital and people within the twelve-nation European Union — by the end of 1992.

Today, there are about five million EU nationals living in other EU countries, including 1.8 million who are in the host country workforce. Italians in France and Germany are the largest group of intra-EU migrant workers, although there are also a considerable number of Irish workers in Britain and persons from all over the EU in Belgium at EU headquarters. Intra-EU migrant workers from southern Europe in northern European countries tend to be un- or semi-skilled workers, while migrant workers from northern Europe in southern European countries are often skilled or professional workers.

Assessment

Most foreign worker programmes are begun to remedy macro or micro shortages. Both types of labour shortages are often directly or indirectly due to government policies, so that governments are inclined to be sympathetic to employer pleas for foreign workers. In Western Europe in the 1960s, macro labour shortages were largely due to government policies that shrank or stabilized the labour force and maintained an export boom that governments were reluctant to risk choking off with high wages.

In the Middle East, governments in the 1970s used higher oil revenues to launch a construction boom that could be completed quickly only with foreign workers. The foreign companies that won government bids thus received a sympathetic ear to their requests for foreign workers. In countries such as Taiwan, the demand for foreign workers also arises largely from government-funded infrastructure construction projects, and from an export boom fuelled by an undervalued currency. However, most twenty-first century foreign worker programmes are likely to respond to micro rather than macro labour shortages. Even in a country such as Malaysia, which has been growing at 7 to 8 per cent per year for the past decade, labour shortages and foreign workers tend to be concentrated in the plantation and construction sectors rather than throughout the economy.

The problem in most countries is likely to be that of dealing with employer requests for foreign workers to fill plantation, construction or service jobs, not requests for workers from the economic sectors that might justify immigration. In this sense, I expect foreign worker programmes in response to labour shortages to be dealt with in a rifle-fashion with micro non-immigrant programmes, rather than in shotgun-fashion with immigration or probationary immigration programmes.

Labour certification

Labour certification is the process through which governments decide whether foreign workers should be admitted, and if so how many and for how long. In most countries, and in response to most micro labour shortages, the need for foreign workers is checked by the Labour Ministry on a case-by-case basis, and foreign workers are tied to a particular job by a contract that spells out the terms and conditions of their temporary stay in the country.

Macro labour shortages are sometimes met by immigration or probationary immigrant foreign worker programmes that admit a number of foreigners who find their own jobs in the labour market. Permanent immigrants admitted to the United States for economic reasons, for example, are not required to go to work for the US employer who petitioned for their entry. For four years the United States had a programme that could have admitted up to one million alien workers as probationary immigrants; if they performed at least 90 days of qualifying farm work annually, they could have converted their status to that of immigrant.

The distinction between certifying the need for foreign workers to fill a particular job and tying them to it, versus admitting immigrants or probationary immigrants to seek their own jobs, is usually captured in the distinction between contractual and non-contractual foreign worker programmes. Contractual programmes are based on the notion that there is a vacant job to be filled, that the employer makes a good-faith effort to find a local worker to fill it by offering at least a government-approved package of wages and benefits, and then, if local workers cannot be found, the foreign worker receives a contract that spells out his rights and responsibilities. Certifying the need for foreign workers on a job-by-job basis is thus a major policy instrument used by governments to determine where and for how long foreigners will work.

Non-contractual or free agent programmes, by contrast, open a country's border gates to foreign workers who can 'float' from job to job. Immigration and unauthorized workers are examples of 'free agent' foreign worker programmes, but there are programmes under which legal foreign workers are permitted to move from job to job without securing government permission after they have satisfied their initial contracts.

Contractual programmes

Before foreign workers are legally admitted to alleviate labour shortages within the country of immigration, employers who wish to hire them must usually demonstrate to a government agency that local workers are not available to fill the vacant jobs for which foreign workers are being requested – a process termed 'labour certification'. Labour certification works smoothest when the rationale for importing foreign workers is a macro labour shortage, there is little illegal immigration, and the government has strong local labour market institutions to determine whether there is a real need for foreign workers.

Employers generally initiate the labour certification process by asking the Employment Services (ES) or a similar government agency to help find workers to fill vacant jobs. (The ES is the logical agency to turn to, since it is the government agency whose purpose is to help workers to find jobs and employers to find workers.) If the ES agrees that local workers are not available, then the employer receives permission to recruit a certain number of foreign workers for a particular work site and a pre-determined period of time, such as 100 semi-skilled foreign workers to fill assembly line jobs at Opel in Germany for one year. Under some programmes, these foreign workers are recruited in any country and by any means the employer chooses. Under other programmes, the employer is required to recruit workers under the auspices of bilateral agreements.

European labour certification

Labour certification has been smoother in Europe than in the United States, largely because there was general agreement in the 1960s that foreign workers were needed, there was proportionately less illegal immigration than in the United States (except in France), and the Employment Service was a very strong government agency. The labour certification procedure in countries such as Germany and Switzerland began with employer requests for workers to fill individual vacant jobs, but the process can be considered practically blanket certification for assembly-line, construction or mining jobs, because the ES routinely certified such requests during the 1960s.

As an example, a German employer wanting 100 foreign assembly-line workers began the process by advertising the vacancies and notifying the local ES. The ES certified that the employer was offering adequate wages and working conditions, and there was rarely any dispute about what was adequate because many of the German employers requesting foreign workers in the 1960s were unionized, and thus offered a fairly standard package of wages and benefits. However, the ES had the right to demand that local workers, including settled foreign workers, be hired first, and that wage or working condition improvements be made before the need for foreign workers was certified.

Employment service agencies in Europe had enormous credibility with employers in making these certification decisions. In Germany, for example, the ES was making 50 per cent of all job matches annually in the 1960s, and private employment agencies were banned, so there was little second guessing about the need for foreign workers. (In the United States, by contrast, the Department of Labour made less than 10 per cent of all job matches in the 1960s, and today makes only about 4 per cent of the 60 million annual job matches; a Department finding that foreign workers are not needed to fill particular job vacancies is often seen by US employers as only the first step to obtaining eventual court permission to import foreign workers.)

There was usually a minimum two or three week waiting period during which the employer and the ES sought local workers. In Germany, the employer had to ask the workplace's works council to approve the need for foreign workers. In some cases, the ES also had to check that the employer did not exceed a quota on foreign workers; for example, in Switzerland and in many Asian countries, employers may not have more than one-third or two-thirds foreign workers.

Germany and most other Western European nations stopped recruiting unskilled and semi-skilled foreign workers under guest worker programmes in 1973–4, however, foreign workers continue to enter and find jobs, especially at the extremes of the job ladder, and there are very different programmes for the high-level Professional, Technical and Kindred (PTK) categories and usually unskilled seasonal workers. In both Germany and Switzerland, the system for admitting PTK workers today is much like that of the guest worker era, but there is practically blanket certification for high-level PTK foreign workers. If a multinational corporation wants to bring foreign workers temporarily into the country, it must apply to the ES on a job-by-job basis, but in most cases, the firm's assertion is accepted that local workers are not available.

There are also programmes under which mid-level foreign workers (such as nurses) are admitted to Germany and Switzerland. These programmes operate similarly to the PTK system, with job-by-job certification in theory but practically blanket certification in practice.

US labour certification

In the United States, labour certification is a major point of contention, largely because US temporary worker programmes aim to fill micro labour shortages on the basis of weak government labour market institutions, continuing illegal immigration, and often polarized employer and worker advocates. For this reason, a common scenario is this: the employer requests certification of a labour shortage, unions and worker advocates protest that 'there is no shortage of workers, only a shortage of wages', the Employment Service makes a determination of whether foreign workers are needed, the 'losing' employer or worker advocate appeals to the courts, and the courts override the Employment Service if the employer can show that there are likely to be economic losses without the foreign workers and more careful analysis can demonstrate that, without foreign workers, economically feasible adjustments would occur.

The US H–2A programme is a case in point. Farm employers wishing to employ H–2A workers must follow an application process set out by law and regulation. This process requires US employers to file a job order with the local Employment Service office that details the jobs, wages and working conditions for the vacancy(ies) for which H–2A workers are sought. This job order must be filed at least 60 days before the anticipated need for H–2A farmworkers. The Department of Labour/Employment Service then has 40 days to determine whether the job order satisfies its regulations and to issue or deny the employer's request to be certified to import H–2A workers.

US employers wishing to convince the Department of Labour that they need foreign workers must attempt to recruit US workers under regulations that include the employer offering at least a Department-stipulated hourly or piece-rate wage. In order to demonstrate that they attempted to recruit American workers, they must prepare an interstate Employment Service clearance system order to seek workers in other states, and they must offer free housing to the US and H–2A workers.[10] This 'clearance order', in turn, requires the employer not to discriminate in recruitment on the basis of race, sex, marital status, etc., so that employers who recruit solo men because they have only barracks housing can be accused of discrimination against family workers.

The H–2A programme has been the subject of much litigation and debate. Growers denied certification by the Department of Labour have often asked federal district judges to issue injunctions to require that their need for H–2A workers be certified to avoid crop losses. In some cases, the Labour Department refused to certify that there was a shortage of US farmworkers, and a grower wishing to import H–2A workers then went to a federal judge to obtain an order compelling the Immigration and Naturalisation Service nonetheless to admit H–2A workers in order to avoid crop losses. In 1977, for example, Mexican H–2A farmworkers were admitted into Presido, Texas, reportedly after the intervention of President Carter, despite the employer's failure to obtain Labour Department certification that there was a labour shortage (Congressional Research Service 1980: 62). According to one critical review of such practices: 'District courts routinely granted requests through preliminary injunctions that prohibited the Department of Labour from denying certification. These injunctions were often issued in circumstances that suggested bad faith by the growers' (Coleman 1989: 197).

European seasonal workers

France, Switzerland and Germany operate seasonal worker programmes that are similar in purpose to the H–2A programme in the United States. In Switzerland, there is a national quota (110,000) as well as cantonal quotas established on the basis of previous admissions and employer requests for seasonal foreign workers. Most seasonal workers are Portuguese, Spaniards or Yugoslavs, and most arrive on 15 March for stays of about nine months.

Swiss employers request seasonal foreign workers at their local ES or immigration office. Employers usually provide housing for the workers and must offer the prevailing wage as established by collective bargaining agreements.[11] The ES, in conjunction with immigration authorities, matches seasonal workers with employer requests by taking into account the previous year's employer experience, the canton quota, and this year's employer requests. There is apparently no formal appeal if, for example, an employer requests ten seasonal workers and is assigned only eight.

The workers are deployed to their employers in the spring, and they depart in the autumn. Many – about two-thirds by one estimate – return year after year. A seasonal worker can become an annual worker by working 36 months within four years, and each year about 10,000, or 10 per cent, of the seasonal workers make this transition to non-seasonal status. In this sense, the Swiss seasonal worker programme is also a probationary immigration system which permits alien workers to convert from seasonal to annual worker and eventually to immigrant status.

Switzerland is a nation of small employers. Nestlé, the country's largest employer, has about 2300 employees. The Swiss system for allocating seasonal workers among its small employers appears to work well because of informal and local consultation and negotiation between employers and government agencies.

The alien workers appear to be extraordinarily dependent on their Swiss employers, since they are dispatched in groups of four or five to an employer. According to one estimate, about one-third of the seasonal workers in Switzerland do not return from one year to the next, one-third return for several years (and some of these returning migrants qualify for the annual immigrant worker status), and one-third are more than one-year but less than committed seasonal workers.[12]

Since 1989, German employers wishing to hire workers for jobs that last 90 days or less have been able to recruit Eastern Europeans by name or anonymously. About 170,000 seasonal workers were employed in German restaurants and on German farms in 1993, the equivalent of over 40,000 full-time employees. The seasonal worker programme was made more employer-friendly in 1994, with a form of blanket certification that permits employers to have their anticipated need for foreign workers certified in advance.

Labour importer/exporter arrangements

There are three major types of arrangements between labour importing and exporting countries. Most common are bilateral agreements between labour importers and exporters that detail recruitment procedures in the labour-exporting country and establish at least minimal contract terms. Some bilateral agreements also deal with remittances and returns. Turkey, for example, was reluctant in the 1960s to permit work contracts to be renewed, preferring other workers to 'have their turn' to work in Germany.

There are also multilateral agreements, such as the freedom of movement clause of the EU's Treaty of Rome, which guarantees nationals of member states the right to work in another member state. The Nordic countries have a similar multilateral agreement permitting freedom of movement without screening to determine whether citizen workers are available to fill vacant jobs.

Most foreign workers today enter labour-importing nations under unilateral agreements. This means that the laws and regulations of the immigration country spell out what a domestic employer must do to receive permission to import foreign workers, and the conditions of their employment in the labour-importing country, but do not specify where or how foreign workers are recruited.

Many countries try to regulate the domestic activities of foreign recruitment agents and those of their own nationals in arranging foreign jobs for their citizens, but in most cases, such efforts are ineffective at best, and may ultimately hurt rather than help workers. For example, the Philippines – the world's second leading country of emigration – has an extensive set of regulations meant to protect its nationals who find jobs abroad, but their effect seems to have been to encourage workers to pay 25 per cent of their wages to a middleman, either a registered recruitment agent or a smuggler.

Recruitment

Once approved to employ foreign workers, employers must find them and persuade them to accept vacant jobs outside their country of origin. In Western Europe, government agencies — usually the Employment Service — played an important role in this recruitment process, while in the United States and Asia, recruitment was typically left to the private sector.

German employers could request foreign workers by name (nominative recruitment) or simply ask for a certain number of workers with or without certain skills (anonymous recruitment). Migrant workers were screened for health, skills and moral character in their country of origin, and they received a translated work contract, their work and residence permits in the form of a visa stamped in their passports, and train or plane tickets to their destination.

Most European employers relied on their own country's Employment Service to recruit workers for them. This means that a request for 100 assembly line workers in Germany would be sent to the German ES office in Istanbul. German officials there would screen Turks who had applied for jobs in Germany, and provide those who had accepted the assembly-line jobs with a train or plane ticket to the German workplace. In the early 1970s, several thousand foreign workers arrived in this manner each day. Some large employers even sent their own recruiters abroad to screen foreign workers.

Foreign workers usually arrived at their German workplaces within one month after the initial request was filed; most of the delay was caused by the two- to three-week period in which the local ES sought local workers. Most employers who wanted foreign workers in the 1960s were at least medium-sized manufacturers, and they could plan their hiring schedules so that the three to four weeks required for certification, recruitment and transportation to the workplace did not interfere with production schedules.

The guest worker system remains on the books in most Western European countries. However, since 23 November 1973, Germany has refused most employer requests for unskilled alien workers from non-EU nations under this system.[13] German employers can recruit workers in other EU nations privately, or in co-operation with the German or another EU country's Employment Service, since wage and salary workers are guaranteed freedom of movement by Article 48 of the Treaty of Rome, but the German ES no longer maintains missions in Turkey and other non-EU nations that have workers ready and willing to work in Germany. In 1991 Germany tried unsuccessfully to recruit Spanish construction workers — before Spanish workers had freedom of movement rights through the Spanish ES.

Worker rights

Foreign workers are usually admitted to fill a particular job for a named employer and for a pre-determined period of time. However, once in the country, their status falls into one of two categories: they are either *non immigrants*, whose rights remain constant regardless of their behaviour, or they are *probationary immigrants*, who acquire more rights if they are still needed and if they are performing satisfactorily. The expansive nature of worker rights under probationary immigrant programmes tends to produce more worker settlement and family unification.

In classic immigration countries such as the United States, foreign workers are typically non-immigrants: successful completion of one or more non-immigrant work contracts plays no role in becoming an immigrant. Non-immigrants may marry citizens or legal immigrants and thereby adjust their status, but their successful completion of work contracts does not in itself give them priority for immigrant status.

Non-immigrant Asian countries similarly aim to prevent non-immigrant foreign workers from becoming immigrants. In countries such as Singapore, not even marriage to a citizen automatically enables a foreign worker to become an immigrant. In Malaysia, foreigners born inside the country are considered non-immigrants who should eventually depart for their country of citizenship.

In Western Europe, most guest workers were probationary immigrants. In most countries, worker rights expanded with each work permit renewal, so that after three to five years a guest worker had the same legal status as an immigrant in the classic immigration countries.

Most European guest workers were initially admitted for one year to fill a particular job with one employer. If the foreign worker was still needed by the employer when the initial one-year work and residence permits expired, these could be renewed at the request of an employer. A renewed work permit enabled the migrant worker to renew his residence permit with city authorities for another one or two years.

Restrictions on the foreign worker were progressively removed with each renewal: in Germany, after the first one-year renewal and proof that the migrant had adequate housing, a migrant could use the usually two-year work permit renewal to secure residence (but not always work) visas for his family;[14] after five years of lawful work and residence (usually two renewals) he usually received an unrestricted work permit that conferred an immigration status similar to that of immigrants or Permanent Resident Aliens in the United States. A 'settled' foreigner could change employers or occupations without securing ES approval, could apply to become a naturalized citizen after eight to ten years of lawful employment and residence, and was not deportable if unemployed or the recipient of public assistance.[15]

International Labour Office (ILO) Convention 143 (1975) recommends that after two years foreign workers acquire what amounts to US immigrant status: the right to live and work in all private and most public sector jobs (Böhning and Werquin 1990: 11); however, few nations have adopted this recommendation. Sweden removes job restrictions after one year, France after three years, Germany after five years, and Switzerland after ten years. In a study of employment restrictions in Western Europe, it was noted that about one-fifth of jobs are in the public sector. The ILO recommended that after two years settled immigrants have the same rights as intra-EU migrants to public sector jobs (Böhning and Werquin 1990: 14).

In the United States, the Replenishment Agricultural Worker (RAW) programme would have admitted the number of probationary immigrants needed according to national calculations of farm labour 'need' made by the Secretaries of Labour and Agriculture.[16] Although calculations indicated no need for this category of workers before the programme expired on 30 September 1993, if they had been admitted, and if these probationary immigrants had done at least 90 days of qualifying farm work in each of three years, they would have become permanent resident aliens or immigrants.

Some of both types of immigrants settle in the labour importing country despite the intentions of employers, workers and governments. The variables that determine settlement patterns include conditions and rights in the host country and conditions in and expectations about the country of origin.

Many diffusion and settlement processes are similar. The first migrants are generally solo men, who tend to return to their families in their countries of origin. But some invariably develop ties to the host country and settle, laying the basis for more settlement. Settlement snowballs, especially if there are expectations of an end to recruitment or an amnesty in the host country, or fears of a coup or recession in the country of origin. Finally, settlement levels off – almost always at less than half of the total migrant flow.

As the pioneering work of Mark Miller (1981), *inter alia*, has shown, foreign workers obtain rights in many ways in industrial democracies that have the effect of permitting more of them to settle than in less democratic states. Many industrial democracies recognize this fact. For this reason, recent legal changes in Germany and elsewhere permit the entry of temporary workers while making it harder for them to settle.[17]

This pattern is important for three reasons. First, governmental control is everywhere greatest in the earliest stages of guest worker programmes. This means that governments should not look at a 5 or 10 per cent 'leakage into permanence' during the first decade of a guest worker programme and assume that the settlement rate will not change; instead, they should assume that settlement rates will rise over time. Second, governments can influence the timing and extent of settlement. The Asian nations appear to be leading the way in the development of economic instruments to discourage settlement. Taiwan, for example, requires foreign workers to deposit 30 per cent of their wages in an interest-bearing government account. These wages must be claimed by the worker at a Taiwanese consulate within 30 days of the end of the contract. Third, government efforts to prevent settlement promise a clash between labour importers and exporters in international organizations. ILO recommendations, for example, call for equal pay and working conditions and immigrant status after two years as a foreign worker. Asian schemes – from calling foreign workers trainees so that they are not covered by such recommendations, to forced savings, which makes wages equal only if the worker returns – may violate these international norms.

Effects on labour-importing countries

Settlement

Between the mid-1950s and the mid-1970s, the European countries that recruited guest workers attracted between 20 and 30 million migrant workers from Southern Europe and North Africa. About two-thirds of these migrants eventually returned to their countries of origin, but those who stayed formed or united families abroad, giving today's Europe a foreign population of 20 to 25 million. The European experience suggests that countries that recruit migrant workers can within a decade or two expect to have foreign populations equal to about half the number of migrants recruited. France and Germany recruited over two-thirds of the migrants to Europe, but dependence on alien workers reached its zenith in Switzerland, where in 1973 one in three workers was foreign. In Germany, France, Belgium, Sweden and the Netherlands, foreign workers made up 8 to 12 per cent of each country's workforce in the early 1970s. In many assembly-line industries, one-third of the unskilled and semi-skilled workers were foreign, and in textiles and construction migrants made up a majority of the unskilled work forces.

Economic effects

There are no definitive models or studies to determine what the trajectory of Western European economies would have been without guest workers; however, there is general agreement on the major economic effects of labour migration in the 1960s. The availability of migrant workers sustained high levels of non-inflationary economic growth; if migrants added 1 per cent to the 10 per cent annual growth in the German GDP in the early 1970s, they would have been responsible for an annual increase of 10 billion DM.[18] They helped to hold down the rate of increase in wages, and their availability permitted employers to expand production by building additional assembly-line facilities that employed unskilled workers. Local workers enjoyed upward mobility as migrants filled the vacant jobs they left behind, and migrants sometimes raised the profitability of investments in machinery because they were willing to work at night and on weekends.

Migrant workers savings also helped to restrain inflationary pressures and to boost exports. While they earned money in Germany, for example, migrants remitted 30 to 50 per cent of their net earnings to their home countries, reducing the demand for goods in Germany and increasing the demand for German goods in Turkey. Because migrants during the 1960s were mostly single men, they made few demands on German society for infrastructure investments in housing, schools or hospitals.

Distortion

The economic benefits of migrants were immediate, and fairly transparent, in the growth of employment, output and profits. The costs of migrant workers are much harder to isolate. Germany provides a classic example. Schiller *et al.* (1976: 3) notes that with guest workers there was expansion instead of automation. The German economy in the early 1960s, he argues, could have adjusted to the shortage of workers by redirecting investment into labour-saving technologies, by investing abroad, or by simply slowing the job creation process in Germany to narrow the gap between jobs and workers. Alternatively, Germany could have developed policies to increase the size of the workforce, such as trying to counter trends towards longer education and earlier retirement. According to Schiller, the path of least resistance was to import foreign workers, and it was adopted without extended discussion of its consequences in relation to its alternatives.[19]

There are few assessments of the economic effects of guest workers on European economies since 1960 that conclude whether or not migration was worthwhile. Lutz warned: 'The dependence of some of the European economics on foreign labour has thus assumed an aspect of permanency which had previously been quite unforeseen' (1963: 5). He further argued that the importation of migrant workers obviated the need to change relative wages or to make other adjustments to eliminate labour shortages. The Lutz model for explaining how migrants make such adjustments unnecessary is straightforward: there is a high-wage Sector 1, which employs mostly or only native workers, and a low-wage Sector 2; low-wage migrants are confined initially to Sector 2 and raise wages in Sector 1 relative to Sector 2, while their presence helps to hold down general wages and thus prices. Some or most native workers in Sector 1 benefit from selective immigration because their relative wages rise and they pay lower prices for Sector 2 migrant-produced goods and services.

Writing in the early 1960s, Lutz recognized that if migrants settle and move into high-wage Sector 1, the relative wage gain to native workers diminishes and the general rule that additional workers dampen wage increases for all workers dominates the short-term benefit of cheaper goods for native workers.[20] Furthermore, she predicted that European governments would not be able to confine migrant workers to the Sector 2 occupations and industries that native workers were abandoning, so that there would be generalized shortages of labour as the employment and economic base of host nations expanded with the help of migrant workers. Lutz concluded that 'over the longer run ... the effects of selective immigration are in many ways the opposite of those achieved in the short run' (1963: 42). Owners of capital and land eventually benefit most from what began as selective immigration, she argued, and 'the position of the native labour force, or of future generations thereof, will be worse than it would have been had no foreign labour been drawn in' (ibid: 43).

Lutz outlined demand and supply changes that she believed distorted relative wages and generated labour shortages in Europe in the 1960s. On the demand side, uneven productivity growth led to faster wage growth in some sectors than in others. On the supply side, the demand for educated workers grew faster than the number of young college graduates, pushing up their wages; if manual workers' wages did not rise, then young people especially would be drawn into education and higher wages. Importing unskilled guest workers was a way to postpone the relative wage adjustments suggested by these demand or supply shifts (ibid: 15).

Kindleberger (1967), in contrast, emphasized how the availability of migrant workers sustained export-led economic growth by suppressing wages and the prices of export goods and keeping up profits and business investment. He argued that the export-led economic growth which began in the 1950s would have been choked off by rising wages and falling profits during the 1960s were it not for the availability of migrant workers, which restrained wage and price increases, raised profits and encouraged investments in additional factories.

Kindleberger (1967: 3) described a virtuous circle in which the migrants who helped to restrain wages in the 1960s permitted export-dependent European economies to export goods to the United States and elsewhere. These exports generated profits and additional local and foreign investment in modern plants in Europe, which in turn lowered European export prices and stimulated yet more exports and employment. Stable wages thus prevented a negative feedback in which labour shortages raise wages and export prices, reducing exports and economic growth.

Economic historians have noted that large-scale immigration encourages capital-widening – the adoption of machines and production processes that make use of the available labour – so that an influx of mostly unskilled and semi-skilled migrants can be expected to promote growth and expansion but not labour-saving change. Schiller *et al.* (1976: 7) reviewed the dependence of particular German industries on migrant workers: employment in the clothing industry rose by 3000 between 1961 and 1970 as 35,000 migrants replaced 32,000 departing Germans, while coal mines added 6600 migrants even as 225,000 Germans became ex-miners. Migrant workers sometimes replaced departing Germans and permitted the industry to expand, as in clothing; in other cases migrants permitted an industry to expand faster than it could have by adding only local workers, as in autos; or sustained declining industries, as in mining and cigarette manufacturing.

The data suggest that importing guest workers allowed immigration policy to act as a counter-cyclical economic policy in Western Europe during the 1960s, before many migrants acquired rights to settle. Migrants could be laid off during recessions, sent home, and re-imported when growth resumed. Normal turnover among foreign workers and the exit of the unemployed from the country kept labour productivity in such industries high when the demand for goods fell, as in 1966–7.[21]

Firms could adjust their work forces to the market for their goods and services, and the government could regulate how many unemployed workers it had to assist by altering its immigration policies. Stopping immigration and sending unemployed guest workers home made it less urgent for Germany to have expansionary monetary and fiscal policies in order to re-employ German workers. Böhning (1972) noted that migrants also eased the pressure on governments to fight inflation. The high propensity of migrants to save helped to reduce inflationary pressures in host nations such as Germany, especially during the 1960s when many migrants left their families at home.

Some of the industries that became dependent on migrants probably faced more difficult adjustments during the 1970s and 1980s than if they had not grown as much during the 1960s, but still most European economists today are reluctant to conclude that importing migrant workers was an economic mistake. Instead, most assert that, given the circumstances of the 1960s, importing workers appears to have been a rational policy, although perhaps they should not have imported as many, and perhaps not from the same countries. Similarly, most German policy makers today endorse the 1960s decision to import migrant workers, but most would have preferred tighter regulations that would have reduced the number and settlement of migrant workers in the country.

Half a century ago American economists recognized that 'the abundance of cheap immigrant labour [causes firms] ... to adapt jobs to men ... [and to increase] output by driving the workers' (Schlichter 1929: 393). This point was made again in the early 1960s, when the United States was debating whether to end the Bracero programme bringing Mexican farmworkers to the United States. To grant special entry permits regularly to certain groups of workers, for whatever reason, is to subsidize their employers and (perhaps) the consumers of their output, at the expense of their native labour market competitors (Reder 1963: 229).

The notion that too many immigrants can reduce an employer's incentive to raise productivity has its modern-day expression in the notion that 'there is nothing more expensive than cheap labour'. An abundance of unskilled immigrant workers can be a double-edged sword: their availability permits firms to expand output at stable wages with current technologies, but the availability of immigrants also dulls an employer's incentive to search for productivity-increasing technologies. And productivity growth ultimately determines economic and wage growth.

As guest workers stream into a nation, they deliver immediate and visible benefits to their employers, some as domestic workers and some as consumers. However, after 30 to 50 per cent of them settle, as experience suggests that they will, the receiving country incurs integration costs, which occur long after the benefits of immigrants have been realized (in Europe, the auto factories began laying off guest workers when the integration costs became apparent), and are paid by a much broader part of society than the group that initially benefited from their presence. Economists have shown that the timing and nature of the benefits and costs of guest workers[22] tends to permit too many such workers to enter industrial nations (Böhning 1984; Straubhaar 1988).

Effects on labour-exporting countries

Economic theory sees trade in goods and the migration of labour as substitutes: the international migration of labour is beneficial to some people in both sending and receiving nations and to the world as a whole because scarce resources (labour) are re-allocated to a more efficient or higher wage use. Labour migration eventually stops because wages rise faster in the emigration country than in the immigration country.

If migrant workers are similar to the workers left behind and similar to the workers in the receiving country, then the average wages of workers in the emigration country rise but the emigration country's total wage bill falls, provided that there is full employment both before and after emigration. In the host country, average wages fall but the total wage bill rises, assuming once again that there is full employment both before and after immigration. The key to this seeming paradox between rising average wages and falling total wages is that migrants are counted as (for example) Turks before they move but as residents of Germany after they move; world economic output unequivocally increases because migrants are made several times more productive by moving from Turkey to

Germany, since economic theory assumes that higher German wages reflect the increased productivity of Turks in Germany.

The alternative theory is one of asymmetries that sees the three Rs of recruitment, remittances, and returns operating in a manner that increases inequalities between emigration and immigration areas. Instead of flowing from theory, most of the asymmetry studies are based on the development pattern of areas that sent migrants to Western Europe in the 1960s. The three Rs produced, in the title of one study, a 'fortune in small change' that reinforced the existing economic structure (Penninx 1982).

Asymmetry studies argue that the existing economic structure did not generate development before emigration began, and remittances and returning migrants reinforced the factors that prevent an economic take-off. For example, returned workers use remittances to speculate on real estate or to imitate a successful service (delivery services or retailing), thereby flooding the market and bankrupting all participants. These studies often criticize emigration because, they assert, governments thought of exporting labour as a development panacea, which it was not (Abadan-Unat *et al.* 1976; Schiller *et al.* 1976).

Asymmetric growth or growing inequality arises from the operation of the three Rs. First, the argument runs, employed and skilled workers are first to be recruited because they are most ambitious and most attractive to foreign employers. Second, remittances tend to be spent on housing, land or imported consumer durables, rather than invested in enterprises that use local inputs or otherwise foster the backward or forward production linkages which would increase local employment. Third, many of the best and brightest do not return, so that 'without vigorous measures many potentially favourable affects of migration on the home country will not materialise, while many adverse ones will' (Abadan-Unat *et al.* 1976: 386).

Balanced growth theories dominate discussions of migration for employment. An OECD report issued in 1978, for example, was critical of European decisions to stop recruiting foreign workers:

> Restrictions on international labour flows are simply an obvious form of protection. The policy is intended to protect domestic jobs, wages, and the 'integrity' of social transfer systems, in the face of cutbacks in demand for labour, public budgets, and medium-term growth prospects. The cost of these decisions − potential inflationary pressures due to continued lack of responsiveness of domestic wages to international competitive pressures, growing job vacancies in certain sectors or occupations, illegal or 'black' markets, the failure of new labour and capital markets to develop within the OECD area, for example − may not have been given adequate consideration.

The report argued that restricting labour migration to Western Europe has reduced or will reduce overall economic efficiency or output.

Teitelbaum and Russell (1994) concluded that it is very hard to generalize about the 'complex and indirect' relationship between fertility, migration and development. Many emigration nations see exporting labour as a source of jobs and remittances, while many immigration countries are alarmed by migrant unemployment and the possibility of an ethnic underclass. Teitelbaum and Russell emphasize that the surest long-run solution for emigration pressures – sustained economic growth – can have the seemingly perverse effect of increasing emigration in the short to medium term, the so-called 'migration hump' phenomenon.

Economic gaps between industrial and developing nations widened in the 1980s, but emigration pressures were often strongest in some of the fastest-growing nations, such as China and Mexico. Remittance flows from migrants abroad to families at home total over $71 billion annually, and over $31 billion from industrial to developing countries, equivalent to almost two-thirds of the official aid provided to accelerate development.

Middle-income developing countries

Thailand ($1800), Poland ($1900), Malaysia ($2800) and Venezuela ($2900) import and export labour. There are also several economies with higher incomes – Korea ($6800), Greece ($7300) and Spain ($14,000) – that have only recently made the transition from exporting to importing unskilled labour. Of these, Malaysia provides an interesting example.

Malaysia is a country of nineteen million with a labour force of 7.5 million. The economy has been growing at an annual rate of 8 to 9 per cent, the labour force at an annual rate of 2 to 3 per cent, and employment at an annual rate of 3 to 4 per cent. One result of rapid economic and job growth are labour shortages, estimated to be 5 to 10 per cent of current employment in plantation agriculture (250,000 employees) and manufacturing (1.4 million employees).

Almost one in six workers employed in Malaysia is an immigrant, and immigrant workers generate an estimated one-eighth of Malaysia's GDP. The Mid-Term Review of the Sixth Malaysian Plan, issued in December 1993, asserted that 'The use of foreign labour should not be regarded as a permanent solution to overcome the tight labour market situation' (Economic Planning Unit 1993: 52). The report described the share of foreign workers in the Malaysian labour force as 'already high', and noted that the Malaysian government will encourage labour-saving production processes, promote the training and promotion of native workers, and encourage women to join the workforce to avoid dependence on foreign workers.

The most widely cited estimate of the number of immigrant workers in Malaysia – reflected in Table 9 – uses Malaysian Trade Union Congress assumptions about the share of foreign workers employed in four

Table 9   Estimated immigrant workers in Malaysia by sector in 1991

	Employment 1991 (000)	Immigrant share per cent	Estimated immigrant workers (000)	Distribution per cent
Agriculture and forestry	1 835	30	550.5	48
Construction	456	70	319.2	28
Manufacturing	1 374	3	41.2	4
Non-government services	2 290	10	229.0	20
Total employment	6 849	17	1 140	100

Source: Adapted from Pillai 1992: 43.

economic sectors. It concluded that there were 1.2 million[23] immigrant workers in Malaysia in 1991, i.e. immigrants made up, on average, 17 per cent of Malaysian employment in 1991, and 19 per cent of the labour force employed in these four sectors (Pillai 1992: 43). Almost half of these immigrant workers were believed to be in agriculture and forestry, followed by construction and services.

If estimated 1991 immigrant shares are applied to 1993 employment data, the data suggest that there were 1.2 million immigrant workers in the country in 1993, and that the number of foreign workers had been increasing by 17,000 per year. This procedure makes employment growth the sole determinant of the estimated number of foreign workers.

There is general agreement that 30 per cent of the plantation estate workers are immigrants, but the share of immigrants in total Malaysian agriculture and forestry employment is less clear. Navamukundan (1993: 24, 32–3) asserts that one-third of 250,000 plantation workers are immigrants, suggesting 82,500 foreign workers. There are additional immigrant workers in smallholder agriculture, such as Thais who work seasonally in northern Malaysian rice farms, and in forestry, but there appear to be no data to suggest that they number 550,000 − 82,000 = 468,000. This means that the number of foreign workers in agriculture obtained by assuming that 30 per cent of *all* those employed in agriculture and forestry may be an overestimate.

Immigrant workers are *not* of declining importance in the Malaysian economy, for three reasons:

(1) Manufacturing and service employers are complaining of labour shortages and requesting permission to employ immigrant workers. If the manufacturing workforce were to have a 16 per cent foreign worker share by 1995, there would be an additional 320,000 immigrant workers in that sector alone.
(2) The traditional immigrant ports of entry − agriculture and construction − are revolving-door labour markets, in the sense that immigrants

enter these sectors from abroad and then move into the informal economy of street hawking and service jobs. So long as these sectors remain dependent on immigrant workers, some of whom move into the informal economy, the number of immigrants will grow faster than foreign worker employment by sector.

(3) The Malaysian government has announced ambitious development projects in Sabah, the province believed to have over 40 per cent of all Malaysia's foreign workers. Development there may draw additional immigrant workers to east Malaysia.[24]

The number of immigrants in Malaysia may also increase if foreign workers marry Malaysians or unite their families in the country. In Europe, the number of spouses and dependants, plus second and third generation foreigners born or raised in the country recruiting foreign workers, typically surpassed the foreign workforce with two decades after the entry of the first foreign workers (Martin 1998).

Malaysia is not a declared country of immigration; the government does not anticipate an annual influx of immigrants. However, Malaysia does welcome business and tourist visitors, and has programmes under which non-immigrants can work in the country temporarily. It is generally believed that the number of illegal migrants in the country exceeds the number legally present.

There need be little concern about the future supply of immigrants willing to work in Malaysia. Malaysia is akin to a small island in a sea of potential foreign workers. Indeed, what distinguishes Malaysia from Western European and North American nations that are grappling with illegal immigration is the fact that Malaysia is dwarfed in size by the countries from which most foreign workers come. The United States, for example, is almost three times more populous than Mexico, France is larger than Algeria and Morocco, and Germany larger than Turkey and the former Yugoslavia, but Indonesia has almost ten times more people than Malaysia, Bangladesh six times, and the Philippines and Thailand three times.

In virtually all countries with foreign workers, employers request them, unions oppose the importation of migrant workers, and the government acts as referee. In the United States and Western Europe, governments have established programmes that admit foreign workers after employers convince the Labour Department that they suffer from labour shortages that are best filled with foreign workers. Union opposition is often pro forma, since most foreign workers are imported when the economy is booming and unemployment is low, and most foreigners are employed at the bottom of the labour market, where there is rarely competition with union members.

Managing labour migration has proven to be a difficult challenge for governments, in part because the benefits occur immediately and the costs are deferred, a point made by Kindleberger: 'the short-run economic benefits ... are positive, although there are social costs. In the intermediate and long run, the economic advantages become less clear ... to rely heavily on foreign labour constitutes a positive risk ... 30 percent is too high. 10 percent seems acceptable... To locate the discontinuities more precisely is probably impossible' (1967: 213).

The leading students of Malaysian migration tend to emphasize its costs rather than its benefits. Most base their arguments on what they perceive to be the negative effects of migrants on what happened in particular sectors. Mehmet, for example, argued that tolerating an influx of unskilled immigrants to work on plantations contradicted one of the major goals of the New Economic Plan (NEP): the elimination of rural poverty. According to Mehmet, 'reliance on imported cheap labour ... tends to reproduce poverty, contrary to NEP objectives' (1988: 26). Pillai seems to agree. He concluded that: (1) immigrants displaced Malaysians and depressed wages in agriculture and construction; (2) relying on migrants to attract Direct Foreign Investment was a false hope because Malaysia cannot hope to compete with Indonesia, Thailand and the Philippines for DFI that requires large numbers of low-wage and unskilled workers; and (3) 'the availability of low-cost foreign labour' may impede the restructuring of the Malaysian economy and labour market (1992: 18–19).

Malaysian immigration policies aim to control the employment of foreign workers through:

- border and interior enforcement to prevent the entry and employment of illegal aliens;
- the provision of a mechanism whereby Malaysian employers can employ foreign workers legally if there are shortages of Malaysian employees;
- regulations on the sectors that can employ each type of foreign worker as well as per-worker levy on employers who hire foreign workers.

Malaysia began to regulate immigration when it achieved independence in 1957. There was relatively little attention paid to immigration or emigration until 1968, when the 1968 Employment Restrictions Act required Malaysia employers to get work permits lawfully to employ non-citizen workers. Sabah and Sarawak retained control over immigration when they joined Malaysia in 1963.

In 1984, the Malaysian government signed the Medan agreement with Indonesia, allowing Malaysian plantations to recruit immigrant workers if there were no Malaysian workers available, and this agreement was soon extended to the Philippines, Thailand, Bangladesh, India and Pakistan. Only agricultural employers could legally recruit foreign workers, and then only after the local employment office agreed that Malaysian workers were unavailable. The process for legally obtaining foreign workers was considered cumbersome, and there was little enforcement, so that illegal immigration continued.

On 4 January 1989, the Malaysian government launched a programme to regularize foreign workers employed in agriculture by requiring the Indonesians among them to be taken to the port city of Malacca and then returned to Sumatra. There they were issued work permits and then returned legally to Malaysia – this 'drying out the illegals' process, which took one week and cost M\$300 per worker, was avoided where possible by both alien workers and Malaysian employers, so that fewer than one-third of the estimated 550,000 illegal alien farmworkers were legalized (Azizah 1991: 23). Relatively few workers were legalized or brought into Malaysia under the programme because the process was too slow and expensive. The list below (adapted from Pillai 1992: 50) shows the process for recruiting legal foreign plantation workers before 1992. As can be seen, there were at least twelve steps involved in the two- to six-month wait between an employer request and the arrival of foreign workers.

(1)   An employer approaches a local agent (LA) with a request for foreign workers for the agricultural sector.
(2)   The LA writes to the Immigration Department (ID), requesting permission to import foreign farmworkers.
(3)   The ID writes to the Ministry of Human Resources (MHR), requesting verification that the type of labour required by the employer is not available in Malaysia.
(4)   The MHR writes to the ID, verifying the need for such workers in Malaysia.
(5)   The ID gives permission to the LA to recruit foreign workers.
(6)   The LA then informs his contacts overseas (CO), who recruit workers.
(7)   The CO recruits foreign workers, and sends their names to the LA in Malaysia.
(8)   The LA sends the list of foreign workers to the ID, to provide them to the police for screening.
(9)   The list of names is then discussed at a meeting of the Jawatankuasa Pengambilan Pekerja Asing (JPPA) or Committee for the Recruitment of Foreign Labour under the Ministry of Home Affairs.
(10) If the JPPA approves the list, the ID issues work permits to the LA.
(11) The LA then asks the CO to get the necessary travel documents for the workers and to send them to Malaysia by air or by boat.
(12) When the foreign workers arrive in Malaysia, the LA transports the workers to the prospective employers.

On 16 October 1991, the Malaysian government revised its immigration policies. The new policy, to be effective for five years, required all foreign workers to have a legal status and to receive the same wages and benefits as Malaysian workers. A three-step procedure for determining whether Malaysian employers truly needed foreign workers, and for regulating their entry and employment, was established:

(1) Labour-short employers first contact the Ministry of Human Resources (MHR) to determine if unemployed Malaysian workers are available and, if local workers are not available, they can have their need for foreign workers certified.

(2) An employer certified to import foreign workers provides a 'registered agent' or broker with the details of the foreign workers needed, and the agent in turn arranges with the Immigration Department to have a Malaysian consul abroad issue entry and work documents to foreign workers.

(3) The foreign workers undergo a medical screening and are brought to the Malaysian work site on one- or two-year temporary work visas, and they or their employers pay an annual levy (from M$360 to M$2400 per worker per year, but M$420 per worker in most cases).

The October 1991 policy change also included Malaysia's third amnesty or registration programme for illegal alien workers since 1984. Unlike amnesties in Europe and the United States, which grant legal immigrant status and the right to eventual citizenship to illegal aliens who met certain criteria, the Malaysian registration programme initially permitted illegal aliens employed in the plantation and construction sectors to register with Immigration authorities between 1 November and 31 December 1991. After a medical exam and payment of the levy, they could obtain two-year legal work permits.[25] Registration was encouraged by the threat of stepped-up enforcement after the end of the registration period. Relatively few illegal aliens registered during the last two months of 1991,[26] and employers, fearing labour shortages, persuaded the government to extend the registration period[27] – and to defer stepped-up enforcement – until 30 June 1992.

Immigration authorities began a well-publicized operation to arrest the estimated 100,000 remaining illegal aliens[28] in Peninsula Malaysia and spent M$10 million for nine detention centres to hold the aliens arrested (Pillai 1992: 31). Between 1 July 1992 and 31 October 1993, about 52,000 illegal aliens were detained: 70 per cent were Indonesians, 15 per cent Bangladeshis. However, fewer than half of those detained during this period were deported.

There are three major issues surrounding Malaysian foreign worker policies today:

(1) Can employers count on the availability of foreign workers? The October 1991 policy was supposed to provide five years of access, but between April and June 1993, and again beginning in January 1994, the recruitment of foreign workers was halted.

Table 10: Illegal aliens apprehended in Malaysia between 1 July 1992 and 31 October 1993

Country	Illegal aliens per cent
Indonesia	70
Bangladesh	15
Thailand	6
Burma (Myanmar)	4
India	2
Pakistan	1
Nepal	1

Source: Malaysian Department of Immigration; total apprehensions were 52,037

(2) Will illegal immigrant workers continue to be available? Many illegal immigrants who registered did not receive work permits, suggesting that they are still in an underground economy in which, while no levy is collected, no worker protections are available.[29]

(3) Will additional sectors, especially in manufacturing, be permitted to employ legal foreign workers?

The Malaysian government has been criticized locally and by foreign firms for intermittently relaxing the ban on foreign workers. In March 1994, 'skilled' electronics workers from Indonesia were admitted despite the fact that they were paid only M$400 monthly, below the average for such workers. In May 1994, the Rural and Development Ministry was permitted to import unskilled foreign workers for FELDA, FLCRA, and RISDA projects, even though the 7 January 1994 ban on unskilled foreign workers remains in effect (*Business Times*, 24 May 1994).

Conclusions

Foreign worker programmes provide substantial economic benefits to sending and receiving areas. They add workers 'instantly' to a country's labour force, thereby reducing production bottlenecks and inflationary pressures, raising returns to capital and increasing rents and other population-driven prices. Sometimes the guest workers are complements to domestic skilled workers, pushing up their wages, as occurs when foreign workers in the fields create or support non-farm processing jobs. Foreign workers benefit from higher wages than they otherwise would earn, and families and friends in the country of origin enjoy a higher standard of living because of remittances.

The major costs of foreign worker programmes are distortion and dependence, especially in the immigrant-receiving countries that initiate the influx. Distortion refers to the fact that unskilled foreign workers will continue to be available, economies and labour markets in both sending and receiving areas can evolve in ways that create and reinforce international labour markets, which become progressively less subject to governmental control.

The major issue in evaluating foreign worker programmes is to determine whether the economic, migration management and development benefits offset the permanence and distortion costs. In an imperfect world in which first-best solutions are not possible, guest worker programmes are often considered the second best pragmatic solution.

Many economic policies are adopted as second-best solutions because optimal solutions seem impossible for political or economic reasons. Wage and price controls, for example, are implemented to slow inflation, even though they eventually distort the economy. Similarly, currency controls are used to prevent 'speculation' in a country's currency, even though they often permit the currency to be over-valued, thus making imports cheaper and choking off exports.

Guest worker programmes adopted to cope with labour shortages are similar, in the sense that their short-term effects differ from their long-run effects. Even though they are adopted to deal with short-run problems associated with labour shortages, immigration controls and low wages and unemployment in emigration areas, foreign worker programmes everywhere tend to become larger and to last longer than originally planned. Expansion and permanence often produce problems such as economic distortions and permanent immigration that may prove more costly to deal with than the short-term problems that the guest worker programme was intended to remedy.

Guest worker programmes should not be thought of as tools to reduce illegal immigration or to accelerate economic development in sending countries. Only under special circumstances can guest worker programmes effectively substitute legal for illegal workers – it is likely that a guest worker programme implemented to channel illegal immigrants into legal guest workers will result in continuing illegal immigration. Also, relieving unemployment and generating remittances do not in themselves lead inexorably to stay-at-home development; there is as much likelihood that labour migration can distort development and increase the dependence of the emigration area on foreign labour markets.

Guest worker programmes may serve useful transitional roles, but they should be undertaken as second-best solutions that everywhere produce at least some distortion and dependence. They will come closest to their aim of adding workers to the labour force and not residents to the population if three conditions are satisfied:

(1) There is little illegal immigration and there are strong labour market institutions.
(2) Employer taxes or levies minimize the distortions due to the presence and availability of foreign workers.
(3) Economic incentives promote the return of guest worker.

If there is any single lesson from the guest worker experience, it is that neither economics alone, nor laws and regulations alone, can regulate what is a dynamic socio-economic process.

Recommendations

In order to manage the immigration and employment of foreign workers better, middle-income developing countries should follow the five guidelines below:

(1) *Improve the immigration database.* It is very hard to discuss how to deal with a problem that is not well understood. International organizations have pioneered techniques to estimate stocks and flows of migrants.

(2) *Buttress immigration controls with economic incentives.* Improving the database and understanding foreign worker incentives to enter, as well as employers' reasons for hiring them, would lay the basis for more effective enforcement of whatever policies the government adopts.

There is a very fine line between the use of temporary foreign workers to overcome labour market bottlenecks and long-term dependence on such workers. The aphorism that there is nothing more permanent than temporary workers suggests that the Western European nations that tried to employ foreign workers without settling immigrants failed.

Two steps are needed to provide the government with the information required to develop appropriate foreign worker policies, and to regulate the foreign workers admitted. First, there is a need for more analysis of the micro, sector, and macro effects of immigrant identified. Better data on the number and distribution of foreign workers, for example, would increase the usefulness of analyses of trends in unit labour costs and capital-labour ratios in sectors that vary in their dependence on foreign workers. Case studies could indicate whether foreign workers are in fact displacing local workers and distorting local labour markets. Finally, a better database would permit analysis of the macro effects of remittances on the immigration country's economy and its external accounts. Second, the government needs to add an economic instrument to regulate foreign worker employment. Current measures have not, by all accounts, prevented the entry and employment of foreign workers. Instead, the current system permits many of the rents that arise from wage and job gaps between countries to be captured by labour brokers. The profits they earn from labour arbitrage may encourage others to enter the labour brokering business, in which violations of labour and immigration laws are common.

The government should also consider an earnings-based foreign worker levy to generate funds to regulate the use of foreign workers, to improve the administration and enforcement of foreign worker programmes, and to involve employers and unions in restructuring the economy and labour market. The key to making such a levy system effective is to encourage employers to hire legal foreign workers and pay the levy. Employers could be encouraged to participate in several ways: first, by establishing a policy that made certain of and expedited the admission of foreign workers; second, some of the levy funds could be used to promote worker mobility and skills acquisition by local workers, helping to overcome acknowledged skill deficiencies; and third, some of the levy funds could be used to strengthen immigration and labour law enforcement, making it riskier to employ illegal foreign workers outside the legal programme.

An earnings-based levy in which the funds collected are used to work with employers to end the dependence of any industry and employer on foreign workers, and to increase enforcement so that employers shun illegal workers, would enable the government to regulate immigration better. The earnings-based levy has another advantage – worker representatives can be added to industry and sector boards that would decide how the levy funds collected are to be spent, so that worker representatives would understand the reasons for importing foreign workers. Labour would have a voice in skills development, immigration and labour law enforcement, and other policies and programmes supported by the funds collected.

(3) *Develop transparent and consistent foreign worker policies.* There is a great deal of confusion over immigration policies in many middle-income developing nations. As a result, there is misunderstanding among employers, unions, and local and foreign workers as to what the government's immigration policies are, and a certain degree of cynicism that arises from contradictions between announced economic and labour market policies and the immigration reality.

(4) *Retain more skilled and professional workers.* There is some irony in importing needed skills when every year individuals with the same skills emigrate. Professionals emigrate for many economic and family reasons, but governments need to understand why skills leave the country – it is much cheaper to retain than to import skills.

(5) *Adopt regional approaches to trade and migration.* Theory and experience in Western Europe suggest that trade and investment can be a substitute for the migration of labour, i.e. the nations in a region can integrate without extensive labour migration. Despite freedom of movement guarantees and policies that encourage migration within the European Union (EU), for example, fewer than two million citizens of one EU country are employed in another, making intra-EU

migration despite earnings gaps of as much as one to five, as between Portugal and Germany, and even larger gaps between, for example, rural Portugal and south-western German cities.

In the first steps towards regional economic integration, growth is often uneven, creating labour shortages in boom areas and displacing workers and peasants in other areas as industries privatize and restructure. Such uneven development within an economic region tends to produce an initial wave of labour migration, as occurred during the 1960s when Italians and Spaniards sought jobs in Germany and France. A similar 'migration bump' is expected in North America as NAFTA accelerates economic integration there.

South Africa, for example, is a leader in promoting African economic integration. Such economic integration may not initially have to deal with migration. Immigrants want to enter South Africa because of its economic successes and, properly managed, foreign workers can contribute to the country's economic growth. However, immigrant workers can also lead to dependence and distortion in some sectors, and the inevitable settlement of some migrants may raise difficult integration issues. Managing migration is not easy, but experience elsewhere suggests that failure to manage migration is worse.

Notes

1. International labour migration was regarded positively by most opinion leaders in the 1960s. A leading economist asserted in 1967 that 'the major factor shaping the remarkable economic growth which most of Europe has experienced since 1950 has been the availability of a large supply of labour' (Kindleberger 1967: 3), implying that restrictions on labour mobility would slow economic growth.
2. The incentive to invest and create jobs in Germany was significant: if the exchange rate was $1 = 5DM when it 'should' have been $1 = 4DM, then a $100 investment in Germany was worth 500DM to the investor rather than its 'true' 400DM value.
3. About 600,000 legal immigrants entered the United States annually during the 1980s, and 50 per cent or 300,000 joined the labour force, including about 5 per cent (150,000 of three million) who had farming occupations (US Department of Labour 1989, 25, 27). About 80 per cent of the 1.8 million general legalization applicants were in the labour force, including 80,000 farm workers, who were 5 per cent of the 1.44 million general legalization applicants in the labour force, and all the 1.3 million Special Agricultural Worker (SAW) applicants should have done farm work in the mid-1980s. The Immigration and Naturalisation Service indicated in February 1992 that it had approved almost 1.1 million SAW applications.
4. This exemption from the 1917 Immigration Law was extended to railroad maintenance workers and coal miners in June 1918. Between May 1917 and

June 1920, some 51,000 Mexicans entered the United States under these exemptions, and 80 per cent were farm workers (Fuller 1942: 19853).

5. Varden Fuller argued that the structure of California agriculture – its system of large farms dependent on seasonal workers – developed because (immigrant) workers without other US job options were usually available. In his words, the assumption was 'that with no particular effort on the part of the employer, a farm labour force would emerge when needed, do its work, and then disappear – accepting the terms and conditions offered, without question' (Fuller 1991: vii).

6. The merits of slavery versus seasonal farm workers were debated extensively, with seasonal workers usually found to be cheaper because: no capital outlay was required to purchase them; they boarded themselves while employed and reproduced abroad; they were available when needed but they were paid only for the time they were actually employed; and at the end of the season they 'moved on, relieving [the] employer of any burden or responsibility for his [workers'] welfare during the slack season' (Fuller 1942: 19824).

7. Illegal immigration increased as Braceros learned they did not pay bribes to local Mexican officials to get on recruitment lists, and then pay additional bribes at Mexican recruitment centres in order to work in the United States. US farmers were pleased because they could employ Mexican workers without government 'red tape', such as having their housing for Braceros inspected and being required to offer them the minimum or government-calculated prevailing wage, whichever was higher.

8. In 1949, for example, about 20,000 Mexicans received contracts from US employers at recruitment centres in Mexico and legally entered the United States as contract workers, while over 87,000 arrived illegally in the United States and then had their status legalized after they found jobs (President's Commission 1951: 53).

9. A job-seeking intra-EC migrant is not entitled to unemployment or other public assistance from the host nation while seeking employment, although such assistance may be paid by the country of origin.

10. Farm workers in over 20 states need not be covered by workers' compensation insurance. Employers in such states wishing to employ H–2A workers must 'provide, at no cost to the worker, insurance covering injury and disease arising out of and in the course of the worker's employment which will provide benefits at least equal to those provided under the State workers' compensation law for comparable employment' (US Department of Labor regulations implementing H–2A programme).

11. Switzerland has no minimum wage system, and even though there may be no negotiated wage for many jobs, e.g. the piece-rate harvesting jobs filled by seasonal workers, the Swiss assert that seasonal workers are paid the prevailing wage.

12. Estimates by Roger Böhning, 16 May 1990.

13. Germany admitted 48,000 and France 12,000 non-EC nationals for employment in 1987, although most of these were skilled and professional workers (Böhning and Werquin 1990: 45).

14. In the mid-1970s, there was a short-lived regulation in Germany which permitted cities to declare themselves overburdened by foreigners and prohibit family unification even if the alien otherwise qualified.
15. All foreigners employed in Germany need a work permit from the ES. The ES issues work permits to foreigners on a case-by-case basis. Three types of work permits are issued. *General* work permits are issued for one year and for a specific workplace. Local ES offices have discretionary authority to give or withhold general permits depending on the labour market situation. German and EC workers get first priority for vacant jobs. *Special* work permits may be given to foreigners who have five years of lawful employment. *Unlimited* work permits are available to foreigners after eight years of lawful employment.

    Note that foreign workers have a right to the five- and eight-year work permits, but a foreigner with a right to a special or unlimited work permit may still find himself unable to work in Germany because he failed to apply for or failed to obtain a residence permit (Mehrländer 1997: 20).
16. These calculations are described in Martin (1990).
17. In Germany, guest worker employment peaked at 2.6 million in 1973, hit a low of about 1.6 million, and is today about two million. The total foreign population in Germany is about seven million.
18. Between 1972 and 1973, the GDP in Germany rose from 826 to 919 billion DM, or 11 per cent. Ten per cent of this 93 billion DM growth is 9.3 billion DM, or almost 10 billion DM. By another estimate, guest workers were responsible for one-sixth of German GDP growth between 1960 and 1966 – the real German GDP rose 31 per cent during these years, but without guest workers it would have increased only 26 per cent (Engelen-Kefer 1990: 102).
19. Discussions during the 1960s and today accept most job vacancies reported by employers as legitimate, assuming that if there were a technological or other alternative, employers would have implemented it and not requested foreign workers. In 1987, the Chief of Staff of the German Chancellor's Office asserted that Germany must, in the long-run, 'offset at least in part the shrinking of the German population with more foreigners [because] the labour market requires them [more foreigners]' (Engelen-Kefer 1990: 133). If jobs are filled at current wages or even with marginal changes in wages, the sometimes non-marginal adjustment necessary to restructure production to reduce labour needs are not pursued.
20. Lutz concluded that: (1) 'a persistent "scarcity" of domestic labour is ... ultimately a wage (or price) question ... I shall argue that the primary reason for the recent large-scale importation of foreign labour by the European countries concerned is that relative wages have been out of line with conditions on the supply side of the domestic labour market'; (2) 'the importation of foreign labour ... may itself lead, unless halted in time, to the development of a generalised shortage of domestic labour' (Lutz 1963: 7); and (3) 'the native labour force ... may, for a certain period, be benefited, and not harmed, by certain forms of immigration ... over the longer run, however, the effect will normally be ... disadvantageous to the native labour force' (ibid: 8).

21. Between 1966 and 1967, migrant worker employment in the FRG fell 30 per cent, from 1.3 million to 904,000.

22. Guest workers provide immediate and measurable benefits that are concentrated in relatively few hands; their integration costs tend to be delayed, hard to measure, and diffuse across a larger part of the population. The timing and nature of the benefits and costs of guest workers helps to explain why most labour migrations expand beyond original plans.

23. Using the same data that appear in Pillai (1992: 43), there were in fact 1.1 million foreign workers in 1991.

24. The state governments of Sabah and Sarawak were given control over immigration in 1963 to prevent peninsular Malaysians from moving there and depriving natives of economic opportunities. The National Front Coalition, which came to power in March 1994, has promised to remove controls on travel between peninsular Malaysia and Sabah.

25. The restrictions on where permanent immigrants – those with red identity cards – could work were lifted in October 1991.

26. Employers complained that illegal Indonesian workers who registered had to be taken to Malacca, where they underwent medical examinations, then they were taken 24 miles across the Strait of Malacca to be issued an Indonesian passport and a Malaysian work permit, and finally, after the levy was paid, the now legal worker was returned to the plantation or construction site. The cost of this was estimated at M$500 per worker, plus two to three weeks of lost employment.

27. Extending the registration period allegedly encouraged additional illegal aliens to enter Malaysia. There were numerous press accounts of aliens who paid smugglers to get them into the country, leading in some cases to tragedy and abandonment (Pillai 1992: 31).

28. During the first week of July 1992, some 1,800 aliens, three-quarters of them Indonesians, were detained.

29. Reportedly, 100,000 of those who registered did not pay their levy (*Straits Times*, 24 November 1993: 19).

3

The quest for skill: a comparative analysis

Gary P. Freeman

This chapter reviews the experience of immigration receiving countries with the migration of skilled labour. I seek to establish what governments have done to identify the skills needs of their labour markets, to select and recruit appropriately qualified workers and place those migrants in suitable employment, and to examine what effect such programmes have had.

A review of theoretical issues produces predictions of the expected direction of skill flows and the impacts of skilled migration on labour markets and productivity in receiving societies. It shows, however, that there is no well-developed, widely accepted theoretical exposition of skilled migration. Fundamental issues relating to the sources and consequences of skill migration are unresolved.

The core of the analysis consists of extended case studies of the skilled migration programmes of three major immigration receiving countries: Australia, Canada, and the United States. These amount to critical cases for the analysis of skilled migration. They are the countries most favourably situated to attract, recruit and exploit skilled migration. If they cannot do so at a high rate of effectiveness, it is unlikely that less favourably situated states can. All three accept immigrants each year for permanent settlement and have done so for a long time. They consequently have long experience – in some cases going back more than one hundred years – in managing immigration and recruiting certain sorts of immigrants, including the highly skilled. Large numbers of people around the world wish to move to these countries, so that the applicant pool is many times greater than the number that can be admitted each year. Selection, therefore, is not only possible, but is also necessary.

The case studies show that any skill migration programme must involve some mechanism for identifying the skill needs of the economy, as well as a procedure for attracting skilled migrants and selecting from the available pool those who fit the needs profile. Migrants must then be integrated into the local economy without disrupting national labour markets and in such a way as to maximize the utility of imported skills. The case studies indicate that Australia and Canada are ahead of the United States in the aggressive recruitment and selection of skilled workers and in managing the integration of such workers into the national economy. Nevertheless, the general conclusion suggested by the case studies and a briefer examination of skills migration to other destination countries, is that skilled migration programmes are difficult to organize and implement. No country has been more than modestly successful in achieving programme goals due to technical, institutional and political obstacles.

Theoretical issues

A recent extensive review identifies over a half-dozen theoretical approaches that can be employed to study international migration and points out that none has been thoroughly validated or disconfirmed (Massey *et al.* 1994). There is no consensus as to the most promising theoretical school, and given the paltry state of the empirical literature that is self-consciously theory-driven, it would be premature to discard any of the existing theoretical enterprises. Consequently, I will discuss several theoretical approaches to international migration from the point of view of what they have to say about the more specialized subject of skill migration.

The most widely employed model of international migration is that drawn from the neo-classical theory of trade (Borjas 1988, 1989; Ethier 1986; Simon 1989: 12–21). It assumes that there is an international market for migration, i.e., individuals make migration decisions on the basis of their expected earnings in destination countries and move to the country offering the highest earnings, net of migration costs (Borjas 1989; Massey *et al* 1993: 433–6).

The key features of the neo-classical model are its predictions with respect to observed and unobserved characteristics of migrants and positive and negative selection processes. Borjas, for example, wishes to predict whether flows between particular countries are likely to increase or reduce the 'quality' of the labour force of the countries involved (where quality is defined as the wage differential between migrants and natives with the same measured skills) (1988: 27). To get at quality, one needs to distinguish between observed and unobserved characteristics of migrants and to understand the separate selection processes at work with respect to these characteristics. Observed characteristics include level of education, measurable skills, age, and other externally visible factors. Unobserved characteristics are measured by earnings differentials between migrants and natives with the same measurable observed characteristics. Although Borjas does not say in so many words, he means for unobserved characteristics to encompass those ineffable traits – ambition, creativity, innovativeness, diligence – that make persons of similar qualifications perform differently in the labour market.

One of the most critical insights of the economic model of migration is that the selection processes for observed and unobserved characteristics of migrants are different and independent (ibid: 29–31). The effects of observed skill characteristics on migration depend on how highly valued those characteristics are in the home and host countries. Persons possessing certain observed characteristics will try to migrate from countries that undervalue their skills to those that value them more highly. On the other hand, the conditions that affect the selection of unobserved skills have to do with the income distributions of the host and home countries. Borjas hypothesizes that 'an increase in the variance of the income distribution in the home country leads to a decrease in the quality of migrants reaching any country of destination' (ibid: 28). Migration from countries of high inequality is likely to be negatively selected, i.e., to involve persons, with below average earnings at home and lower earnings in their new country compared to natives with similar skills. However, 'an increase in the variance of the income distribution in the country of destination leads to an increase in the quality of migrants choosing to migrate there' (ibid), yielding positive selection. Finally, 'immigration policies that stress family reunification are likely to generate a migrant flow that has lower earnings capacities than immigration policies stressing skills and occupational characteristics' (ibid) because family members cushion migrants from the effects of poor labour market outcomes and create migration incentives for persons who would not have otherwise migrated.

Thus the economic model suggests that positive selection occurs when migrants have above average earnings in their home country and higher earnings than comparable natives in the host country. Positive selection is likely, according to Borjas, when the home country 'taxes' high-ability workers and 'insures' low-ability workers against poor labour market outcomes. Therefore, positive selection, or what is often referred to as 'brain drain' takes place when the host country's income distribution is more unequal than that of the home country (ibid: 24). Negative selection, on the other hand, involves the movement of persons with below average incomes in the country of origin to the host country where, holding characteristics constant, they perform comparatively poorly in the host country's labour market. Negative selection is predicted when the income distribution in the host country is more egalitarian than that of the home country. In other words, in this scenario the host is 'taxing' the high-income workers relatively more than the country of origin and providing better 'insurance' for low-income workers against poor labour market outcomes (ibid: 24).

If confirmed by empirical research, this model has profound implications for governments trying to recruit skilled workers. It identifies structural factors that shape the incentives of individuals to move and that affect the available pool of migrants from which particular countries may draw. It suggests that governments may 'control immigration primarily through policies that affect expected earnings in sending and/or receiving countries' (Massey *et al.* 1993: 436). Moreover, this analysis indicates that a migration of workers, highly skilled in terms of education and formal job training, may not necessarily be the most qualified highly skilled workers from the source countries, if quality is defined as relative earnings capacity and if the conditions for negative selection are present. Borjas recommends, therefore, that comparisons between migrants and natives must be standardized, holding education, age and other observable characteristics constant in order to develop 'measures of the types of selections in unobserved characteristics' taking place (1993: 32).

The economic theory of migration, whether pitched at the micro or macro economic level, has been faulted for ignoring a number of factors thought to shape the migration process. Massey and his associates, for example, advance theoretical propositions drawn from the 'new economics of migration', the thrust of which is to take the family as the basic decision-making unit rather than the individual (1993). They also explore such structural issues as dual labour market theory (Piore 1979), world systems theory (Wallerstein 1974; Portes and Walton 1981; Castells 1989; Sassen 1988; Zolberg 1989), network theory, institutional theory, cumulative causation (Massey *et al.* 1990), and migration systems theory (Fawcett 1989). The authors observe:

> Theories developed to understand contemporary processes of international migration posit causal mechanisms that operate at widely divergent levels of analysis. Although the propositions, assumptions, and hypotheses derived from each perspective are not inherently contradictory, they nonetheless carry very different implications for policy formulation. (Massey *et al.* 1993: 463)

Moving beyond the literature on the sources of migration flows, I wish to consider a number of arguments dealing with the effects of migration. My purpose is to suggest that many of these issues are more open to dispute than one might gather from the mainstream economics literature.[1]

One of the chief presumed benefits of skill migration is what some economists refer to as spillover. This 'spillover' is identical to the effects of unobserved characteristics of migrants. Immigrants are believed to possess certain traits that cause them to work harder or to be more innovative and dynamic, and, therefore, to raise either the level or rate of growth of total factor productivity (Withers 1991; Nevile 1991). The logical appeal of the argument is undeniable. Nonetheless, it may be a mistake to over-interpret as beneficial the simple fact that immigrants earn more than the native-born of similar education and training. As the Economic Council of Canada puts it:

> If immigrants do work harder, have more ideas, are better entrepreneurs, and so on, all of this will surely show up in their earnings, according to both common sense and standard economic theory. Immigrants will then add to national output more than seemingly similarly qualified native-born workers, but ... economic theory ... asserts that *there is no reason to expect that the hosts themselves will earn more as a result*. Putting it technically, there is no reason to expect spillover according to standard production-function analysis. (Economic Council 1991: 33, emphasis in original)

Many economists argue that skilled migration is a net positive benefit to the economy whether or not the migrants are more productive than similarly situated natives. According to this line of reasoning, skilled immigrants contribute to the overall stock of human capital in an economy and, thereby, contribute to greater efficiency and higher incomes. It is widely believed that in the newly emerging global trading system, those economies whose workers possess the highest level of training and skills will enjoy a competitive advantage that will be reflected in higher living standards (Reich 1983). Skilled immigrants, in this view, make special contributions because they arrive already educated and trained so that the receiving economy experiences a net increase in human capital without having to subsidize its creation.

One possible flaw in this argument, as the Canadian report sees it, is that it talks vaguely about the economy when what is really at stake are the economic circumstances of individuals, both hosts and immigrants. Arriving immigrants retain title to their human capital and all the benefits this capital earns; host workers gain nothing from the migration. Only in cases where a very small economy lacks a critical mass of skills would the hosts receive any benefit from the migration of human capital, other than avoiding paying taxes for the education of the immigrant worker (Economic Council 1991: 34).

There are similar counter-arguments to the claims that immigration contributes to financial capital expansion and entrepreneurship. All three of the major immigration countries have introduced special economic admissions categories for 'investors' or 'business migrants' that are effectively designed to lure those individuals with financial capital to invest in the host country. The assumption behind such policies, presumably, is that any expansion of the sum of capital investment in the country is beneficial; therefore, special migration incentives are needed to attract sufficient investment. The Economic Council, however, is pessimistic regarding the utility of such programmes. Again, the immigrants retain ownership of their money capital and any earnings therefrom, whether they invest it in their own businesses or lend it to hosts. The Council argues that 'the hosts get nothing, unless either capital markets are so imperfect that an additional domestic source of loanable funds is needed (in today's global world, that seems overwhelmingly improbable) or unless immigrants are obliged to accept a lower-than-market return on their investment' (1991: 34). The report concedes that there might be pockets of capital shortage in an economy, and a programme that could identify and address such shortages through targeted migration might make some minor contribution.

The Economic Council report also investigates the argument that migrants improve the overall capital/labour ratio (if they own more capital on average than natives). The Council rejects this argument on the grounds that it assumes that the international capital markets are insufficient to permit a country to reach the optimal capital/labour ratio, regardless of the part of the capital stock that is immigrant-owned. This presumption is dubious, especially in an age of increasing globalization (ibid: 35).

Claims are frequently heard that immigrants are more likely than natives to be entrepreneurs who can jump-start lacklustre economies by creating new businesses and developing new products. Here, the Economic Council report introduces the problem of incrementality: it is necessary to prove, rather than assume, that immigrant entrepreneurship contributes to the growth of business above what it would have been in the absence of immigration. The report's authors conclude that 'logic and economic theory suggests' that the answer is 'no' (ibid).

Finally, there is the issue of whether immigration might play a peculiar role in bringing into a country the highly specific skills, such as language, cultural familiarity, and personal networks that aid in the development of emerging regional markets. This, as we shall see, has become a major issue of public policy in Australia. There is, as yet, scant evidence on the validity of this proposition, however.

Case studies[2]

Australia

Australia provides a wealth of experience and data with respect to the possibilities and pitfalls of embarking on a programme of skilled migration recruitment. No country has tried harder to benefit from the importation of skilled professionals and business entrepreneurs. Still, the effort has been marked by severe controversy and debatable success.

The principal legislative bases for the Australian immigration programme are the 1958 Migration Act and the 1989 Migration Legislation Amendment Act. These laws establish three main categories of migrants: family, humanitarian and economic.[3] The category of most direct interest for this inquiry is the economic or independent class, which is devoted to persons who have special skills or a business background that will make an economic contribution to Australia. There are four kinds of economic migrants:

(1) Persons may be admitted under the Business Migration Programme if they can demonstrate a successful business background and sufficient capital to invest in a productive enterprise.
(2) Persons may be designated for admission for either a specific approved job or a job covered by an industry agreement by employers under the Employer Nomination Scheme.
(3) People whose background, youth, education, skills and ready employability will contribute to the Australian economy are also eligible. These individuals are subject to the 'points test'.
(4) People who have distinguished themselves internationally through their special creative or sporting talents, or who have outstanding abilities that would represent a clear gain for Australia, are admissible under the special talents category.

The relative importance of these various categories is shown in Table 11.

There are two strong short-term trends in the planning levels for the Australian immigration programme over the last four years: the overall level of the intake has been reduced by about one-third and the economic category has been slashed in half, with the independent (points-tested)

Table 11 Migration programme planning levels, Australia, selected years, 1990–1 to 1994–5

	1990–1	1991–2	1993–4	1994–5
Family migration	64 000	56 000	45 000	47 000
Preferential family	44 000	37 000	34 000	36 500
Concessional family	20 000	19 000	11 000	10 500
Economic migration	50 000	42 500	17 000	25 000
Employer nominations	9 500	7 000	3 000	4 600
Business migration	10 000	5 000	1 500	1 600
Special talents	500	500	200	200
Independents	30 000	30 000	12 300	10 300
Humanitarian	11 000	12 000	13 000	13 000
Special eligibility	1 000	500	1 000	1 000
Total	126 000	111 000	76 000	86 000

Source: Department of Immigration, Local Government and Ethnic Affairs (DILGEA), Media release, 30 April 1991; Birrell 1994b, Table 1: 42

subcategory falling by two-thirds. These are but the latest in a string of fluctuations in the size and character of the Australian immigration intake.

Background

The most important factor in Australian immigration has been the cost and difficulty of getting to Australia. This, in turn, has put great pressure on governments attempting to attract the right kinds of migrants. Until recently, a large share of those who arrived in Australia benefited from government subsidy. One estimate is that, of the 3.35 million post-war migrant arrivals through 1980, 2.02 million, or 60 per cent, received government passage subsidy (Wooden *et al.* 1990: 307). Even so, an assessment of the assisted passage scheme concludes that it was not adequate either to attract sufficient migrants to meet government targets or to 'promote a more selective immigration flow' (Lloyd 1970: 15). In any case, the great need through the 1960s was for manual labour, a type of migration for which selection was less essential.

In the 1970s and 1980s, two things happened to alter the policy calculus significantly. With the elimination of the White Australia policy between 1968 and 1973, the sources of immigration shifted away from Europe and towards Asia and other parts of the developing world. Second, changes in the structure of the Australian economy and in its position in an increasingly global economy, brought about a rethinking of the role skilled labour and high technology professions might play in maintaining competitiveness. The first change increased significantly the potential pool of migrants to Australia so that inflows would be more supply-driven than they had been in the past; the second provided the impetus for a more self-consciously selective migration programme that would focus on bringing in economically useful professional, scientific and business skills.

The government reacted to these new circumstances by altering the immigration policy rules and tinkering with the established procedures for selecting immigrants.[4] Rapid programme change makes it difficult to evaluate the efficacy of particular permutations of the selection system. Before 1958, when the dictation test was eliminated (Immigration Act 1901, section 3, paragraph 1; Palfreeman 1967), immigrant selection was arbitrary, and considerations of ethnic and national origins dominated admissions decisions. Even after the Migration Act of 1958, the objectives of ethnic selection were achieved, though through different means. The Act, which was a modestly revised version of the Immigration Act of 1901, retained for administrators the wide discretion they had always exercised in the admission of migrants and avoided spelling out explicit selection criteria. When the White Australia bias of the programme was eliminated in 1973, a more rationalized system of selection was required.

From the mid-1970s on, a spate of reports and inquiries eventually spurred the government to revamp the immigration programme to accentuate the recruitment of skills. The National Population Inquiry in 1975, for example, raised the spectre of a no-growth population within 30 years and warned that this might 'tend to reproduce the cycle of labour shortages (particularly in skilled and professional areas) that were apparent in the "fifties" ' (NPI 1975, Vol. 2: 734). Two years later, a Green Paper on immigration and population issues called for the recruitment of skilled and professional workers to meet labour market needs through a new general eligibility category based on a 'points system' (Australian Population and Immigration Council 1977). This call was subsequently heeded.

The 'points system' became the centrepiece of the Australian selection process in the late 1970s. It applies to certain subcategories of the general economic class and to the concessional family category as well. In its first incarnation, it went under the title of Numerical Multi-factor Assessment System (NUMAS) (Wooden *et al.* 1990: 308). It has been in more or less constant change since it was introduced.

The most significant contribution to the debate over skill selection was made in 1988 by the Committee to Advise on Australia's Immigration Policies (CAAIP). It pointedly recommended a more tightly organized economic focus for the migration programme. Concerned that the skills levels of certain classes of migrants were falling and that the median age of migrants was rising, CAAIP argued for an increase in the independent category and an adjustment of the points system to reward those migrants most capable of contributing to the economy. However, the report also insisted that immigration should not become a substitute for developing a highly skilled native labour force and called for redoubled efforts to train the local population.

The chief objective of the 1989 Migration Legislation Amendment Act was to reduce ministerial discretion by including in the statute the requirements for admission under various categories. Many of the personal appeals to the minister had been coming from individuals from the migrant community who wished to be joined by family members. Some critics had charged that the growing predominance of family migration was contributing to a decline in migrant skill levels and reducing the potential economic benefits of migration.

The period from 1978 to 1992 saw sharp swings in Australia's recruitment of skilled immigrants, reflecting both political and economic considerations. The percentage of total intake included in skills categories rose rapidly in the last years of the Fraser government (1978–9 to 1981–2) as the significance of the family category was deliberately reduced. This continued in 1982–3, before the Hawke Labor government came to power, with 44,973 entrants in skilled categories, or 48 per cent of the total intake (Hawthorne 1994). The new Labor government cut the total intake by 25 per cent in 1983–4. A renewed emphasis on family reunion meant that the skills categories dropped by nearly half (47 per cent), with the skills intake about 23 per cent of the total in 1983–4 and 28 per cent in 1984–5. But this gradually changed over the next six years, as can be seen in Table 12.

One element in the discussion about the skill level of the labour force at this time involved a broader national economic strategy. As Australia's traditional economic relationship with Great Britain flagged with the latter's entry into the European Community, as her trade with Japan and other countries in the Asian Pacific region expanded, and as the economic dynamism of regional economies promised, finally, to turn Australia's geographic location from a problem into an advantage, the country's leaders began to see her prospects tied to Asia. Immigration, it was argued, could play a role in cementing economic, social and political ties with the region. More specifically, through migration Australia could acquire the technical, linguistic and entrepreneurial know-how that she needed to penetrate Asian markets and to develop collaborative economic ventures (Garnaut 1990; Foley 1989; Inglis and Wu 1990; Lary *et al.* 1993). The Asian economic gambit therefore emerged as a justification for an expanded immigration programme and an intensified effort to improve skills recruitment.

Recent changes in the skilled migration programme

In 1984–5, the Labor government, which was cutting back on the total annual intake, introduced a new mechanism for linking the admission of skilled workers more closely to national labour market conditions. The Occupational Share System (OSS) restricted the recruitment of skilled migrants to those occupations in short supply over the medium term. The Department of Employment and Industrial Relations (DEIR) set annual occupational 'shares' or programme numbers for specific occupations which were, in turn, supposed to determine the recruitment decisions of overseas immigration officers. Shares were based on labour market conditions and were limited to occupations where shortages could not be

Table 12 Skilled migrants as proportion of total intake, Australia

Year	Per cent skilled
1986–7	48.0
1987–8	52.0
1988–9	49.4
1989–90	51.8
1990–1	58.3
1991–2	57.4

Source: Hawthorne 1994: 6–7

readily filled by Australian training institutions. The Department of Immigration and Ethnic Affairs (DIEA) received explicit instructions as to the qualifications acceptable under each share. Typically, these instructions stipulated that the applicant's professional qualifications have utility and be recognized in Australia and that the individual be fluent in English. OSS helped DEIR (or DEET as it was later renamed) keep strict control of skilled migration. The largest number of principal applicants in any year (1988–9) was 2,900, of whom 2,000 were professionals (Birrell 1994a).

The OSS was gradually eclipsed by other admissions ventures, however. The concessional family category (in effect, the sibling class) had been introduced in 1982. Siblings at first were required to pass a points test that included skill, education, occupation and English. But in 1983, under pressure from ethnic organizations, the test was modified so that points were awarded to the semi-skilled and to those without tertiary education. In addition, DEIR began recruiting professionals through other channels at the same time that OSS was in place so that the overall number of skilled admissions was considerably larger. In 1986–7 recruitment began for independent applicants other than those under OSS. By 1988– 9 there were 25,000 accepted in this programme and in an expanded employer nomination programme. These figures rose to 30,000 in 1989–90 and to 40,000 in 1990–1. The selection system for independents was the same as that for siblings, except that family sponsorship was removed. Unlike OSS, moreover, the selection system for independents did not contain any mechanism to debar applicants with occupations in surplus or with poor English or qualifications that were not recognized in Australia, nor did it target particular occupations (Birrell 1994a).

These circumstances resulted in the CAAIP report's critical assessment of the selection system as unable to select for skills adequately. A new selection system was duly implemented in mid-1989, although not all the CAAIP recommendations were followed in detail. The OSS was eliminated. However, the DIEA resisted reforms linking selection to occupational demand, and there was no entrepreneurial factor (this was left to the Business Migration Programme). The new system did give preference to (1) skills or professions recognized in Australia, (2) English language proficiency and (3) job experience. The modified rules diminished the significance of tertiary education unless it led to professional credentials recognized in Australia. Moreover, an applicant received extra points if his or her occupation was designated as a 'priority' by DEET. The sibling, or 'concessional' category was reformed along the same lines, but with no language factor. This system was in place during the peak years of 1989–91, when 50,000 independent and concessional migrants were admitted and 11,500 persons entered under the Employer Nomination Scheme.

In May 1992, the government introduced further changes in the skilled migration programme that indicated a fear that professional migrants were not faring well in the Australian labour market. The selection system was altered to include a vocational English language test for independent applicants and a requirement that applicants in certain occupations (including engineering) pass this test, whether they were in the independent or the concessional categories. A partial about-face occurred in December 1993, when, apparently because overseas posts were not receiving enough qualified applicants to meet the 1993–4 programme targets, the pass marks for the independent and concessional categories were reduced by 10 and 5 points, respectively. As one observer notes, under the old system one had to have professional or trade credentials recognized in Australia and at least a working knowledge of English. With the reduction in the pass mark, any applicant with the professional or trade credentials and three years of post-qualification work who is in the 18–29 age group would pass (Birrell 1994b: 41).

In early 1994, moreover, the new Minister for Immigration also made public statements indicating that an intensification of the skilled migration recruitment effort was envisioned (*Sydney Morning Herald* 5 March 1994; *Australian Financial Review* 21 April 1994). Events proved otherwise. In May, Prime Minister Paul Keating told Parliament that 'in this recovery the complement to skill formation in the labour market is not going to come from migration. This time it has to come from training our own people, including those who are presently unemployed' (quoted in Birrell 1994b: 42). This view is implicit in a White Paper issued in 1994 (*Working Nation*) which concludes that the provision of employment opportunities for the resident unemployed must become a national priority and which assumes that 'the substantial decline in net migration since 1988–89 mean[s] that Australia can no longer rely on new entrants to the workforce to meet the skill needs of industry' (Birrell 1994b: 98). These new considerations have not yet significantly affected government migration targets. Planning levels for 1994–5 differ only marginally from those of the previous year (see Table 10).

Have the various programmes implemented by the Australian government had the intended effect of selecting and recruiting skilled migrants in the numbers desired? Data indicate that the share of migrants possessing skills has gone up, as Table 11 shows. Borjas, for example, finds that Australia (and Canada) recruit a higher quality migrant stream than the United States, offering implicit evidence that a points-tested system has discernible effects (1988). In addition, Withers (1988) has argued that the average skill level of migrants is higher than that of the Australian-born population, though the differences are not great, and his findings have been challenged (Wooden et al. 1990: 125).

On the other hand, a number of critics have argued that many of the migrants admitted under the independent and concessional programmes have not been able to find appropriate employment or, in many cases, any employment at all. Although this appears to be a general problem across all skill groups (Mitchell W. 1992; Mitchell B. 1993), and was exacerbated by the recession of the early 1990s, it is an especially serious problem for engineers. The most common complaints are that the selection process is insufficiently attentive to demand in the Australian labour market and fails to ensure that migrants have credentials that will be accepted in Australia (Birrell *et al.* 1992; Birrell 1994a).

Smith (1994a) found that among people claiming qualifications in civil engineering, those from non-English-speaking backgrounds (NESB) were four to seven times more likely to be unemployed than Australian-born civil engineers. In a more extensive follow-up investigation which attempted to exclude the effect of applicants who might have inflated their qualifications, Smith (1994b) focused on applicants claiming qualifications in selected professional fields who also held tertiary-level qualifications. Even among these migrants, evidence from the 1991 census shows that those who arrived in Australia between 1986 and 1991 with tertiary training and professional qualifications have been far less successful in gaining professional employment than Australian residents, including 20–24-year-old recent graduates. Smith, moreover, reports that the level of unemployment for recent arrivals holding tertiary qualifications is typically six times that of residents and that the level of professional employment is about one-half that of residents (cf. Smith 1993; Murphy 1994b).

A recent study based on a longitudinal analysis of 81 immigrant engineers drawn from Victoria and Western Australia sheds important light on the employment experiences of immigrant professionals (Hawthorne 1994).[5] These migrants entered Australia at a relatively propitious time, both in terms of the unemployment rate in their profession (which rose from 1.1 in 1987 to 4.4 per cent in 1991) and in terms of the settlement services available to them. Individuals from non-English speaking backgrounds (NESB) were targeted for priority language resourcing within Australia's Adult Migrant English Programme. Moreover, purpose-designed engineering vocational-access courses were available to facilitate labour-market entry (ibid: xv).

Nevertheless, 'by late 1991 these immigrant engineers were experiencing acute labour market disadvantage' (ibid). All the migrant engineers from English-speaking backgrounds acquired engineering employment within five months. The NESB engineers, on the other hand, had much more difficulty. Although 69 per cent had anticipated finding a job within three months after arrival, none were able to do so. The NESB engineers in the Victorian sample took vocational access courses which led to employment for one-third of the sample. But there were fourteen job offers to the 27 Europeans and only three to the 25 non-Europeans. No offers were made to those from the Middle East. In the Western Australia sample, by late 1992, only 18 per cent had gained full-time work, and only 36 per cent of the total NESB sample was fully employed by late 1992.

Hawthorne found that employers and co-workers imposed exacting standards for English proficiency, demanded local professional experience, and preferred NESB engineers of East European background. Hawthorne's data show that ethnicity is critical to overall employment outcomes. Of the 24 NESB engineers in full-time work in 1992, 63 per cent were European, 25 per cent were from Asia, and 13 per cent were from the Middle East. Racial origin was the only factor that was statistically predictive of employability.[6]

Canada

In late 1994, the Canadian government announced a new long-range immigration strategy entitled *Into the 21st Century: A Strategy for Immigration and Citizenship* (Citizenship and Immigration Canada 1994d). At the same time, the Minister of Immigration issued as his annual report to Parliament a five-year plan called *A Broader Vision: Immigration and Citizenship, Plan 1996–2000* (Citizenship and Immigration Canada 1994a). Taken together, the two documents, which are the outgrowth of a change of government in the previous year and a broad consultative process undertaken during 1994 (*Immigration Consultations Report*, Citizenship and Immigration Canada 1994c), constitute a significant reshaping of the Canadian immigration programme – both to reduce numbers and to reinforce the economic orientation of the programme.

The government promised that 'a greater share of immigrants will be selected on the basis of their ability to contribute to Canada's economic and social development, reducing demand on integration services' (Citizenship and Immigration Canada 1994b: 1). The government also announced that 'recruitment and promotion strategies for economic immigration will be integrated with the government's economic agenda and with foreign relations plans for particular countries, regions and emerging export markets' (ibid: 2). To ensure migrant access to the labour market, a national clearinghouse on accreditation for the recognition of foreign credentials will be established with the co-operation of the provinces and professional associations. The plan also called for 'placing an immediate moratorium on new private immigrant investor funds, pending redesign of the programme' (ibid).

In order to focus on economic migrants, some tightening of the family category will take place, including strengthening of sponsorship obligations, with the possible introduction of a financial guarantee mechanism or sponsorship bond. Moreover, parents and grandparents will be put in a newly established immigration category and 'the size of the category will be managed to safeguard the share of other categories in the programme' (ibid).

The plan promises that the management of specific categories, and the share of total immigration, will respect 'the programme's goals rather than some arbitrary target. Thus, a shortfall in, for example, the economic category will not be made up by increasing the family class, or vice versa' (ibid: 5). The 1995 plan sets an overall target of between 190,000 and 215,000 (Citizenship and Immigration Canada 1994a: 6). The economic category retained its 43 per cent share, but total admissions in the category were down from 1994.

The planning levels for 1996–2000 are given as shares of programme classes in Table 13. The total number of immigrants to be admitted each year will be determined annually but will reflect long-term strategic objectives. The goal to restrict immigration to approximately 1 per cent of Canada's population will be applied over the long term, 'keeping in mind Canada's absorptive capacity' (ibid: 13). Beginning in 1996, as the table indicates, the balance between the classes of immigrants will place greater emphasis on economic migrants.

The Canadian immigration programme is, like its Australian counterpart, divided into three main classes: family, economic and refugee.[7] The economic category includes individuals admitted as skilled immigrants or as business immigrants. Skilled immigrants are selected according to criteria outlined in the immigrant selection (points) system, largely on the basis of their labour market skills. Their dependants, who are not subject to any selection criteria, may also accompany them. In 1993, the points system was altered to increase the value of education and skill levels and to toughen the assessment of English and French language skills. The five-year plan and other documents released in autumn 1994 promised that additional changes in the points system would be forthcoming to 'enhance both the short- and long-term contributions by newcomers to the Canadian economy' (ibid: 10). The plan notes that the number of applicants in the skills category had fallen in recent years, reflecting the rate of unemployment in Canada.

The points system as it stood in November 1994 provided for a maximum of 105 points, plus 5 bonus points if the applicant was an assisted relative.

Table 13   1996–2000 Immigrant Plan, Canada (planned percentages)

	1994	1995	1996	1997–9	2000
			(Projected)		
Economic	43	43	47	52	53
Family	51	51	47	44	44
Other	6	6	6	4	3
Total	100	100	100	100	100

Source: *A Broader Vision: Immigration and Citizenship, Plan 1995–2000.* Citizenship and Immigration Canada, Ottawa 1994: 13

The pass mark was set at 70. The criteria that could earn the highest points were education (16), specific vocational preparation (18), and knowledge of English and French (15). Intermediate points could be earned for the occupation of intended employment (10), for having arranged employment or a designated occupation (10), for age (10) and for personal suitability (10). Finally, one could earn up to 8 points for experience and a criterion labelled 'the demographic factor', which is applied equally to all applicants and has been used to adjust the overall flow of immigrants. This last criterion is effectively a way to float the pass mark.

The Business Migration class includes three sub-categories of immigrants: entrepreneurs, investors, and self-employed migrants. Entrepreneurs must demonstrate their intention and ability to establish, purchase, or invest in a business that will create or maintain employment for at least one Canadian. Investors, on the other hand, must have a successful track record and a minimum net worth. A prescribed amount must be invested for a fixed period of time. Smaller investments are required in provinces which receive fewer business immigrants. Self-employed migrants must demonstrate an intent and an ability to keep themselves employed, and their endeavours must contribute to the economy or to the country's cultural and artistic life.

The Business Migration programme was reviewed during the 1994 consultations, and a number of changes are being introduced. The government hopes these changes will allow the programme to make a greater 'contribution to business development, export market expansion priorities, to provide venture capital to small and medium sized business and minimize abuse' (Citizenship and Immigration Canada 1994d: 30). Among the changes foreseen are an improved selection process to ensure that business migrants are qualified and know what is expected of them. The criteria for selection will be clarified, with basic criteria to be established by the federal government while the provinces 'customize' these to suit local circumstances. The self-employed category will be collapsed into the skilled class (for a critique of the programme, see Nash 1991).

As was already noted, a moratorium was placed on the investor programme as of 1 November 1994 until the programme could be redesigned. A private sector expert panel is being established to advise this process. A new programme, directed towards providing a source of risk capital to small- and medium-sized businesses, should be in place by 1996 (Citizenship and Immigration Canada 1994d: 32). The entrepreneur programme will also be revised. Applicants will be encouraged to visit Canada as often as necessary before immigrating in order to familiarize themselves with local economic circumstances. Once admitted as permanent residents, entrepreneurs will be expected to establish a business and maintain it for a specified period of time of between six months and two years. Finally, Citizenship and Immigration Canada will establish or improve the services offered by specialized business centres at key missions abroad. The chief aim is to attract potential business migrants from both traditional and emerging markets.

Background

Contemporary Canadian policy may be traced from the pivotal year of 1957, when the Diefenbaker government shifted the focus of immigration policy away from a broad range of low-skill occupations to a narrow range of high-skill professionals and entrepreneurs with capital.[8] Planners concluded that the skills needs of the economy could not be met from either domestic supply or from the traditional sources of immigration (largely Britain). A process was put in train, therefore, to reduce the emphasis that had previously been placed on country of origin. By 1962, regulations had been tabled in Parliament that effectively eliminated the White Canada policy. As the Economic Council puts it:

> With this change in policy, and a strong recovery of the economy, the average annual inflow of professionals more than doubled from roughly 7,000 during the years 1958–61 to 20,000 during the years 1962–69. By the late 1960s, professionals accounted for one quarter of the immigrants entering the labour force. (1991: 14)

In 1967, the law was amended again to introduce the points system to be applied to applicants who did not qualify as close family members or refugees. These immigrants became the independent or economic class. Relatives who were not immediate family were also subjected to the points system. The chief objectives of the points system were to select those applicants who would make the greatest economic contribution to the Canadian economy and to do so in a completely non-discriminatory manner. The points system in its present form has already been described. Although the particulars have been changed frequently, the general structure of the system has remained constant since its introduction.

The changes in immigration regulations in 1962 and 1967 had profound effects. The proportion of immigrants coming from Europe and the United States declined precipitously. Immigrants from the West Indies, the Middle East, Asia and Africa made up only 20 per cent of all immigrants in the late 1950s and early 1960s, compared with over 40 per cent in the late 1960s and early 1970s (Economic Council 1991: 14).

The Canadian immigration programme got its current structure through the Immigration Act of 1978. This legislation laid out formally the three categories of immigrants already being admitted in fact: family, independent and refugee. The Act tried to rationalize immigration policy by requiring that target levels be integrated with Canada's demographic and labour market conditions. Responding to a deep recession, the law stipulated that temporary workers could not enter Canada unless the employer could show that no Canadian citizens were qualified to perform the work. Immigrant applicants who did not score at least one or more points for occupational demand on the points system were automatically barred, no matter what their scores on other criteria. An applicant who was unable to make prior arrangements for employment was assessed a 10 point penalty. As economic malaise continued, controls over independent migrants were tightened. After May 1982, no independent migrants could be recruited unless they had prearranged employment (ibid: 17).

In 1985, with the economy recovering, the government authorized a gradual increase in the intake by expanding the number of visas available to economic migrants selected by the points system, which was adjusted to emphasize training and employment-related factors. At the same time a House of Commons report recommended that 'every effort should be made, beginning today and continuing for at least 30 years, to consider using immigration policy to smooth out the current age imbalance in the Canadian population' (cited in Economic Council of Canada 1991: 17). Hence, immigration targets were set for 1986 and 1988 at 105,000 and 135,000 (ibid: 19). This general policy direction was reaffirmed in 1990 when the Mulroney government produced its first five-year Immigration Plan covering 1991–5. From 215,000 entries in 1991, the government intended to reach 250,000 for each of the years 1993–5 (Canada 1990).

However, in 1992 there were major changes, in part sparked by the asylum crisis, but also stemming from a more general concern that the government under existing law lacked the 'authority to manage the admission of immigrants in such a way as to achieve the levels in the plan and to realize other policy objectives' (Press release, EIC June 1992: 1; cf. EIC 1992). The problem as the Minister outlined it was that, whatever the programme targeted, if more people than anticipated applied and met basic eligibility standards, they had to be accepted for eventual landing. This led to settlement and financing problems, backlogs and client frustration.

The new 1992 programme created three immigrant applicant streams as a means of circumventing the problem of applicant backlog. It stipulated that qualified persons in the first stream would all be processed and admitted as quickly as possible. These would include immediate family members of people living in Canada, Convention refugees and business persons applying under a revised Immigrant Investor programme. Stream 2 applicants would be processed on a first-come, first-served basis. For each category in this stream, admission ceilings would be set in the immigration plan. These applicants include parents and grandparents of Canadian residents, government-assisted or privately sponsored refugees, and applicants with arranged employment. Stream 3 applicants 'would be selected on the basis of excellence because they are the best in their category'. All categories in this stream are subject to limits and, once these are met, no further applications are accepted. The categories in Stream 3 are independent immigrants, people qualified in certain designated occupations and qualified entrepreneurs with business experience.

Bill C–86, incorporating the changes described above, was passed in February 1993. Ruddick and Burstein provide insiders' accounts of the thinking that lay behind these changes and a sanguine view of their likely effects (1993). They note that the rationale behind the economic component of the immigration programme has been gradually changing. Before, it was based on the notion that immigration would produce scale economies as it increased the size of the Canadian market (ibid: 24; cf. Economic Council of Canada 1991: 22–31). Increasingly, the government has moved to the view that 'independent immigrants must contribute to higher productivity through their skills, knowledge and experience. This view is consistent with the new economic theories of growth which emphasize knowledge and creativity and the ability to produce small runs of specialized tailored products rather than large runs of the same product (scale economies)' (Ruddick and Burstein 1993: 24). The authors note that more and more family reunification and humanitarian classes have tended to dominate the programme:

> The existence of a large backlog of family class cases with vested rights, poor economic conditions which make Canada a relatively unattractive destination for highly skilled applicants and a lack of effective management tools to implement desired changes to levels and components have frustrated the Government's ability to influence the makeup of its annual immigration flow. (ibid: 24)

Lastly, Ruddick and Burstein observe that, in 1992, more than 25 per cent of the principal applicants selected in the Independent and Assisted Relative categories (excluding business immigrants) have only secondary education or less. Twenty-three per cent spoke neither English nor French.

One of the most important changes in the selection process is that skilled workers must now meet one of three criteria in order to be assessed further by the points system: (1) their intended occupation must be on the General Occupation List,[9] (2) their intended occupation must be on the Designated Occupations List (a smaller list of occupations in shortage); or (3) they must have arranged employment in Canada with a job offer validated by a government employment centre. If applicants qualify through one of these means, they move on to the points system. As noted previously, the points system has been modified to place more emphasis on criteria which provide labour market participants with transferable skills and with flexibility – what the government calls 'selection for excellence' (Ruddick and Burstein 1993: 26). Or, 'the skilled worker movement will ... change moving the focus away from an applicant's intended occupation, and concentrating instead on "generic" attributes that will contribute to Canada's productivity and competitiveness' (ibid: 29).

Birrell views these changes with alarm. In his opinion, they take Canada in the direction that Australia went in the late 1980s when independent migrants were selected according to occupationally related qualities but without reference to the state of Australia's labour market. 'This system,' he warns, 'delivered thousands of engineers, nurses, teachers, and other professionals in the early 1990s into some of the fields worst affected by the recession. It is currently being dismantled' (1993: 30).

The Strategic Research and Analysis Branch of Citizenship and Immigration Canada produced a study (Citizenship and Migration Canada 1994e) of the relative labour market performance of independent and family class immigrants that sheds considerable light on the effectiveness of their economic selection programme. The database consists of linked immigrant landing and tax records for all immigrants who landed between 1980–8 and who filed a tax return in any one of those years. The unit of analysis is the immigrant taxfiler. The data provide a comprehensive information set on immigrants, including their employment and other earnings, their place of residence, and their use of unemployment insurance – all of which can be categorized by immigrant class, age, gender, and other relevant characteristics at landing. As the report puts it: 'The objective of the independent immigration programme is to increase Canada's productivity, by selecting skilled individuals who will earn more than the average, pay more in taxes, and have less cause to resort to social programmes such as unemployment insurance' (ibid: 1).

The analysis in this study builds on independent migrants who are principal applicants selected for their skills and who have not benefited from any of the special programmes which have, at various times, been available to independents. The comparative group is usually family class immigrants (principal applicants and dependants). The study focuses on the labour market experience of immigrants three full years after landing, i.e. the economic performance of those who landed in 1985 and 1981 is examined in 1988 and 1984, respectively. Among the important findings of the study are the following:

(1) Independent immigrants have higher employment earnings than family class immigrants, even when compared to family class immigrants with the same linguistic and education level. Independent immigrants also earned more than the average employment earnings for Canadians, while family immigrants earned less. These differences can be attributed to the fact that independents, on average, have higher skills and greater attachment to the labour market.

(2) Independents earn two-and-a-half to three times more, on average, than family class immigrants, both on arrival and three full years after landing.

(3) Family class immigrants tend to be over-represented in industries with low average earnings and under-represented in industries with above average earnings, while independents tend to be more highly concentrated where earnings are at or above average.

(4) Independents are much better educated than family class immigrants. In 1988, 13 per cent of independents and 61 per cent of family class taxfilers who landed in 1985 had less than thirteen years of schooling. Fifty-eight per cent of independents and 14 per cent of family class had a university degree.

(5) Of independents who landed in 1985, 64 per cent had over four years of occupation-specific training, as compared to only 6 per cent of the family class.

United States

United States immigration policy differs in a number of ways from that of both Australia and Canada. There has typically been much less emphasis in US policy on selection for skills, although this appears to be changing. Family reunion is the principal goal of American policy, dominating the programme to a greater extent than in Australia or Canada. Furthermore, US policy is chiefly the responsibility of the legislative branch rather than the executive. Specific details of policy, such as the number to be admitted in a given year and a given category, are part of immigration law and cannot be changed readily by the Congress, or changed at all by the administration. American policy is, consequently, less flexible than that of other receiving nations. In addition, the United States employs different tools for choosing among applicants within its broad classes of admissions. The preference system, rather than a points mechanism, is employed for both family and skills admissions. In addition, the labour certification system has been a central feature of American policy since 1952.

The Immigration Act of 1990, along with the Immigration Reform and Control Act of 1986, constitute the basic framework of American immigration law. The former addressed levels of immigration; the latter dealt mostly with illegal immigration, imposing sanctions on employers who knowingly hire undocumented workers (Miller 1992). At a time when Australia is cutting its annual intake significantly and Canada is moving in the same direction, US policy makers substantially increased US entries by over one-third. The 1990 law set an overall ceiling for admissions during FY 1992–4 at 714,000. This figure is expected to fall in succeeding years to 675,000. These numbers are to be allocated among several classes of admissions through the preference system and among countries according to a formula that sets the total number of entries from any country in a given year at 25,000. With some oversimplification, the American programme can be described as having the same three chief classes of admissions as those of Canada and Australia: family, humanitarian and refugee, and employment.[10]

Under the 1990 Act, employment-based visas increased nearly three-fold to 140,000 annually. These are distributed across five preferences. Visas unused in one preference during the previous fiscal year 'spill down' to the next preference. Unused visas from the fourth and fifth preferences are passed to the first preference, from which they pass on, if not used, to the second, and then to the third. Beginning in FY 1994, the unused visas from employment-based categories pass to family-sponsored and unused family-sponsored visas pass to employment-based.

The five preferences with their corresponding visa allotments are as follows:

- First (40,000): priority workers (aliens with extraordinary ability, out-standing professors or researchers, and certain multinational executives and managers. Not subject to labour certification.
- Second (40,000): professionals with advanced degrees and aliens of exceptional ability in the arts, science or business who will benefit the United States. Requires US Labor Department certification.
- Third (40,000): skilled workers, entry-level professionals and 'other' (formerly called unskilled) workers. The 'other' category may not receive more than 10,000 visas.
- Fourth (10,000): special immigrants (primarily ministers of religion and persons who work for religious organizations).
- Fifth (10,000): investors who create full-time employment for at least ten US workers and invest at least $1,000,000 in a new commercial enterprise.

Annual immigration data for fiscal years 1989–93 are shown in Table 14. The data indicate that the numbers entering under the family class have risen steadily throughout the period. Family-class migrants constituted 55 per cent of all admissions in FY 1993. Employment-based entries doubled from 1991 to 1992 and increased again in 1993. Even in the peak year of 1993, however, employment-based entries made up only 15 per cent of the total, and this was about double the share of such entrants during the years 1989–91. However, only about half the persons in this category are workers or professionals themselves; the remainder are their family members. As a result, only 8 per cent of all admissions to the United States were persons selected on the basis of their employment-related characteristics.

Table 4 also reflects the rapid growth in the asylee category. For comparative purposes, it includes estimates of the illegal immigration rate as developed by the Center for Migration Studies (300,000). These estimates are higher than the Census Bureau's figure of 200,000.

Table 14 Annual immigration, 1989–93 (000s)

Category	1989	1990	1991	1992	1993
Family	341.6	446.2	453.2	500.9	539.5
Employment	52.8	56.7	58.0	119.8	149.2
Humanitarian	179.5	186.4	168.1	220.8	246.9
Refugees	107.2	122.3	112.8	132.1	119.5
Asylees	61.3	58.9	49.6	83.2	120.3
Cuban programme	11.0	5.2	5.7	5.5	7.1
Special	29.1	42.0	32.0	41.6	36.3
Total	603.0	731.3	711.8	883.1	971.9
Illegal (estimate)	250.0	250.0	300.0	300.0	300.0
Total	853.0	981.3	1 011.8	1 183.1	1 271.9
IRCA legal	478.8	880.4	1 123.2	163.3	75.0*
Total	1 331.8	1 861.7	2 135.0	1 346.4	1 346.9

* INS data not yet available, estimated at between 50–100,000
Source: INS Statistical Yearbooks 1989–92 and 1993 data; State Department for refugee data. Reprinted from *Backgrounder*, Center for Immigration Studies May 1994

Background

The educational and skill characteristics of immigrants to the United States have fluctuated in response, primarily, to economic and political conditions at home and in sending countries, rather than in consequence of changes in national policy. Thomas Archdeacon (1983) characterizes immigration in the first hundred years since the ratification of the Constitution in 1789 as displaying relatively advanced economic traits: migrants included independent farmers, shopkeepers, tradesmen, and an important component of professionals and the 'better-off'. But by 1890, the continent had been settled from coast to coast and the frontier had been declared officially closed. Migration over the next 40 years helped to fill the jobs of a growing industrial economy. These new migrants were drawn increasingly from eastern and southern Europe, were often single men intending to stay only temporarily, and were overwhelmingly of working-class origin.

Between 1830 and 1860, the United States received 4.7 million immigrants; in the subsequent 30 years, 10 million arrived; and between 1890 and 1920, another 18.2 million entered. This last period was the high water mark of the American immigration experience, and it provoked the Congress to enact the first systematic national immigration regulations in 1924. The national origins quota system, which focused on the sources of migration and, by extension, on the ethnicity of migrants, was a transparent attempt to favour immigration from the traditional source countries of northern Europe. This approach was retained in the 1952 Immigration and Nationality Act, although for the first time Asian countries were allotted a token share of visas (100 a year per country in the region).

The combined impact of the 1924 and 1952 Acts, along with the Great

Depression and World War II, sharply reduced overall entries. Only 1.8 million immigrants arrived between 1925 and 1948. As numbers declined, immigrant communities aged, and Americanization was stressed, towards the middle of the century the United States became much less an immigrant country.

New immigration legislation in 1965 changed all this. In a move to eliminate discrimination from the selection system, Congress abolished the quota system and allotted visas to countries in the eastern hemisphere on an equal basis. For the first time, it established an overall ceiling in the western hemisphere as well, but without individual country limits. The results of this new policy were profound. By removing the bias that had favoured northern Europe, the reforms opened the country to mass immigration from dozens of poorer countries around the globe whose citizens had previously been effectively excluded. The immediate result of this policy, therefore, was a sharp increase in the overall level of immigration, accompanied by a massive shift in source countries away from Europe and towards Asia, the Indian sub-continent, and other developing areas. Finally, by placing a ceiling on western hemispheric immigration, Congress created the legal framework for a vast explosion of illegal migration from Latin America.

Recent developments on skilled migration

The Immigration and Nationality Act of 1952 was the first serious attempt to select immigrants by skill. This law included two major innovations in US policy: the preference system and the labour certification process. Originally, there were four preferences. The first, or highest priority, was for those with the education, technical training, special experience, or exceptional abilities that were designated by the Attorney General (because the Immigration and Naturalisation Service is located in the Justice Department) to be beneficial to the United States. As Briggs notes, 'By creating this category, Congress gave official recognition to the idea that immigration policy could be used as a human resource instrument to select immigrants on the basis of their training and in accordance with the needs of the nation's labour market' (1992: 101). Half of all visas were reserved for applicants qualifying under this category. The remaining three preferences assigned priorities to various categories of adult family relatives of citizens or permanent-resident aliens.

The law also authorized the Secretary of Labor to certify that the admission of non-family-related immigrants would not adversely affect the wages and working conditions of citizen workers who were similarly employed. Because of staffing shortages, implementation of this feature was erratic (ibid: 105).

When the immigration programme was amended in 1965, the

preference and labour certification procedures were maintained for immigrants from the eastern hemisphere, but in altered form. (Those from the west were free from such constraints.) One critic of these changes writes that 'the adoption of the new preference system represented a dramatic shift in policy emphasis away from the human resource development considerations (that had been in place since 1952) toward one that relied largely on family reunification as its priority concern' (ibid: 109). The amendments continued the practice of not counting the migration of spouses and minor children as part of the hemispheric or individual country ceilings (and added parents of US citizens over the age of 21 to this category). Moreover, the amendments stipulated that 74 per cent of available immigrant visas each year should go to persons with family ties to US citizens or permanent resident aliens. The preference system, moreover, was reordered to reduce the priority of occupational visas (the previous first preference was split into two parts and downgraded to the third and sixth preferences). Even more significant was the creation of a new, fifth preference, for adult brothers and sisters of US citizens and the assignment of 24 per cent of the available visas to this group (Borjas 1989).

We have already seen that the 1965 reforms had the largely unintended consequence of greatly enlarging the share of immigrants coming from Asia and other developing nations. The concurrent shift in emphasis from work to family reunion was arguably intentional, although it emerged from a highly complex political struggle in which the motives of the principal players were exceedingly mixed (Briggs 1992: 110–13). By the late 1970s, therefore, the policy wheels were turning again.

The most important analytical step in the reform process of the late 1970s and early 1980s was the Report of the Select Commission on Immigration and Refugee Policy (SCIRP) in 1981 which urged that the admissions systems be modified to increase the number of visas available for so-called 'new seed' migrants, i.e. those without existing family ties to the US (SCIRP 1981b). The national policy discussion that led eventually to the passage of the 1986 Immigration Reform and Control Act, which dealt with illegal migration, and the 1990 Immigration Act, which re-organized the legal programme, was neither so vigorous and open as that in Australia nor as systematic and deliberate as that in Canada. Both long-term, theoretical interpretations of the American economy and much more short-term responses contributed to policy change. As one keen observer, who was himself a high-level participant in the process, tells us:

> The passage of IRCA was in many respects the US Congress' immigration response to an ideology of limits. The 1970s and early 1980s had given rise to, and had subsequently fuelled, perceptions of extreme US vulnerability to foreign political and economic events. These perceptions had reinforced a US self-image

of eroding ability to control its own fate ... In contrast ... the (1990 Immigration Act was an expression) of a new attitude. This attitude reveals a more economically and politically confident United States with a sense of itself, and of its ability to control its destiny. (Papademetriou 1991: 5)

In the debates of the late 1980s, this new confidence was perhaps most directly reflected in the increasing concern about potential labour shortages as unemployment fell, birth rates were below replacement levels, and IRCA threatened to shut off access to illegal workers (Meissner and Papademetriou nd: 9).

Of probably more importance than the fear of labour shortages was the broader concern over international competitiveness. Immigration reform was thought necessary for two reasons: first, to redress the fall in average skill level of immigrants consequent to the 1965 legislation, and second, specifically to recruit persons possessing the high-level scientific and technical know-how essential in a modern post-industrial economy (Hudson Institute 1987; National Center of Education and the Economy 1990; Commission on Workforce Quality and Labor Market Efficiency 1989).

Despite these concerns and the fact that employment-based admissions were expanded in the 1990 Act, it is hard to conclude that the reforms really moved immigration policy in the direction of a more carefully calibrated contribution to the labour market. First, non-employment based admissions did not decline as a result of the legislation. In fact, although it had been proposed that family admissions be reduced to make room for skills migration, the family category was increased by almost 20 per cent in the first three years and by 10 per cent afterwards. However, the amount of total legal immigration consisting of employment-based admissions increased substantially, both in actual numbers and as a share of the total.

It is too soon to know the impact of the 1990 Act, but a recent overview of the economic literature on immigrants to the United States (Borjas 1994) draws pessimistic conclusions that differ considerably from the more optimistic conclusions economists were advancing a decade earlier. Borjas argues that new research has established that the relative skills of successive immigrant waves declined over much of the post-war period and that it is unlikely that recent immigrants will reach parity with the earnings of natives during their working lives. He goes on to note that there is a strong correlation between the skills of immigrants and the skills of second-generation Americans, 'so that the huge skill differentials observed among today's foreign-born groups become tomorrow's differences among American-born ethnic groups' (ibid: 1713). Finally, he notes that immigration policy 'matters, so that host countries which filter applicants in terms of observable skills "attract" immigrants who are more skilled, have higher earnings, and are less likely to participate in public assistance programs' (ibid).

Other pertinent experience

Australia, Canada and the United States are the most important examples of skill migration policy, but theirs is not the only relevant experience. Constraints on space prevent a systematic review of the other countries, such as those in Latin America (especially the Southern Cone), that have long histories of accepting immigration. Recent evidence suggests, however, that the bulk of contemporary international migration in that region is non-professional (Lattes and de Lattes 1994: 118).

The Western European states present a quite different picture. With few exceptions, these were never countries of immigration. Governments there are mainly preoccupied with controlling inflows from outside Europe. Their efforts focus on developing better means for excluding or deterring asylum-seekers and illegal entrants, while at the same time admitting the family dependants of foreign residents who settled before the doors were closed in 1974. These efforts are undertaken in the context of the realization of free movement of labour within the European Union, which has recently expanded to fifteen states (Freeman 1992). The evidence is that intra-EU migration is stable or even declining. There were, in 1991, an estimated 4.9 million EU nationals residing in other member states (Koslowski 1994: 369). For all the furore immigration has provoked in recent years, there is little evidence that intra-EU migration has caused much concern. Even more striking is the fact that a considerable migration from outside Europe (mostly temporary) of highly skilled professions, managers and technical personnel is admitted routinely. Around 85 per cent of all work visas granted by the UK government, for example, go to such individuals (Salt 1989). These admissions, however, are for the convenience of multinational firms rather than being part of a general immigration recruitment strategy.

A number of countries in the East and South-east Asian region have in recent years become immigrant receiving states at the same time that they remain significant sources of emigrants. As two keen observers put it, the investment policies of Japan and the ASEAN NIEs have stimulated the creation of international labour markets:

> The migration flows that have been activated include both legal and illegal immigration into the NIEs, trainees from subsidiary companies to the investing countries, and growing numbers of Japanese, Korean, Taiwanese, and Hong Kong managers, professionals, technicians, and other qualified workers accompanying the capital flows. (Lim and Abella 1994: 225)

The situations of the states in the region differ significantly, depending on the extent of industrialization or stage of modernization (Appleyard 1992). Many are experiencing influxes of illegal workers, especially in the unskilled and manual sectors. Some states organize and recruit unskilled migrants, but generally these governments are trying to orient their migration policies towards the selection of skilled workers, who are the only persons welcomed and permitted to settle (Skeldon 1992). This is the case in Japan, for example, where most of the legal foreign workers in the country are business executives, entertainers and language instructors. Singapore admits both skilled and unskilled workers, but only the former are allowed to bring their families and may be permitted to settle. Taiwan only permits the entry of skilled workers (20,000 in 1990). Malaysia has half the foreign workers in the region (an estimated 340,000 legal workers in 1995), with perhaps an equal number of illegals. However, in 1994, the Malaysian government banned the recruitment of unskilled and semi-skilled foreign workers and created numerous disincentives to discourage employers from hiring foreigners. Yet the government anticipates skill shortages by the year 2000 and admits professionals and expatriate executives who earn above a certain salary (*Migrant News* February 1995).

A general and very tentative proposition that can be made about the East and South-east Asian record is that, while states there often have the administrative capacity and political space to engage in highly interventionist labour market and immigration policies that would be unacceptable in Western liberal democracies, their relatively limited experience in dealing with migration pressures means that they are engaged in a game of catch-up and have not yet demonstrated a clear capacity to manage immigration for state purposes.

Conclusions

The records of the skilled migration programmes considered in this chapter are mixed at best. All of the principal cases have endeavoured to attract skilled workers, to expand the share of migrant streams composed of the highly qualified, and to connect the recruitment of skills with conditions in local labour markets. As I have argued, these countries are in comparatively advantageous positions in the international trading system to accomplish these goals. Yet, they have encountered serious problems.

The broad trends among the three countries are in the direction of convergence on the desirability of admitting skilled migrants, but there is continuing disagreement on the basic policy tools by which this should be done. As one pores over an accumulating mountain of government documents and reports, one is struck by the overweening conviction of policy makers that using immigration to develop a more highly skilled labour force is worth expenditure of considerable administrative and political effort. The only qualification to official enthusiasm is uncertainty as to whether skill recruitment should be closely tied to occupations for which shortages are evident or anticipated or whether recruiters should be instructed to search for 'excellence' wherever they find it, regardless of the particular occupation of the applicant.

Canada has embarked on a quest for excellence, very generally defined, after hewing to a 'tap-on, tap-off' policy closely reflecting the domestic unemployment rate throughout the post-war period (Veugelers and Klassen 1994). Australia has flip-flopped on this question. At present, there seems to be disagreement at the top of the Labor government on how best to proceed. Nevertheless, it is evident that disillusion has set in about the wisdom of admitting large numbers of professionals if they are destined to be jobless. Given that Australia does more than the other governments to assist skilled migrants to adjust to their new setting, the spectacularly bad labour market experience of some professionals, especially engineers, is notable. The United States is formally reorienting its policy away from the overwhelming concern for family migration that has predominated since 1965. Even as the size of the economic class is increased, however, the selection mechanisms in place (the preference system and labour certification) appear unlikely either to be sensitive to domestic employment conditions or to produce 'the best' in the meaning the Canadians give the term. Moreover, such extraneous political objectives as the 'diversity' category that was inserted into the 1990 legislation promise to water down the American programme (Bean and Fix 1992: 50).

Is the consensus on the wisdom of skills recruitment supported by the evidence? In all three cases, the levels of skills and income among the economic or independent class migrants are higher than for persons recruited under the family and humanitarian categories. One view, therefore, is that as long as there is going to be a migration programme of some considerable size, it ought to have as large a skills component as possible. This is the fallback or default position for many of the critics and defenders of immigration. Critics insist that migration must serve the national interest, defined typically in terms of economic performance. Advocates of mass immigration make their case on the grounds that migrants play a role in fostering economic growth.

It appears that the skill level of immigrants in Australia and Canada is comparable to, if not higher, than that of the native population. This supports the view that immigration has resulted in a modest improvement in the overall stock of human capital. This is not the case in the United States, where the skill level of immigrants has declined over the last thirty years (Dawkins *et al.* 1992: 113–15). Easy access to imported skills may also result in the atrophy of national educational and training efforts and may therefore contribute to a gradual decline in the skills levels of the native population. I have found no empirical evidence for this (see ibid: 115), but Australian officials fear this prospect (see the words of PM Keating quoted above).

Do skilled immigrants adversely affect the employment of native workers with comparable skills? The general answer one finds in the economic literature is a resounding 'no', reinforced by evidence that 'immigrants create more jobs than they take'. In Australia (and Canada) there has been little empirical research on the impact of immigration on native job prospects, but this topic has received considerable attention in the United States. A recent review concludes that:

> while immigration may cause some decrease in employment and wages among low-skilled non-immigrants, depending very much on the region or industry examined, these effects are small. Immigrants (and illegals) tend toward only weak substitutability or complementarity with non-immigrant groups, with the overall result being essentially benign. (ibid: 118)

A more recent reappraisal by Borjas, however, draws a more tentative conclusion. He finds that immigration has a small effect on wages but none on employment in local labour markets, while it may have a significant impact on employment at the macro-economic level. He observes that:

> a fair appraisal of the literature thus suggests that we still do not fully understand how immigrants affect the employment opportunities of natives in local labour markets; nor do we understand the dynamic process through which natives respond to these supply shocks and re-establish labour market equilibrium. (1994: 1700)

The possibility that professional migrants themselves might face unemployment in their new economic environment is amply demonstrated by the data from Australia. One contributing factor in migrant unemployment is the 'transferability gap', which may be defined as the disjuncture between the pre-migration experiences and qualifications of migrants and the assessment of those experiences and qualifications by employers (Hawthorne 1994). The gap appears to result from (1) problems with the recognition of overseas qualifications, (2) issues of linguistic and other cross-cultural factors and (3) discrimination. The pervasiveness of these problems raises serious questions for government recruitment and settlement programmes.

Recognition of qualifications has received extensive attention in Australia. Even the requirement that workers selected overseas must show that their qualifications meet national standards does not insure that these qualifications will be recognized by the appropriate governmental or professional organization once the migrants are in the country. It seems undeniable, given the research of Hawthorne (1994), Woldring (1994), and Castles *et al.* (1989), that elements of racial or ethnic bias enter into patterns of recognition. In Australia, Chapman and Iredale (1993) found that in a sample of skilled migrants, only 39 per cent presented their qualifications for direct recognition, and of these only 43 per cent achieved formal recognition at the level desired. They note that most skilled migrants in their sample did not apply for formal recognition at all

(Chapman and Iredale 1993: 379). Much can be done to ease the process by which migrants apply for and receive recognition for their educational and experiential qualifications. Hawthorne recommends that the Australian government put as much emphasis on educating employers to the possibilities of immigrant qualifications as it does on training and educating migrants to make their credentials fit the local situation. Clearly, Australian efforts to vet qualifications at overseas posts are currently inadequate.

All three countries are experimenting with business migration or investor recruitment schemes, which have been among the most problematic of all employment-based immigration programmes. In both Australia and Canada, the programmes have come under heavy criticism – because of fraud and other unintended consequences, quite apart from the perception some have that they allow the rich to 'buy' their way into the country. Both countries have had to suspend and revamp their programmes. Yet, despite the unpopularity, bad press, and questionable economic logic of business migration schemes, policy makers appear to be fatally attracted to them.

A skilled migration programme must determine need, select migrants and integrate them into the national economy, and conduct subsequent evaluations of programme effectiveness. Although all the governments surveyed have made impressive efforts to carry out each of these activities, it is evident from the speed and often contradictory direction of programme changes and from the sharp criticism levelled against such programmes, that policy makers have found these challenges exceedingly difficult. More effort has been directed at selection and, secondarily, at linking selection to need. Less effort has been devoted to adaptation, although Australia is something of an exception in this regard. Critics often assume that it is possible to get accurate, up-to-date and meaningful measures of the manpower 'needs' of industrial sectors and trades. In practice, governments tend to rely on official unemployment rates, and these are not necessarily accurate at the level of specificity the programme requires. The Economic Council of Canada's 1991 survey of immigration concludes that immigration policy is rarely a useful tool for filling particular 'gaps' in the labour market. They recommend that the selection process should cease even to develop 'open lists' of occupations because they are unreliable (Economic Council 1991: 32).

One can only admire the determination and creativity of those bureaucrats in Australia and Canada who have devised, revised, fine-tuned, and polished the points system since it was invented about three decades ago. The Canadians, in particular, seem committed to enhancing the objectivity and scientific rationality of their selection mechanism and appear undeterred by their own evidence that previous prototypes, much ballyhooed, have failed to perform to standard. How does one interpret the maddeningly complex trail of adjustments, retreats and overhauls that characterizes the histories of both countries' selection systems? Is it evidence of impressive flexibility and bureaucratic learning or disappointment, confusion and disorder? The US preference system, with its spill-downs and carry-overs, is even less a model of administrative clarity.

Some of the difficulties are technical. Initiatives may founder due to inadequate data or insufficient analytical tools. Technical problems derive, at base, from economic uncertainty. The most significant uncertainty involves predicting the unemployment rate, nationally and in specific sectors, nine to eighteen months in advance, because this is when the migrants being recruited today will be on the job market. In addition, planners must project how large the stream of applicants for particular classes will be and what characteristics they will have. Even the United States cannot be sure that there will be more qualified applicants than places in its economic categories. The problem is much worse for Canada and Australia, both of which were shaken by the substantial increase in the US intake legislated in 1990 because they feared it would wreck their own much smaller migration programmes.

More serious and pervasive obstacles to effective skill recruitment are administrative and political. These have been touched on in the three case studies. Burstein's lucid accounting (1992) of the administrative and political difficulties that managers in Canada face also applies, with minor adjustments, to the other countries as well (cf. Birrell 1994b). The basic problem is that administrative control over the various classes of migration varies systematically, running from weak to strong as one moves from on-site asylum-seekers, to family migrants, privately sponsored migrants, investors, other business migrants, independents with relatives, independents with no relatives and finally to government-selected refugees (Birrell 1990: 8). For those categories over which the government has little control, the primary immigration decision originates with private individuals. The targets, ceilings, or levels plans for those categories are 'predictions' rather than policy choices grounded in 'reasons'. Government tries to figure out how many qualified persons will apply and sets the category targets accordingly to avoid backlogs. The only effective controls over these categories are the numbers of potential applicants and the administrative capacity to process them.

The discretion left to the government over the remaining programmes is quite narrow. It is limited, in effect, to residual categories which have levels that can be contracted or expanded as necessary to complement changes in the 'uncontrollable' categories. A predictable policy dynamic emerges. Programme expansions can occur due to government decisions or because of spontaneous changes in the behaviour of private individuals. As Burstein puts it:

Whatever the reason, after a period of varying length, the new arrivals begin to sponsor their families from abroad thus extending the competition with other applicants for limited immigration slots. (Limited either by policy or by processing capacity.) Generally, the contest is one-sided where the economic flows are concerned. Because family or asylum migration is based on relatively inflexible statutory rights, the independent and business categories, which are more easily contracted (by government), end up being squeezed out. (1992: 9)

The fact that the immigration train is pulled along by the engine of family reunion, asylum-seeking, and other demand-driven categories does not mean, however, that the economic categories cannot exhibit long-term growth. On the contrary, there is, according to Burstein, a 'political bias that favours generous admission criteria over more restrictive ones — or, put a little differently, that favours errors of commission over errors of omission' (ibid: 5). Moreover, as the family category grows at the expense of the economic class, concerns begin to surface about 'balance' in the programme. To restore balance, one can either reduce the size of the family component (by changing the rules or manipulating processing capacity) or by increasing the volume of the economic category. The case studies indicate that the latter is the most politically palatable choice.

Taken together, the technical, administrative, and political difficulties of mounting a successful skilled migration programme suggest that governments so inclined will need to make major commitments of finances, personnel and time. Even then, the odds appear to be against anything more than an erratic, episodic and modest success.

Notes

1. Two of the chief arguments for immigration, scale effects and shortages, make no assumptions as to the skill level of the migrant stream. It is a staple of economic theory that increases in the size of domestic markets are accompanied by economies of scale that result in greater unit output (Nevile 1991: 22–5). All three of the traditional countries of immigration reviewed in this chapter have used immigration to increase the size of their markets, most prominently in the post-World War II immigration programmes of Australia and Canada. A recent overview (Economic Council of Canada 1991) reports that the evidence of scale effects in Canada is only modestly positive; other data suggest that rapid population growth may have side effects that offset the advantages of scale economies.
    Immigration is also commonly thought to be an important means of filling gaps in the labour market that occur periodically in certain industries or regions. Shortages can drive up the price of labour, causing inflation, and contribute to production bottlenecks. Labour shortages, actual or projected, have often been the impetus for calls for expanded immigration in the countries studied. They were the principal force behind the massive guest

worker recruitment schemes in post-war Europe (Kindleberger 1967). The actual implementation of programmes to meet specific labour shortages is quite difficult, as will be argued, though there are examples of highly targeted efforts such as the US programme to recruit nurses (Papademetriou 1991).

2. The following case analyses will focus primarily on the skills aspects of national immigration programmes. However, in order to place the matters in an appropriate context, it is necessary to give at least a truncated overview of general immigration policy and history. To conserve space I deal only with permanent immigration categories and leave aside the important category of 'temporary' entrants.

3. Within the category of family migration there are two sub-categories: preferential and concessional. Preferential family migrants are those who have a spouse, a fiance(e), a child under 18, or other close relative who is living in Australia and willing to sponsor them. The concessional (or extended) family category applies to persons who are non-dependent children, a parent who does not have the balance of his or her family in Australia, a brother or sister, or a niece or nephew. Concessional migrants, unlike those in the preferential family rubric, are subject to the points test. Points are awarded for a person's skill, age, relationship to the Australian sponsor, citizenship of the sponsor, capability of the sponsor to provide settlement support, and location of the sponsor in Australia. The humanitarian category includes refugees and other persons admitted on special compassionate grounds.

4. One tries in vain to trace the evolution of these aspects of the immigration programme over even a few years. As one survey concludes: 'There is no accessible, single source which describes clearly, simply and chronologically these regulations and incentives, to whom they applied and how they were administered' (Wooden *et al.* 1990: 306).

5. These represented the elite of professional migrants. They had all been recruited under either the independent or concessional categories between 1987 and 1992; they had (with one exception) received immediate and full recognition of their qualifications; they enjoyed substantial pre-migration professional experience (five to fifteen years); they were of prime workforce age at time of arrival; and they were intermediate to native speakers to English at the time the study began.

6. Hawthorne's findings are consistent with earlier data reported by Jones (1988). Drawing on an analysis of the status and income returns to education, qualifications and labour force experience for a sample of males in the labour force in 1982, Jones concludes that schooling obtained overseas counts for less than Australian schooling, that pre-migration labour force experience is heavily discounted in Australia, and that migrants from some countries get jobs with significantly lower status than Australian-born persons with similar qualifications and experience (1989: 11; cf. Woldring 1994).

7. Migrants in the family class generally fall into one of two sub-categories: immediate family members, and parents and grandparents. Immediate family members include spouses, fiance(e)s, and dependent children. Between July

1988 and April 1992, the definition of dependent children included all never-married children regardless of age. In 1992, regulations redefined dependent children as those under the age of 19 and unmarried, as well as those adult children who are supported by their parents either because they are full-time students or have disabilities. All sponsored spouses and dependent children who apply will be processed, subject to the usual medical and security requirements.

Persons admitted under the refugee rubric enter Canada either through the in-Canada refugee status determination system, or through the resettlement of refugees from abroad. Refugees selected abroad for resettlement are brought to Canada either through government assistance, or through private sponsorships.

8.   This discussion draws heavily on Economic Council of Canada 1991.

9.   The General Occupation List is derived from the Canadian Classification Dictionary of Occupations. From that list are removed those with low skill levels, with citizenship requirements, with unemployment rates in excess of the national average, with occupations for which promotion is through internal job ladders, and those to which special considerations apply (i.e. physicians are excluded).

10. Family admissions are governed by the preference system. Within this class there are six preferences in descending order of priority, roughly mirroring the closeness of the family connection. The family category was increased by almost 20 per cent in the first three years and by 10 per cent thereafter. For the first time family admissions were 'capped' at 520,000 for FY 1992–4 and at 480,000 thereafter. But Congress set a floor of 226,000 annual admissions under the preference system. This means that the admission of immediate family of US citizens (spouses, fiance(e)s, minor children), which are outside the ceiling, will not be allowed to crowd out admissions under the preference system because preference admissions will be allowed to rise above the cap. Admissions of refugees and asylees is governed under the Refugee Act of 1980. The annual intake is limited by a ceiling established by the administration in consultation with Congress. The authorized level in FY 1994 was 121,000, down from 132,000 for the previous year (Center for Immigration Studies 1994: 13).

4

International trade, capital flows and migration: economic policies towards countries of origin as a means of stemming immigration

Robert E.B. Lucas

The dominant international movements of people are south–south. Nonetheless, one of Ravenstein's (1889) famous laws of migration still holds: substantial migrations also occur when relatively poor and rich regions are in close geographical proximity. These latter flows generate responses within and among the wealthier, destination countries ranging from open hostility to recognition that immigration can prove beneficial, both economically to the indigenous population as well as to the migrants, and more generally through effects on international relations and cultural diversity.

The purpose of this chapter is not to join this debate. Instead, the focus is on a set of issues which are under discussion in several of the higher income, immigration countries as a means of stemming immigrant flows, irrespective of the desirability of such reductions. Frustration with inefficacy and costs of restricting the number of legal and illegal migrants from a given pool of aspiring entrants has promoted interest in measures to reduce the pool of aspirants. Expanded trade, investment and aid are the three principal instruments typically considered as vehicles through which the countries of destination may be able to limit the supply of immigrants.

These broad strategies have been debated in the context of NAFTA (US Commission 1990; Cornelius and Martin 1993), east–west migration into

Western Europe from the transition economies (Layard *et al.* 1992), and from the Maghreb into the EEC (Faini and de Melo 1994). Yet no clear resolution as to the efficacy of alternative strategies and instruments has emerged (see Russell and Teitelbaum 1992; Böhning and Schloeter-Paredes 1994).

The nature of this debate is sketched here under three main headings. The first section addresses the role of international trade. Are trade and migration substitutes or complements? What are the differences between the short run and long run in this regard? What part can the destination country play in expanding trade for the sending country? The second section turns to international capital flows. Does direct foreign investment (DFI) enhance labour market conditions and increase incomes in developing nations? Why does more DFI not occur in low-wage countries and what policies are available to the immigration countries to encourage such investments? Does Official Development Assistance (ODA) typically create or displace jobs? Whose incomes are enhanced by ODA? How could ODA be targeted to increase employment and incomes of groups more vulnerable to emigration? The final section takes up a more general discussion of the importance of home country employment opportunities in affecting the desire to migrate.

The answers to many of the issues posed in the following sections hinge upon the policy framework imposed by the countries of migrant origin. In contrast, the central questions posed in this chapter touch upon potential policies which might be considered by the destination countries. However, in certain contexts it may be conceivable for the receiving countries to influence policies of their lower-income neighbours. This may be feasible either in an advisory role, or because of some bargaining power permitting imposition of conditionality. Bilateral ODA is probably far too small in most contexts today to offer any real bargaining strength with respect to conditionality, and international competition among direct foreign investors probably renders curtailment of DFI without policy reform a threat which is not credible. On the other hand, it is noteworthy that several of the low–high income country pairs with high migration flows are members of some form of customs union, within which negotiation of a mutually acceptable trade policy is normal.

International trade and employment

In discussing the role of international trade in making the country of origin more attractive for potential migrants, a number of distinctions need to be made. First, this section takes up a fairly general discussion as to whether trade expansion is a substitute for or complement to migration, both in the short and long runs. The narrower question of the effect of destination country trade strategies in influencing origin country trade is then considered.

Are trade and migration substitutes?

The short run

Even in the short run, when no additional investments in skills or capacity occur, expanded trade opportunities may have an important impact upon employment. In particular, at least two types of effect may be distinguished.

First, expanded exports can serve as a stimulus to an economy constrained by deficient aggregate demand. However, the standard Keynesian story of multiple income expansion from a surge in exports is probably of limited relevance to most less developed countries (LDCs) as countries of migrant origin. More typically, production in the developing countries is restricted by limited (and inappropriate) investments; open unemployment of the type familiar to the industrialized nations is rarely substantial in the LDCs (though search unemployment by school leavers and graduates is common).

The second, and perhaps more relevant, short-run effect arises from attempts to reallocate resources as relative prices shift across sectors. The price shift may, for instance, be in the form of a rise in the relative price of exportables. Alternatively – as in the case of a currency depreciation – the prices of tradables generally (both exports and import substitutes) may rise relative to the price of non-traded goods. In the short run, when investments in capacity or skills are unfeasible, the only way the export or tradables sector can increase production is to bid away mobile resources from other sectors. In most contexts, the most mobile resource is comparatively unskilled labour, and in the process of attracting these workers, their nominal wage rises. Does this leave the country of origin more attractive to unskilled workers? The answer to this is less clear-cut, for it depends upon the relative importance of traded goods in the consumption basket of workers. If exports or tradables are an important component in the consumption of workers, then real earnings will fall despite the rise in nominal wages, leaving the home labour market even less attractive.

Some employees will prove less able or willing to make a transition into the newly competitive sectors. Does this imply an expansion in the pool of potential emigrants? Even if real wages increase in expanding domestic sectors, workers displaced from declining activities may still find emigration more attractive than internal relocation. On the other hand, if the reason that workers are locked into a declining sector is a reluctance or inability to move, then emigration will not result despite relative deprivation.

This latter distinction may be illustrated with reference to two examples. Mexico is undergoing a major adjustment in relative prices as a result of the

NAFTA agreement. Corn production in Mexico has been very heavily protected and is a major employer. Substantial labour displacement from this labour-intensive activity will occur as a result of the trade reforms. No doubt some of the displaced workers will be attracted by the newly competitive industries in Mexico, but others will probably swell the flow of emigrants to the US. Emigration is presumably the more likely choice, to the extent that prior experience in agriculture can be deployed in US agriculture but not in Mexico's newly competitive manufacturing sectors.

The stagnant Malaysian agricultural sector offers a contrasting experience. The tremendous growth in labour-intensive electronics exports in Malaysia has resulted in rapid growth in real earnings in manufacturing. Many rural inhabitants of Malaysia have benefited from this process, making the transition into industrial work. Those agricultural workers who have been less willing or less able to switch to the Malaysian industrial sector have enjoyed little of the benefits of Malaysia's extremely rapid growth. Yet this latter group of workers has not emigrated – the ultimate reason for this relative deprivation is lack of mobility, either internally or internationally.

The long run

Most of the discussion as to whether migration and trade are complements or substitutes has been conducted within a long-run framework in which investment patterns can alter.

It is probably fair to characterize the standard view as one in which trade and migration are substitutes. The factor endowments (Heckscher–Ohlin–Samuelson) theory of international trade predicts that free trade will lead relatively labour-abundant countries to export relatively labour-intensive goods and vice versa. Free trade will then result in a tighter labour market in labour abundant countries as investment proceeds in the more labour-intensive activities. Conversely, the labour market will slacken in the less labour-abundant countries. To the extent that the labour-abundant countries initially experience lower wages or more unemployment, free trade will then lead towards international wage equalization and hence substitute for migration. (This is the basis, for instance, of the recommendation to rely on trade as a substitute for east–west migration from the former Soviet Bloc, made in Layard *et al.* 1992.)

Common as this proposition is, it is by no means the only logical possibility (Markusen 1983; Razin and Sadka 1994). Indeed, there are several contexts in which free trade may well exacerbate the international gap in real earnings. Only a few of these need be mentioned here.

First, once we abandon excessively simplified stories, based only on labour and capital endowments, to incorporate natural resources, the initial predictions may well be reversed. Suppose, for instance, that a low-wage country happens to possess large deposits of a mineral whose extraction is capital-intensive. In this case expansion in export of the mineral, in which a comparative advantage exists, may well result in unemployment (the Dutch disease problem) or reduced wages. Rents from the mineral extraction may offer the potential to compensate workers losses, but if no such compensation actually occurs, then incentives to emigrate are enhanced by expanded trade. Botswana, for example, very clearly has a comparative advantage in diamond production, though extraction is very capital-intensive. As a result of the exchange rate appreciation, Botswana has not developed many other export or import competing activities. In this case, government has used the rents from diamond exports to offer substantial public sector employment, without which the incentives to consider emigration would have been even greater.

A second possibility arises when economies of scale, rather than factor endowments, are the source of cost differences and hence competitive advantage in trade. Suppose that the industry in which scale economies are important is also quite labour-intensive. If the higher-wage country initially has a larger established base in this sector, prior to trade, the scale economy effects may be sufficiently strong as to leave them with a cost advantage despite the higher wage. Expanded trade then results in growth of the labour-intensive sector within the higher wage economy, and the wage gap widens. This possibility has attracted some interest on theoretical grounds recently (Helpman and Krugman 1985; Razin and Sadka 1997), yet it is not clear how relevant it is empirically. How many labour-intensive industries have strong scale economies? Moreover, proponents of the scale economy theories of international trade may have over-stated the importance of scale effects, surmised on the basis of large volumes of inter-industry trade among the industrialized countries with relatively similar capital–labour endowments. Such large volumes can be readily understood in the context of differential skill endowments and capital structures (Davis 1994).

Perhaps a more important departure from factor price equalization occurs when productivity differences exist between nations. When a high-wage country enjoys a productivity advantage in the labour-intensive industry, as compared to the low-wage country, trade expansion may readily result in a widening of the real wage gap (Razin and Sadka 1997). One source of such productivity differences might be gaps in the state of technology. However, one might suspect that, in today's world of rapid communications and technology transfers through royalties and direct foreign investment, sustaining a technology gap is difficult. On the other hand, productivity advantages may also reflect the critical role of infrastructure, raising a potential link with aid projects to enhance infrastructure, productivity and hence trade (see Razin and Sadka 1997). In this context, infrastructure must be viewed in a broad sense, for productivity gaps can as readily result from differences in institutional capacity and market organization as from availability of physical forms of infrastructure.

Yet another important reason that relatively labour-abundant countries may not, in fact, export labour-intensive goods is because of their own distortionary import and domestic regulatory policies. Import duties and quantitative restrictions levied on material inputs used by potential labour-intensive exports may well render these exports uncompetitive. Drawback schemes rarely succeed in achieving full compensation to exporters for the cost of import protection. In addition, various domestic taxes and regulations can hurt labour-intensive exports. For instance, in India, the job security regulations imposed by law significantly raise the effective cost of labour, while until recently industrial licensing prevented capacity creation in textiles, leaving a formerly competitive export industry with antiquated technology. When the combined effect of such self-imposed policies is to tilt exports away from more labour-intensive activities, expansion of existing exports has limited potential for employment creation.

Most existing evidence suggests that the simple Heckscher–Ohlin factor endowment story is inadequate. There is some agreement that south–north net trade does tend to conform to the factor endowment prediction. However, individual, relatively labour-abundant countries do not necessarily export the more labour-intensive goods or vice versa. There are significant departures from the norm (Deardorff 1984). When low-wage countries do not export a labour-intensive range of goods, expansion of existing exports is unlikely to act as a substitute for migration except in so far as it stimulates a demand deficient economy.

If the range of consideration is extended beyond merchandise trade to incorporate trade in services, any tendency towards factor price equalization through trade may be inadequate to resolve whether trade and migration are substitutes. For many service activities it is inherent to current technology that migration is essential to delivery of the service.

Efficacy of trade policies in deterring migration

What range of policy instruments is open to the countries of migrant destination to improve the trade position, and employment in particular, in the countries of origin? A critical distinction must be maintained between changes in the destination country's own policies versus ability to affect origin country policies.

Destination country policies

Even within revisions to destination country trade policies, a further distinction must be made between providing imports to the countries of migrant origin on a preferential basis versus direct attempts to enhance exports from the countries of origin.

In principle, the higher-income destination countries could improve the terms of trade for their lower-income neighbours by subsidizing the flow of imports into the countries of migrant origin. Indeed, food aid represents precisely such a strategy, which could be replicated more generally with other forms of subsidized trade. However, any such strategy is a mixed blessing for the recipient nation. A general improvement in the terms of trade through lower import prices normally leaves any country better off and the enhanced incomes at home may deter migration. However, selective reductions in import prices depend critically upon which imports are affected. Any reduction in prices of the more labour-intensive, import-competing industries can obviously displace labour and hence potentially exacerbate the desire to emigrate. This criticism is frequently levelled at food aid, which may hurt the small farmers and agricultural labourers. On the other hand, improved access to key materials used in the production of labour-intensive exports can tighten labour market conditions. (The sensitivity of these predictions to local policies should, however, once again be noted: if the latter materials are subject to a quantitative restriction imposed by the origin country, then the improved import price will simply translate into a windfall gain for import licence holders, with no direct stimulus to exports.)

Similarly, in principle, a number of methods exist for offering preferential access to origin country exports. These range from selective lowering of import barriers against the specific countries of origin but not others, to lowering import protection against the specific goods exported by the country of origin, to overt preferential buying of origin country goods despite less competitive prices (through government procurement schemes or otherwise). Lowering import barriers is never easy, even for higher-income countries, and will naturally incur resentment from domestic import-competing industries. The US Caribbean Initiative met effective US domestic opposition on precisely these grounds. More costly procurement programmes may also be difficult to justify to tax payers. Yet this may be a part of the price to be paid for reducing immigration.

Lowering protection against labour-intensive imports from the country of origin may be particularly potent in reducing emigration pressures. Not only should such a strategy help to provide jobs in the country of origin, but it should also eliminate jobs attracting immigrants to the destination country. Thus, both in the US and in Europe there is evidence of immigrant concentration in the more labour-intensive industries protected from import competition (Abowd and Freeman 1991; Faini and Venturini 1993). If the higher-income countries lower import barriers in such cases, both the supply of and demand of immigrants can be reduced.

A further complication in the use of bilateral trade policy to avert migration is that such strategies may either be inconsistent with, or at least undermine the process of, multilateral negotiations. One of the guiding principles of GATT, for instance, is the avoidance in use of preferential trading policies. On the other hand, the formation of customs unions is seen as an exception to this principle, and negotiations to lower trade barriers among union members more generally offers an opportunity for migrant destination countries to influence the trade policies of the countries of origin.

Influencing trade policies of origin countries

Altering the trade policies of many developing countries could do much to make the local labour markets more attractive. When this involves lowering import barriers, opposition from owners and employees in previously protected sectors is apparent and is often accompanied by bureaucratic opposition to loss of discretionary controls. To the extent that emigration is reduced, some additional elements of cost must be borne by the country of previous emigration. The loss in remittances can be substantial (see Russell and Teitelbaum 1992). Moreover, at least in some instances, emigrants themselves provide an important demand for home country exports, resulting in a further loss in foreign exchange flows as emigration is curtailed.

Given these elements of cost, the country of origin may well prove reluctant to pursue change without compensation, such as in the form of improved access to export markets. In essence, trade and migration become part of a multifaceted bargaining situation. In particular, as already noted, there are several regions where customs unions have been formed between juxtaposed higher- and lower-income countries. It is not uncommon to see such unions involving some elements of understanding with respect to labour mobility as well. Within the EEC, the lower-income countries such as Greece, Spain, Portugal and Ireland have traditionally been major sources of labour for higher-income neighbours, and the EEC now has agreements on labour mobility as well as goods within the community. Turkey and the Maghreb countries have been major sources of migrants to Europe and are continuing to negotiate their trade privileges with the EEC. Consideration of the consequences for migration was an important component in the discussions with respect to NAFTA. The South African Customs Union members include countries which have been critical sources of mine workers and other labour to South Africa. On the other hand, Eastern Europe's trade privileges with the EEC (other than the former East Germany) remain a matter of dispute.

Gains from the formation of a customs union are never unambiguous. Tariff free imports from the union partner may be preferred by local consumers because they command a lower price on the domestic market than do tariff-ridden imports from a third, non-member country. Although this private choice is quite rational, for the country this may mean a switch to buying from the higher-cost union partner rather than the low cost third country. Such 'trade diversion' can hurt.

The formation of a customs union is only a partial move towards free trade; limiting this freedom to member countries can produce more harm than good. Moreover, even if a move towards free trade results in a net gain for each country, by no means will every individual person gain. As already discussed in the context of whether trade and migration are substitutes, who gains and who loses may differ between the short run and the long run.

Any sudden liberalization of trade by the country of migrant origin is likely to escalate unemployment and, perhaps, to result in declining real wages in the short run. This is likely to be the immediate effect of NAFTA on Mexico, proved to be the case in Chile following their major liberalization phase, and is a major point of contention in the transition economies of Eastern Europe and the former Soviet Union. Removing import barriers permits rapid entry of competitive imports, rendering jobs in many import competing activities obsolete. On the other hand, creating capacity in the newly competitive spheres takes time, workers need to be trained and retrained, and foreign markets must be penetrated.

The situation is made far worse if the changes in policy are not expected to survive. Investors (in new capacity or skill acquisition) will postpone decisions if the new policy environment is not credible. Moreover, such beliefs are likely to be self-fulfilling – if no investments occur in the export sector, balance of payments constraints will almost certainly promote a return to protectionism.

In the short run, then, one can expect considerable slack in the labour market with rapid liberalization in the country of origin. The only mitigating factor is that skills required in the newly expanding sectors will be at a premium and the resulting windfall may prove sufficient to deter emigration at least by those with the relevant skills. Conversely, those whose skills are suddenly made redundant at home may well elect to transfer their skills abroad (witness the emigration of professionals from the former Soviet Bloc).

Most liberalization episodes are soon reversed. If this does not occur, then with a little more time new export sectors will emerge and expand. If these exports are relatively labour-intensive then labour market conditions will tighten. Not very much is known about the real time required for this turn around. Obviously, things will improve more quickly in economies with substantial investment levels, where the new policies are more credible, and where elements restricting entry and exit are fewer. Meanwhile the depth of the recession will tend to be deeper where declining sectors monopolize most of the employment in a region, where financing for retraining poses a barrier, or where elderly workers are displaced with little prospect of retraining.

Liberalization of trade by the country of migrant origin may thus result in considerable labour market slack initially, followed by later improvements. The effects on emigration are not obvious. Perhaps the initial phase will exacerbate the rate of departure. On the other hand, if later improvements are correctly anticipated, then perhaps fewer people will move even in the short run, choosing instead to remain and position themselves for the later opportunities. Alternatively, anticipation of later improvements may accelerate temporary emigration by individuals wishing to accumulate skills and savings for deployment at home after trade liberalization has taken hold. We have little evidence either way.

Where does this leave the country of migrant destination in terms of the trade policy they would like to see the origin country adopt? To delay trade liberalization may defer the initial worsening in labour market conditions at origin, but it also postpones improvements. There may, of course, be a discrepancy between the time preferences of the countries of origin and destination with respect to the phasing of these effects, though it is not apparent which is more likely to want to postpone. Moreover, if the destination country has a limited window of opportunity within which to influence the commercial policy of the sending country, deferring may imply abandoning.

The capital account

If international trade fails to realize factor price equalization, does capital move to the low wage regions and hence potentially substitute for the movement of people? To consider this, let us first review some basic patterns in capital movements before distinguishing issues with respect to direct foreign investment and official development.

Patterns

Figure 1 shows 1990 income levels of various countries (in logarithmic form) on the horizontal axis and their current account surplus (positive) or deficit (negative) on the balance of payments account as a per cent of GDP on the vertical axis. On average, the current account deficit is much larger, relative to GDP, for the lower-income countries. Nor is this observation driven by a few outliers, for a significant positive relationship holds even if the high-deficit, low-income countries, as well as the five countries with obviously high current account surpluses relative to GDP, are excluded.

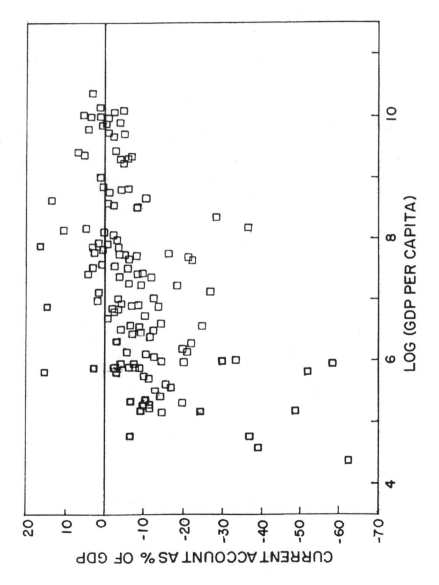

Figure 1 Current account and income levels – cross-country data, 1990

Since these deficits must be largely financed by capital inflows, the implication is that the lower-income countries are indeed receiving large amounts of foreign capital in some form, relative to their current production levels. It is also clear from Figure 1 that the countries with the largest surpluses relative to GDP, and thus providing large capital outflows relative to income, are in the middle-income range. Indeed, according to World Bank estimates, the high-income countries (with incomes in excess of US$7,000 in 1990) had a very substantial, combined current account deficit, largely reflecting the massive US capital inflows. The upper-middle-income group, in contrast, recorded a combined current account surplus.

For the low-income countries, a major source of financing for their current account deficits is official development assistance. Most of the low-income countries receive little by way of private direct foreign investment, despite the fact that in some cases, direct foreign investment includes investments from emigrants abroad. This is illustrated in Figure 2, which shows GDP per capita (again in US dollars on a logarithmic scale) on the horizontal axis and direct foreign investment relative to GDP on the vertical axis, for a number of countries in 1990.[1] Such high-income countries as Sweden, Finland, France and Japan generated significant net outflows of direct foreign investment in relation to the size of their economies. However, very little DFI is hosted by the lowest-income countries. Rather there is an inverse u-shape which may be discerned in Figure 2, though the scatter of countries displays considerable departures from this average pattern.

Several explanations have been offered as to why the low-income, low-wage countries fail to receive more significant inflows of private capital. The explanation which has received by far the most attention from economists in the last few years stems from the 'new' economic growth theory literature. The main theme of this literature is that the returns to physical capital may exhibit increasing returns over some ranges: in particular, the higher-income economies generate better returns to capital by virtue of their size. What drives this unconventional story (revived from a much earlier literature) are technological improvements, generated through private investments in human capital (education or training), which spill over to benefit other producers within the particular country. Since these spillover effects are not captured in any market prices, the social returns to capital can readily differ substantially across the globe despite a well-integrated international financial market (Lucas 1990).

There is not much evidence either for or against the position that countries with more highly developed education and training systems attract more foreign investment. It is true that some of the East Asian economies have emphasized education, but the extent to which the relatively high levels of direct investment in those countries are caused by

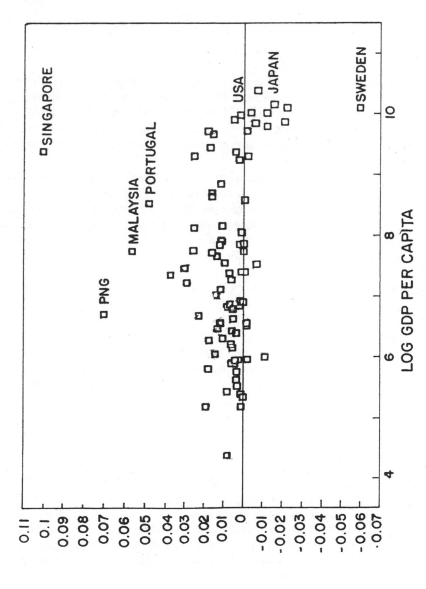

Figure 2 Direct foreign investment in a number of countries, 1990

this strategy, as opposed to the possibility that direct investment has raised incomes and hence both the demand for and capacity to provide education, or indeed whether the association is simply spurious, remains to be disentangled.

The East Asian economies have competed to attract footloose direct investors, such as in the electronics sector, through tax incentives, easing regulations, containing labour costs (including industrial disputes), and by maintaining a stable financial environment (until recently). In addition, political stability has been an important factor in reassuring foreign investors, and there is evidence to indicate that any episodes of disruption, in the countries of this region, have led to diminished direct investment from abroad (Lucas 1993).

No doubt, perceptions of risk have played an important role in other regions which have hosted less DFI. In some countries, and notably in Latin America, the debt overhang from the 1980s made both direct and portfolio investors nervous. Elsewhere, the threat and reality of political instability and of policy reversals have probably deterred foreign investors (Grossman and Razin 1984).

However, self-imposed policy constraints also represent a major barrier to direct foreign investment in a number of developing countries. Most LDCs impose a permission requirement for direct foreign investment and restrict the maximum permissible equity participation. In several of the East Asian economies which have attracted substantial flows of direct investments, the permission requirements have been either effectively abolished or considerably streamlined. A contrasting environment is presented, for instance, by India. Until very recently, the government of India has been openly hostile to foreign investors, frequently requiring several years to review applications, denying entry to many and even reversing admission approvals after substantial investments occurred.

It is not always easy to reverse such stances and to begin to attract foreign investments. Furthermore, denying access to foreign investors may not be irrational. Whether direct foreign investment benefits the host country, and more specifically whom it benefits within these economies, is contentious (Encarnacion and Wells 1986).

Does DFI generate jobs and raise incomes?

If private foreign investment is to substitute for international migration it presumably does so by improving the economic situation for potential emigrants. Several factors influence the likelihood of benefiting from DFI.

First, profit is shifted from domestically owned, monopolistic firms to transnational corporations (TNC) which produce competing goods (Levy and Nolan 1991). In consequence, of course, domestic competitor firms form an important lobbying group to deny entry to the TNC. Domestic manufacturers protected by quantitative restrictions on imports may well possess some monopoly influence in the domestic market, and profit shifting can then result from protection-hopping DFI. This has been the case in India, at least until 1991. Similarly, foreign investment in the US automobile industry has been induced in part to bypass voluntary export restraints. Yet profit shifting need not be confined to protection-hopping DFI. Since exporters from most LDCs have negligible impact on the world price of their output, domestic exporters' profits remain largely unaltered by additional foreign investments. Only if DFI displaces domestic manufacturers from a foreign quota is profit-shifting then likely to matter for direct competitor, domestic firms. However, local providers of materials to the export industry may well find themselves bypassed in favour of imports if part of the inducement to establish a low cost export base is lower protection on materials or drawbacks on duties paid on these materials. Profit shifting may then occur in the provider industry.

More broadly, any reduction in profits of domestic firms may lower the expected returns on domestic investment and savings. In contrast to such 'crowding out' effects, foreign investments may complement domestic undertakings. This latter case is frequently made when foreigners invest in critical forms of infrastructure, for instance, relieving bottlenecks which previously constrained the performance of domestic investments. Indeed, the potential benefits from complementarity in foreign and domestic investments offer a rationale for the common process of admitting foreign investors to a select group of industries (though implementation does not always meet this goal).

To the extent that DFI displaces domestic investment there is an issue — especially important in the debate over consequences for emigration — as to which form generates more jobs. TNCs do seem to adopt less labour-intensive methods than do local firms, though it is less clear that this is true within specific product lines. There may be several reasons why TNCs retain more capital-intensive methods: because their technology is developed in higher wage settings; because TNCs have greater difficulty identifying reliable local workers; because TNCs have access to cheaper sources of capital; or because TNCs pay higher wages. To the extent that the last of these is true, this is again of relevance to emigration consequences — the rate of pay may influence decisions to leave, and not merely the number of jobs. However, the sparse evidence which exists suggests that any differences in pay by TNCs, given employees' skill levels, are insignificant (Knight and Sabot 1983).

The initial inflow of DFI improves the foreign exchange situation, provided that the TNC is restricted from borrowing on the local capital market (which is normally the case). For LDCs where foreign exchange is at a premium, this infusion can act as a general stimulus to the economy, again rendering the country of origin more attractive to potential migrants. However, the net effects of direct investment on foreign exchange are less clear. Some portion of profits is repatriated and typically TNC production is more import intensive, if only because of parts and equipment provided by their own subsidiaries abroad. On the other hand, where direct investment is used to establish a low-cost export base, or where export requirements are imposed as a condition for entry, the resultant export earnings help to tip the balance.

The net consequences of direct investment for tax revenue to the host government are similarly ambiguous. Foreign investors' profits are taxed and, to the extent that DFI stimulates the economy more generally, other forms of revenue are enhanced. Yet it may be necessary to compete for DFI by offering tax holidays, and if the effect is to displace domestic investment, profit tax revenue may actually decline. Moreover, tariff-hopping DFI obviously results in a loss of import duties.

Other potential benefits to the host economy include lower consumer prices of goods generated and a transfer of technology. In most contexts, however, the latter is limited. TNCs are understandably reluctant to share technologies, and concentration of TNCs in export processing zones may limit direct contact and, hence, learning. Some transfer does, however, occur, especially when the TNC upgrades local manufacturers of parts (which is sometimes a requirement of entry).

Besides any net creation of jobs or enhancement to earnings, the other consequences of DFI for emigration are perhaps less immediate though nonetheless relevant. Any relief in the foreign exchange constraint may enable more activity and more jobs elsewhere in the economy; higher tax revenues may either relieve the tax burden on (middle-class) potential emigrants or enable provision of better public facilities; and lower consumer prices raise the real value of potential emigrants' earnings at home. Thus, if DFI offers some of these forms of benefit to the host country it can indeed render the home country a more attractive setting.

In part, the issue of substitutability may depend on the geographical location of DFI within the host country. For instance, it has been argued that DFI in the *maquiladoras* along the northern border of Mexico has accelerated step migration − first internally for employment in *maquiladoras*, then onwards into the United States.

Instruments for promoting DFI

Even if some types of DFI are deemed to be substitutes for migration, only a limited range of instruments is open to the country of migrant destination to promote DFI in the region of origin. Most of the relevant policies are in the hands of the host country.

In the context of broader trade negotiations, it may be in the interest of major immigration countries to bargain for revisions in access for their investors. However, a conflict may well exist between interests in trade reform and conditions which would attract more DFI. If trade liberalization and associated export expansion are targeted as critical to emigration reduction, it should be recognized that tariff-hopping DFI will tend to diminish (which may not be a bad thing), while conditions may still be insufficient to attract export-oriented DFI in a highly competitive global tournament.

In principle, the destination country could offer tax credits to encourage specific forms of DFI by its own firms in particular countries. However, this assumes both sufficient knowledge of the impact of these investments to discern appropriate cases, and a legal capacity to discriminate in this manner with respect to taxation. Providing better information about investment opportunities in the neighbouring LDCs may also help, though it is unlikely to have any dramatic consequences.

Another route open to the destination country is to facilitate infrastructure investment in the neighbouring country. This can help to encourage private foreign investment to the extent that such facilities have been a bottleneck to trade, to production, to communication with headquarters, or to travel by management. In other words, aid can become a vehicle to promote private foreign investment.

Official development assistance

Most empirical studies agree that the allocation of bilateral aid among LDCs is dominated by the interests of the donor countries, either in terms of perceived security issues or economic feedback (Jay and Michalopoulos 1988). Per capita aid receipts initially rise with GDP per capita across countries then turn down at higher incomes. Across countries, therefore, aid is not focused on the poorest.

Whether aid benefits the recipient countries remains a matter of contention (Cassen 1987; Krueger *et al.* 1988). In principle, aid can certainly prove immiserizing in the presence of economic distortions and may encourage domestic policies which prove detrimental to growth (Eaton 1989). The inflow of foreign exchange also defers depreciation of the exchange rate and hence export expansion.

How might aid be redirected to help with job creation, to raise incomes of potential emigrants and, more generally, to diminish international migration?

Most of the job creation in the developing countries is in agriculture, services and the small- to medium-scale factories within manufacturing. Some forms of aid — notably food aid and capital-intensive irrigation schemes — may well hurt job creation in agriculture. The expansion of services is usually tied to overall economic growth and the small-scale industrial sector is notoriously difficult to help (despite the efforts of

USAID and of many LDC governments). Even aid to expand infrastructure can have mixed effects: whether better rural roads permit agricultural expansion or destroy the more labour-intensive forms of farming by allowing easier food imports depends on the context.

Designing project aid to generate jobs is therefore not easy. Partly in consequence, a number of contributors to the ILO-UNHCR meeting on aid and migration in 1992 concluded that structural adjustment loans, which permit a transition to recipient country policies more consistent with job creation, had a greater chance of succeeding in tightening labour markets (Böhning and Schloeter-Paredes 1994). This position ignores, however, the political economy underlying the reluctance of many states to liberalize and move towards more labour absorbing strategies; as already described, there are typically some major losers in this process who naturally resist change. Probably, only the multilateral aid agencies have sufficient influence to condition receipt of their assistance upon adoption of such adjustment policies.

The other major theme which emerges from the ILO-UNHCR workshop is the UNHCR position that aid can be effective in encouraging refugees to return to their country of origin, if that aid is directed towards resettlement. In practice the return rate of refugees is not high. Nor is there clear evidence to indicate that the return rate would be significantly greater with more aid, especially if that aid is placed in the hands of the authorities from whom the refugees initially fled.

Nonetheless, the issue of refugees does raise a more general point – that most of the foregoing discussion on trade, foreign investment and aid focuses on economic migrants. Indeed, the conventional wisdom on trade and capital movements as substitutes for international migration is founded upon an assumption that the greater the difference in earnings opportunities, the more migrants move. How important are economic motives for moving? Does the supply of migrants rise monotonically with the gap in earnings capacity? To these and related questions, the final section now turns.

The determinants of international migration reconsidered

Obviously there are many reasons why people wish to migrate: to escape violence, to reunite a family, for education, to benefit from improved social facilities, to take up a new job and so on. Most of the discussion so far in this chapter has focused on the last of these – the rewards of alternative employment. Even in this context, risks associated with alternatives, and not merely the level of earnings, may play a crucial role.

Nonetheless, what matters in the efficacy of trade, aid and investment as substitutes for migration is the responsiveness of migration flows to changes in home employment opportunities. This influence does not need to be the sole determining factor or even the most important component, but the direction and extent of response are central to these issues.

Evidence on employment at origin

There is a very considerable body of evidence, consistent with internal migration for employment, indicating that higher pay and less unemployment in the place of origin can deter the decision to move (for a review see Lucas, 1997). There is far less evidence on international migration in response to earnings differentials, and indeed, the issues are more complex. Whereas internal migration (in all but a few countries) is generally a matter of personal choice (albeit individuals occasionally move to flee local violence), most immigration authorities and a few emigration authorities seek to control movements. International migration is not merely a matter of choice.

Despite this, the few existing econometric studies of international migration generally suggest that a tighter labour market at origin does retard the supply of emigrants. In the context of emigration from Greece, Spain and Portugal, Faini and Venturini (1993, 1994) find the gross flow of migrants from 1962–88 responded positively to differences in earnings at destination and origin. Their result for Turkey proves less conclusive. Lucas (1987) finds that the supply of workers to South Africa's mines, at least prior to the switch in the Chamber of Mines' recruiting strategy in 1974, was reduced by the development of alternatives in home country wage employment and subsistence agriculture. Similarly, Lucas (1975) shows, in a cross-country analysis, that applications for labour permits to work (legally) in the United States were more common, relative to origin population, the lower the wage at origin (given distance from the United States).

Faini and de Melo (1994) offer some important additional insights in the context of emigration from Morocco to Belgium, France, Germany and the Netherlands during 1977–88. Growth in formal industrial sector jobs in Morocco significantly limited the extent of realized emigration, and shifts towards export orientation in the industrial sector significantly contributed to job creation. In other words, trade and migration indeed operated as substitutes, according to these results.

Yet the picture is not entirely clear-cut. Several historical studies have noted that emigration from particular countries initially rose and then, at a later stage, declined (Akerman 1976; Gould 1979; Massey 1988). This emigration transition may, of course, reflect myriad factors. The initial rise in emigration may simply reflect an episode of more rapidly rising employment opportunities abroad than at home. However, the work of the US Commission (1990) has focused considerable attention on this initial rise in emigration by suggesting that the process of development at origin may actually accelerate emigration. The mere observation that, in historical perspective, emigration rose as income at origin increased is clearly insufficient to disentangle this issue. So what are the potential factors contributing to this observation, and what is the evidence?

Issues and evidence on income at origin

Before turning to the evidence, it is worth deliberating whether sensible arguments can be made to anticipate a positive effect of local development on emigration. At least six potential contributing factors may be identified in the literature.

(1) Enhanced incomes at origin can permit easier financing of costly moves (which may involve not only transport, but initial job search, education and training to enable migration, and perhaps facilitating payments in the context of restricted international migration).
(2) As development proceeds, the institutional nature of asset ownership frequently changes. Titling of land may, for instance, free families to quit their rural origins.
(3) Structural shifts in the patterns of production also accompany development. This may well result in declining demand for specific labour categories while wages for others are driven up. It is then entirely possible that the average wage at origin rises, even though labour conditions are deteriorating for some and, hence, emigration is magnified.
(4) As income rises, a demographic transition occurs with an initial phase of rising population growth, followed by slower expansion. Population growth can (with a lag) put downward pressure on local wages. However, it is also possible that demographic pressures may independently accelerate emigration. For instance, young adults are the main source of emigrants, and a rise in birth rate (or lower child mortality) increases their proportion in the population after two decades.
(5) Rising incomes offer new experiences and it is probable that attitudes and tastes shift in the process, perhaps rendering an international move more attractive.
(6) Emigrants offer information, financing and easier access for the next generation of emigrants from their own families or communities. As the stock of emigrants rises, one might therefore expect to see more emigration for any given difference in earnings opportunities. Thus, it is quite possible that the rate of emigration will continue upwards (for some time) despite a closing in the gap in earnings opportunities.

These (and any other factors) are difficult to disentangle empirically. Indeed I know of no serious evidence addressing the difficult issue of changing attitudes (point (5) above) but some partial evidence does exist relevant to the other components.

Part of this evidence may be gleaned from cross-sectional studies — snapshots at a single point in time. In particular, these studies may be able to contribute to our understanding of the role of any financial barrier to migration (point (1)). To mirror the historical picture, the argument would have to be that at low incomes the financial barrier is binding, but at higher incomes other factors dominate. In their review of village studies, predominantly from India, Connell *et al.* (1976) actually support the reverse of this hypothesis: they report high propensities to migrate out of rural areas by the children of the rich and among whole families of agricultural labourers. Combined with some evidence that the very poorest may again not migrate, this suggests a bimodal pattern of rural departure. Despite this suggestion of a dip in migration rates among middle income groups in India, Banerjee and Kanbur (1981) find that migration by men from rural areas of one state to urban areas of another state of India, prior to the 1961 Census, initially rises with rural income then turns down at higher incomes. However, the turning point, according to their estimates, occurs at a very low income level (somewhat in excess of US$100 (1990) per person per year). The only other systematic study which I have been able to find of this issue with respect to internal migration is by Stark and Taylor (1991). This is an analysis of 423 adults from the Patzcuaro region of Mexico in 1983. In this instance, no statistically significant pattern emerges with respect to the influence of family income on the propensity for internal migration. This latter result could be a consequence of also including the education of each person because income effects may work through education. Yet one must conclude that there is not much evidence to support the n-shape hypothesis among internal migrants.

Perhaps this is because internal migration is relatively cheap compared to international migration. Indeed, in the aforementioned analysis by Stark and Taylor, the n-shape is supported among international migrants: the probability of moving to the US rises up to a household income level of some US$3,100 (1983) per year. However, once one adjusts for household size, it seems this estimated turning point is again at such a low income level (apparently less than US$250 (1983) per person) as to render the lower arm of the n-shape of very limited relevance. (In 1983, GNP per capita in Mexico was $2,410).

Time series studies (of annual or intercensal emigration and income growth) offer an opportunity to disentangle the role of other factors which change as development proceeds through time. However, such studies present some problems of their own. Of necessity, most time series studies look at average wages or income at origin and destination, and hence cannot discern the effects of structural shifts mentioned above in point (3).

Table 15   Turning points in emigration from Greece, Spain, Portugal and Turkey, 1962–88

	Greece	Spain	Portugal	Turkey
Estimated emigration turning point	2 300	2 208	1 922	2 944
Actual GDP per capita in 1962	2 112	3 382	1 787	1 750
Year in which turning point was reached	1962–3	–	1963–4	1974–5

Source: Derived from Faini and Venturini 1994, Table 1[2]

Faini and Venturini have examined emigration from Greece, Spain, Portugal and Turkey between 1962 and 1988. They have found that, given the difference in average incomes between origin and destination, emigration indeed rises and then declines at higher incomes. This might be interpreted as (the first) significant support for the US Commission position. However, if one simply holds the income at destination constant and asks at what origin income level the emigration transition is estimated to occur, the answers are, at GDP per capita in 1985 US$, as shown in Table 15.

Again, the estimated turning points occur at a very low income level, occurring in the first two years of the sample for Greece and Portugal and well before the start of the sample period for Spain. The lower arm of any n-shape relationship between emigration and income is therefore of limited relevance according to this study.

Finally, Hatton and Williamson (1994) re-examine the European historical emigration patterns which started much of this debate. These authors once again support the conventional position that the difference between origin and destination earnings opportunities significantly added to emigration pressures over an extended period. They find no evidence to support the notion that rising earnings at origin contribute to an n-shaped pattern in emigration with respect to incomes. Instead, they attribute the long-term emigration transition to three main components: the indirect effect of the demographic transition; the structural changes in the economy (and specifically the declining fraction of the labour force in agriculture); and the lagged effect of the stock of prior migrants.

A summing up of income and employment

The US Commission on International Migration (1990) accepted the proposition that raising incomes in low-income countries may serve to stimulate emigration up to some turning point in income per capita. In policy terms, this has raised considerable concern about strategies to diminish the supply of immigrants in the short run through any means aimed at stimulating the sending country economies. The evidence on which this is founded is tenuous at best.

There is little or no ambiguity regarding the role of local labour market development: tighter labour markets at origin serve to diminish the drive to emigrate. Other correlates of development may underlie the historical emigration transition. In particular, it seems that the structural shift out of agriculture and the demographic transition played important roles, yet these are very long-term effects.

In the shorter run, there are two potential 'humps' in the time pattern of emigration. The first, which is of dubious relevance, is the hypothesis that emigration initially rises with income per capita because of relief in the ability to finance migration. The data do not offer much support for this notion, and if there is such a hump, it appears to occur at very low-income levels. The second is the difference in direction of effect of a trade reform in the short run and the long run: sudden liberalization may well promote emigration, followed by job creation and reduced emigration. This, however, is precisely because the job market initially becomes worse and then improves, not because of any hypothesized income hump.

Closing remarks

Improvements in economic conditions and tighter labour markets, in particular, in the sending countries probably do serve to limit the pressure to emigrate, both in the short and long runs. For destination countries to play a significant role in achieving such improvements is more difficult: most often the major constraint is the policy framework in the sending country.

Of the three principal instruments available to the destination countries – trade, investment and aid – trade is normally the most potent, if only because in negotiating trade conditions there is some room to influence the sending country's policies. Lowering barriers against labour-intensive imports has the double advantage of stimulating employment abroad while reducing the attractions of the high-income country's labour market to less skilled immigrants. Such reductions can be used to bargain for other reforms in both commercial policy and domestic regulations that are likely to create jobs in the sending countries. Despite the fact that such reforms may be in the general national interest of these lower-income neighbours, coalitions of protected industries and government officials frequently resist change because of the potential for personal losses.

Enhanced flows of direct foreign investment play an ambiguous role both in generating jobs, more generally, and in raising incomes. Such investments are more likely to succeed on both counts where they are cost induced to establish an export base, as opposed to penetrating a protective wall to access the domestic market. Thus, the success of direct investment is often tied to trade strategy, as well. Moreover, trade negotiations have increasingly been tied to issues of access for foreign investors.

Aid can help, if it is in a form appropriate to job creation. However, this is not always easy to achieve. Many forms of aid destroy job creation capability and can even lower incomes for critical groups. Investments in infrastructure are, perhaps, one of the better bets, yet even these are not without negative connotations. However, in the end – and despite the current practice of most donor countries – one should continue to advocate the use of aid for poverty relief, and not as a tool to stem migration.

Reducing and reversing refugee flows is more difficult even than addressing labour migration. In the absence of profound alternations in the political environment or violence which pushes refugees from their homes, I remain sceptical as to the efficacy of aid or other economic incentives to return. Few refugees actually return, and the real issue is therefore one of addressing the consequent pockets of poverty within the destination countries, particularly those which are not members of the industrialized world. One exception in which aid may have some impact occurs when the industrialized world is the target – as in the recent attempts to enter the United States from Haiti. Aid may then become a critical component in bargaining for reform in the refugees' country of origin to contain and reverse the flow, although few nations are able to promise aid on a sufficient scale to enable such bargaining.

In general, it seems that aid, investment and trade policies on behalf of the migrant-receiving countries are likely to prove blunt instruments for diminishing the potential flow of migrants. Both in theory and from our limited evidence, there is considerable ambiguity as to their combined efficacy. And where there is agreement that reform could prove more potent – as in reducing protection against labour-intensive imports in the receiving countries – the political economy costs of such reforms frequently seem to outweigh the perceived costs of continued migration and deterrent efforts.

Notes

1.   The data are taken from the World Bank's World Tables and include only countries with populations of more than one million.
2.   The estimated turning points are derived from Faini and Venturini (1994), Table 1. The estimates here differ from those in the original paper by virtue of including the effect of home country growth in diminishing migration by lowering the income differential relative to destination. Faini and Venturini report turning points *given* income difference between home and destination. GDP per capita here refers to revised estimates by Summers and Heston (1988).

5

Issues in contemporary refugee policies

Astri Suhrke and Aristide R. Zolberg

Throughout the world of open societies, refugee policy is clearly distinguished from immigration policy. Whereas immigration policy is designed primarily to serve the interests of the receiving country by admitting selected categories of foreign nationals and preventing unauthorized entry by all others, refugee policy arises from the legal and moral obligations incumbent upon open societies by virtue of their membership in an international community. Most fundamentally, international law obligates states not to reject foreign asylum applicants if such rejection entails their being returned to a place where they are in danger of being persecuted (the non-*refoulement* principle). Additional obligations are incumbent upon states that are signatories to the 1951 UN Convention on the Status of Refugees and the 1967 Protocol, which modifies the Convention in a more comprehensive direction, or to regional bodies of refugee law. The statutes of the United Nations High Commissioner for Refugees (UNHCR), laid down in 1950, provide a broad mandate for the international community to assist persons in need of protection and assistance.

In practice, signatories of these and related instruments must establish procedures for the consideration of asylum claims and be willing to admit those who qualify as refugees and have no other place to go. In addition, numerous members of the international community – at varying levels of development – have responded to perennial emergencies either by agreeing to take some share of a particular group of refugees for temporary protection en route to permanent resettlement, or by opening their doors to a wave of refugees from a neighbouring state. Finally, among the more affluent states, refugee policy also encompasses the provision of assistance for refugees through the UNHCR and other international organizations, or on a bilateral basis.

Within these broad parameters, there is considerable variation in how individual states interpret their obligations. After World War II, in the wake of the tragic consequences of their restrictive stance during the inter-war period, the industrial democracies generally adopted more generous refugee policies. This openness was further reinforced by foreign policy considerations arising from the Cold War. However, from the late 1970s onward, with the onset of a refugee crisis in the Third World — which coincided with a severe economic downturn in the international political economy — they returned to a more restrictive position (as will be discussed below). This increased after the end of the Cold War, when the erstwhile foreign policy motives for admitting or even encouraging refugees disappeared, while upheavals in the former Communist world raised the prospect of large additional waves, particularly in Europe. While rejecting a majority of asylum applicants on the grounds that they do not meet the criteria for awarding refugee status, all the states in question acknowledge their continuing obligations towards refugees, and insist that they *would* admit them if and when they knocked at the door.

Two considerations should be kept in mind in formulating refugee policy. First, this process provides a special opportunity for a state seeking to overcome its past and achieve legitimacy in the eyes of its neighbours and the international community, more generally. For example, after World War II, the German Federal Republic included in its Basic Law a special provision regarding political asylum, which it retained until very recently, when the adoption of a common refugee policy by members of the European Union made German (and French) exceptionalism in this regard problematic. The states of Central and Eastern Europe are now adhering to the basic international instruments noted as part of their demonstration that they possess the qualifications for admission into such organizations as the Council of Europe. The second point applies particularly to states that border countries or regions likely to generate refugees. These countries must give thought to the development of a comprehensive policy, involving not only the deterrence of massive flows, but also provision for meeting their international obligations if and when qualified 'Convention' refugees appear. In addition to this, proactive regional policies might help to reduce the onset of such flows.

With these considerations in mind, this chapter provides some of the elements necessary for preliminary reflections on a realistic and morally appropriate refugee policy. Starting with a brief account of the historical development of the international refugee regime, we will discuss the refugee challenge in contemporary Africa - which has the largest number of refugees and internally displaced people - and conclude with an overview of how refugee issues are defined and addressed.

Development of an international refugee regime[1]

Since World War II, an international refugee regime has taken form and developed a differentiated capacity to respond to refugee problems on a global scale. This is evident above all in the changing definition of 'refugee' and its application by international institutions, as well as in the growth of the United Nations High Commissioner for Refugees (UNHCR) – the organizational centrepiece of the UN system specifically mandated to assist refugees. One result is that policy options and dilemmas of the state in refugee matters have increasingly been shaped by developments in the international refugee regime as a whole.

Definition of beneficiaries

While much contemporary discussion focuses on increasingly restrictive national asylum policies, in a historical perspective it is evident that the statutory definition of 'refugee' in international law has widened.

The refugee mandate of the League of Nations in the interwar period was temporary and limited to specific nationalities. The 1951 UN Convention, by contrast, defines 'refugee' with reference to a state of affairs rather than the identity of the country of origin. Nevertheless, universal application was ruled out by the clause which restricted the Convention to victims of events that had occurred before 1951. An optional clause further limited the geographic scope of qualifying events to Europe. The move from particularism to universalism was not formally completed until 1967, when the Euro-centric restrictions of the Convention were removed by the addition of a protocol. For the first time, the legal foundation for a truly global international refugee regime was established. Regional instruments in Africa and Latin America subsequently formulated even broader categories of beneficiaries.

The principal legal documents defining 'refugee' in international law are the 1951 UN Convention on the Status of Refugees and its 1967 Protocol, the 1950 Statutes of the Office of the UNHCR and subsequent authorizations by the UN General Assembly, the 1969 Convention Governing the Specific Aspects of Refugee Problems in Africa of the Organisation of African Unity (OAU), and the 1984 Cartagena Declaration on Refugees (in the Latin American region). The critical elements in these instruments are:

(1) *Persecution*: a refugee is defined as a person persecuted, or having a well-founded fear of persecution, 'for reasons of race, religion,

nationality, membership of particular social group or political opinion' (1951 Convention, Art. 1 A(2)). Since several defining elements of the 1951 Convention are open to interpretation, a large and complex jurisprudence has developed. Suffice to note that the Convention is commonly taken to exclude refugees fleeing from war. The meaning of 'persecution', however, is controversial: does it mean that a particular person has to be singled out for harm, or does vulnerability as a result of membership in a particular group suffice? There is more agreement on the role of the state. Persecution does not necessarily mean that the state has to be the agent inflicting harm; public inaction can amount to persecution if this means failure to protect from the harm of non-state agents (Goodwin-Gill 1983; Grahl-Madsen 1966; Hathaway 1991).

(2) *War and generalized violence*: the 1969 OAU Convention includes additional qualifying causes, namely: 'external aggression, occupation, foreign domination or events seriously disturbing public order in either part or the whole of [the] ... country' (Art. 1(2)). Similarly, the Cartagena Declaration supplements the 1951 Convention by including 'generalised violence, foreign aggression, internal conflicts, massive violation of human rights, or other circumstances which have seriously disturbed public order' (Conclusion 3). These events, moreover, have to be of a kind that threaten the 'lives, safety and freedom' of the persons in question. Since the categories are so broad as to include almost any kind of political or public violence, UNHCR has subsequently offered authoritative interpretations.

Grounds for protection similar to those codified in the OAU Convention and the Cartagena Declaration have variously been used to bestow *de facto* refugee status in North America and in Europe (protection on humanitarian grounds, and temporary protection being the most common).

UNHCR and mandate expansion

The mandate of UNHCR is to protect and assist various populations in addition to Convention refugees; in practice this has been a flexible and expanding mandate. From the time of its establishment in 1950, the office of the High Commissioner had a legal basis for operating globally. Yet, the agency did not do so until the late 1950s, when decolonization and state formation in Latin America, Africa and Asia led to the emergence of 'The Third World'.

In many respects, this was also a turbulent world which generated numerous refugees. Given the uneven international distribution of wealth, the richer states were called upon to fund assistance programmes through the UN system and other channels, including non-governmental organizations (NGOs) and bilateral aid. As the division of Europe at the same time stabilized into a polarized status quo which generated few refugees, the focus and activities of the international refugee regime as a whole shifted towards the developing world.

Even so, geographic expansion of the High Commissioner's operation required a series of legal-diplomatic manoeuvres which were to have far-reaching consequences for the expansion of the international refugee regime as a whole. The first step was Resolution 1167 (1957), in which the UN General Assembly asked the High Commissioner to use his 'good offices' to aid Chinese refugees in Hong Kong. The next was the now historic Resolution 1673 (1958) which generalized the intent of Resolution 1167 into a 'good offices doctrine'. The High Commissioner was empowered to 'pursue his activities on behalf of refugees within his mandate or those for whom he extends his good offices' (cited in Holborn 1975: 439). In effect, this gave the organization authority to assist internationally displaced persons without regard to their formal status. An even more general formulation was employed in Resolution 2956, which was adopted by the UN General Assembly in 1972. Upon the invitation of the UN Secretary-General, the agency was empowered to assist 'in those humanitarian endeavours of the United Nations for which his [sic] Office has particular expertise and experience' (Res. 2956 (XXVI) 1972). The resolution gave UNHCR a virtually open-ended mandate to assist persons regardless of their status and location, subject to the request of the Secretary-General and the consent of the country(ies) concerned. Whether the Office also had 'particular expertise and experience' to assist internally displaced persons did not become a major issue until nearly two decades later.

Behind this expansionary process were, first and foremost, the 'new states' in the UN General Assembly which needed international assistance to cope with refugee inflows. But Western states were also interested in a mandate expansion that formalized assistance to a wide category of *de facto* refugees. During the 1960s and the 1970s, Western governments viewed 'order and stability' in the Third World as a bulwark against communist expansion. Large populations of displaced persons who lacked even minimal care or regulation would clearly be inimical to order and stability. By their sheer number, refugees could thus become involuntary agents of new conflict – a notion that was revived in the early 1990s when refugees were subsumed under concepts of 'expanded security' in the post-Cold War world (Weiner 1993). Also UNHCR itself became an important actor in the political process that shaped its role. Probably more significant, and arguably what made mandate expansion possible at all, was its separation from the budgetary process. The UN General Assembly could widen the agency's mandate at will without imposing equivalent financial obligations on its members. Only a small part of UNHCR's budget (US$20 million in 1993) is covered by assessed contributions through the UN, and these are applied towards regular administrative expenses. The main structure of financing is emergency-driven: annual budget projections are based on existing and anticipated case loads, while *ad hoc* appeals are issued to meet sudden emergencies. The relationship between UNHCR and its donors thus is the equivalent of spot contracts, where financing of one situation carries no commitment of future funding. Lacking sequential obligations, these are the most limited kind of contracts, as Kratochwil has pointed out (1993).

Characteristics of the international refugee regime

As it turned out, UNHCR's capacity to respond generally seemed to keep pace with a growing global refugee population. The agency's budget increased from US$8.3 million in 1970 to 500 million in 1990. Measured in constant (1970) dollars, and compared to UNHCR's count of population 'of concern' to the agency, this is equivalent to an increase in per capita expenditure from 3 dollars in 1970 to around 17 dollars in 1990 (UNHCR 1993a). The staff expanded also, especially during the 1980s when 'work years' tripled in the course of the decade (EXCOM 1982, 1993).

The most marked budgetary expansion occurred in the mid- to late 1970s, and again in 1991–2. The 1970s growth – from 69 million in 1975 to 496 million in 1980 – reflected the considerable increase in the world's refugee population, as wars and revolution seemingly coincidentally produced huge outflows in many parts of the world: Afghanistan, the Horn of Africa, Indochina, Southern Africa and Central America. In what came to be known as 'the regional conflicts' of the Cold War, these centres of protracted violence produced long-term refugee populations, mostly in neighbouring countries, that were critically dependent upon UNHCR for channelling funds for care and maintenance. As these refugee situations persisted throughout the 1980s, UNHCR's budget stabilized around $500 million annually.

The end of the Cold War permitted a resolution of most 'regional conflicts' and consequent repatriation of refugees. Yet, the Superpower competition that exacerbated instability and violence in 'the periphery' also served to freeze conflict in 'the centre'. As the Cold War ended, and with it the existence of the Soviet Union, a disintegrative process set in that refocused the attention of the international refugee regime on Europe and its neighbouring regions. It is indicative that it was a European crisis – the war in former Yugoslavia – which sparked the next doubling of UNHCR's budget, which reached $1.2 billion in 1992. The Yugoslav crisis also brought on a step-level change in the functions of the agency. For the first time in its history, UNHCR undertook an unprecedented range of activities to protect and assist internally displaced, besieged and vulnerable groups in the theatre of war itself. Traditional asylum cases formed only a very small portion of its activities.

As indicated earlier, geographic changes in the focus of the international refugee regime reflected the structure of international politics as well as the incidence of violent displacement of people. The main functions of the regime, i.e. protection and assistance, developed according to a related pattern.

The care-and-maintenance assistance provided to refugees during asylum and for what in UN-language are called 'durable solutions' (local integration, resettlement and repatriation) was augmented, channelled and, to various degrees, co-ordinated through a central agency (UNHCR), and delivered with considerable efficiency to refugees when these were located in the developing world. External assistance was a powerful leverage to induce receiving countries to grant asylum. In cases of mass inflows, a receiving country was often unwilling or unable to restrict inflows, and hence was compelled to appeal for international aid to reduce pressure on its own resources. This was especially common in Africa, where traditional forms of asylum and cross-border movements often combined with limited state power and international pressures to produce *de facto* asylum. By contrast, the consistent limitations on asylum which South-east Asian governments imposed on Indochinese inflows in the late 1970s and 1980s stand out as an exception in the developing world.[2]

By the early 1980s, it had become conventional wisdom that only refugee situations in the Third World of special interest to the West, notably the Cubans and the Vietnamese, would be solved through resettlement in the industrialized states. Recognizing that most refugees originating in the South were destined to remain in the region, either as long-term asylees or through some form of resettlement scheme, developing countries countered that the responsibility of the North must be to provide financial assistance. For Africa, reeling under both a huge refugee load and oppressive poverty, this point was critically important. Initially presented through a conference approach, the demand was made at the International Conference on Assistance to Refugees in Africa (ICARA), a much-publicized and twice-held meeting (1981, 1984), where African countries solicited assistance for relief and development on the grounds that a humanitarian and legally defensible refugee policy would otherwise become an obstacle to development. As it turned out, African countries were generally disappointed by the amount of aid generated through ICARA (Stein 1987; Adelman and Sorensen 1994). The conference approach was used more successfully by South-east Asian states to press their demands in refugee matters on the international community.[3]

While the Statutes of UNHCR mandate the agency to provide both assistance and international protection, its authority in asylum matters is the weaker of the two. According to international law, the decision to provide asylum is the prerogative of states, and the ambiguity of contemporary international refugee law – including key concepts such as *non-refoulement* – gives states considerable latitude in legal interpretation. UNHCR can advise, exhort and solicit states to provide asylum as it deems proper, but its power is only that of diplomacy and legal persuasion. UNHCR routinely pronounces on asylum matters, both on substantive decisions and procedures. The pronouncements of the High Commissioner constitute international soft-law on refugees, assembled in the Handbook on Protection and supplemented by the annual Conclusions of the Executive Committee of the High Commissioner.

Given the legal-diplomatic nature of the High Commissioner's power in matters of asylum, it is not surprising that this power has been exercised unevenly. With support from UNHCR, poor states usually provide *de facto* asylum for mass inflows of refugees. UNHCR has typically less influence, in matters concerning individual asylum-seekers in urban areas. This applies, in particular, to African states, which customarily distinguish between these two type of refugees.

In the industrialized world, the relationship between states and UNHCR is characterized by the economic power of states and their role as financiers of UNHCR activities elsewhere. Western industrialized states, moreover, are only receiving, and are not themselves generating, refugees, and have, for at least a decade, been reluctant hosts or destination countries for numerous spontaneous asylum-seekers. UNHCR tries to wield a diplomatic but liberalizing influence on practices that appear to abrogate international legal norms of asylum; the states, for their part, mostly safeguard their freedom of decision making in national asylum policies. Yet, the relationship is not entirely uneven. Even the industrialized states appreciate the importance of a central UN agency to assist and protect refugees elsewhere.

Regional refugee systems

Apart from the links to the international refugee regime, the United States, Western Europe and southern Africa have become receiving poles in regional refugee systems. Central policy dilemmas will be discussed below; here it is useful to sketch their main characteristics.

In these regional systems, traffic is one-way and potentially very large. The patterns of forced migration reflect the presence of zones of war or massive human rights violations alongside countries of relative peace and civic order. To vastly complicate refugee policy for receiving states, there is also a parallel division of economic wealth and migration flows. For such structures of conflict and inequality to become a 'refugee system' requires, in addition, an infrastructure which permits the movement of potential refugees, supportive social networks from previous migrations, a body of international refugee law which accords refugees specified rights, and, most importantly, effective communications. Where these have not been contractually accepted and/or incorporated in national legislation by receiving states, we can say that *de facto* refugee systems develop instead.[4]

As increasingly recognized, refugee systems also function within a framework of international strategic relations (Zolberg *et al.* 1989; Loescher 1993). During decades of Cold War, Western receiving states formulated refugee policies to accommodate the victims of communist regimes and oppose the spread of communist influence. Severely restricted exit from these countries made it particularly incumbent upon the West to receive those who escaped, especially fellow Europeans from the Soviet Bloc. Concurrently, strategic competition between the Superpowers and their local clients typically served to support repressive regimes and exacerbate conflict else-where – both conditions that produced large-scale movements of people who sought protection and assistance from 'the refugee system'. When these people turned up in the countries that contributed to their predicament, however, they were often not welcomed, as was the case with most Central Americans who sought refuge in the United States. Similarly in southern Africa, refugees from the war in Mozambique (1972–92) flocked to South Africa, which itself was an important protagonist and participant in the conflict.

Not surprisingly, changes in the international political system generated by the end of the Cold War also affected the policy dilemmas of receiving states. For Western Europe, the post-Cold War world meant greater turbulence in its neighbouring region, dramatized by the demand for asylum for thousands of refugees from war-torn former Yugoslavia.[5] The end of the Cold War also meant free emigration from neighbouring regions. This came on top of a sharp increase in asylum-seekers from the Middle East, Asia and Africa during the second half of the 1980s, and fears of future large-scale outflows from combined economic and political upheavals in North Africa and the Middle East. Even a reasonably strict definition of 'refugee' under prevailing international law could easily require the industrialized West to admit a very considerable number of beneficiaries. At the same time, and mainly for economic reasons, all West European states sought to strictly control and limit immigration. Although family reunification and skilled migrants were still permitted – and constituted a much larger intake than Convention refugees – the demand for immigration clearly outweighed the supply of places.[6] The result was that would-be migrants also entered the refugee queue in the hope of getting entry. For the first time since the end of World War II, Europe was facing large flows in which refugees mixed with quasi-refugees, and it lacked a compelling political rationale to receive them.

As will be discussed in more detail below, the European Union formulated a common response based on a triad of *control* (to separate refugees from migrants and limit the intake of *bona fide* refugees), *social integration* (of those who were allowed in), and *policy intervention* (to modify the causes of outflow or provide protection in the source country) (CEC 1994). In addition, schemes for temporary protection to accommodate refugees from the war in the neighbouring former Yugoslavia were discussed and partially implemented. Often referred to as a 'comprehensive refugee policy', these innovations transformed the conventional refugee policies pursued by Western Europe during the preceding four decades. In the process, European receiving states came to recognize that a 'comprehensive refugee policy' required greater co-operation both with the regional states and with UNHCR.

For the United States, the end of the Cold War likewise meant a new context for refugee policy.[7] Perhaps more explicitly than European governments, the United States had largely subordinated its refugee policy to foreign policy considerations during the Cold War. As is well documented (Loescher and Scanlan 1986; Zucker and Zucker 1987; Zolberg 1990; Mitchell C. 1992), foreign policy interests had significantly influenced the determination of which refugee populations should be supported in place – with care and maintenance support for the civilians, and sometimes also with weapons for the armed wing of 'refugee warrior' communities – which would be allowed into the United States (either under direct asylum procedures or under resettlement through UNHCR), which would be ignored, and which would be rejected. The underlying principle was simple: persons leaving from, or fighting, communist regimes were likely to be considered refugees worthy of support; opponents of friendly regimes generally were not.

The disintegration of the Soviet Union removed anti-communism as an ideological rationale for US foreign policy and permitted refugee policy to be based on other considerations. Concerns over sharply limiting the number of spontaneous asylum-seekers, regardless of the regime or political conditions in the state of origin, became paramount. One striking result was the decision of the Clinton administration (1994) to treat Haitian and Cuban asylum-seekers similarly – a marked loss for the Cubans, who for decades and by law had benefited from preferential access to the United States.

Another important departure from the past was the use of military intervention to restore order in the country of origin and reduce the outflow of asylum-seekers. In a complete *volte face* of earlier practice – when military intervention typically was undertaken to promote conventional national security concerns and the resultant refugees were considered an unintended, or at any rate, unavoidable side effect – national security policy was now linked to refugee policy as means to an end. Recognizing what critics had long urged, and what the term 'comprehensive refugee policy' sought to formalize, the Clinton Administration sought to develop an effective 'root cause' strategy to solve refugee problems by intervening in Haiti in 1994. As of early February 1995, the policy seemed to be achieving its objectives.

As a concomitant to intervention, Washington established temporary safe havens for several thousand asylum-seekers from Haiti and Cuba. These havens were initially 'off-shore' (at Guantanamo base in Cuba). Recognizing the advantages of developing a regional approach in this type of situation, much as the European Community had done, Washington sought the co-operation of UNHCR to involve neighbouring states in establishing arrangements for burden-sharing. The scheme met with limited success (only Panama signed on in September 1994 to house 8800 Cubans for six months), but the idea received applause from some in-dependent experts and, indeed, from UNHCR.

The above discussion of the development of the international refugee regime, as well as the characteristics of some regional systems, suggests several issues that are salient to the development of refugee policy. These concern:

- asylum;
- the relationship of national refugee policy to regional and international forms of institutional co-operation;
- the relationship between refugee policy and foreign policy.

Before returning to these, an assessment of the nature of the refugee situation in contemporary Africa – and hence the challenges facing major African states – is appropriate.

Africa's enduring refugee crisis

General developments

In the past 30 years, sub-Saharan Africa has become a leading source of refugees. By the end of 1993, nearly six million Africans – or about one-third of the global refugee population – were outside their country and considered in need of protection and assistance; they originated in 22 coun-tries, all but one of them sub-Saharan, and were scattered among 38 countries, all but two also sub-Saharan. In addition, nearly three million were internally displaced (US Committee for Refugees 1994). To these figures must be added the consequences of the Rwandan catastrophe of 1994.

By contrast, as the decade of the 1960s opened, only a few hundred thousand refugees were assisted by the UNHCR in Asia, Latin America and Africa. Many of these were Europeans – remnants of World War II and even the 1917 Bolshevik Revolution. Apart from the Palestinians, who were cared for separately by UNRWA, the only significant non-European refugee populations were Algerians displaced by the war of independence against France and the Chinese who had fled to Hong Kong after the revolution on the mainland.

To many observers – especially in the rich Northern states – these figures symbolized the essence of the refugee problem in the developing world: a population growing faster than the worst run-away demographic increase in the South, produced by obscure and unpredictable causes and defying permanent solutions, since no sooner had a relief camp been erected or repatriation completed in one place, than a new column of refugees appeared elsewhere on the horizon.

In reality, the picture was more complex, but also more ordered. Refugee movements reflected the unfolding pattern of social conflict and international relations in the second half of the twentieth century. Decolonization in Africa and Asia served to enlarge the international system of formally independent states and hence the pool of potential refugees. The decolonization process itself was in some places violent; elsewhere, it set in motion new social conflict. As the victims turned up in neighbouring states, the hitherto European-oriented international refugee regime started to assist and recognize beneficiaries in the developing world.

In addition, two structural conditions accounted for the dramatic increase of refugees in the Third World. One was the underlying demographic growth which, like the expansion of the formal international system, enlarged the universe of potential refugees. From 1950 to 1990, the world's population increased from 2.5 billion to 5.2 billion, most of it in developing countries. The equivalent inflation of refugee numbers is strikingly illustrated by the small African state of Burundi. In 1972, widespread ethnic pogroms generated some 150,000 refugees; when events repeated themselves twenty years later, the outflow was at least 700,000.

The other main factor lay in the international political arena. For more than 40 years, the globalized conflict between the Soviet Union and the United States constituted a determining principle of international relations throughout the world. Originally focused on Europe, the Cold War spread outwards as the dividing lines in Europe became firmly drawn and made the costs of altering the status quo in the centre prohibitive. Conditions in the developing world were more fluid, enabling the two bloc leaders to intervene directly or indirectly to gain incremental power advantages.

In Africa, the United States established itself early on in Zaire, Ethiopia and Liberia, leaving the French-speaking territories to be 'managed' by Paris and the southern part of the continent to be 'managed' by Portugal and South Africa. The Soviet Union put down bridgeheads in ex-French Guinea, as well as Somalia, and invested in the future by sponsoring promising insurgent movements in the Horn, Portuguese Africa and Namibia. For a time, even the People's Republic of China entered into the fray. These probes and confrontations were usually accompanied by vast flows of weapons. Wherever these deadly supplies landed, conflicts between rulers and ruled, as well as between contending regional or ethnic groups, expanded in both space and time. In its most extreme form, the logic of competitive intervention led to warfare by proxy, as happened in southern Africa and the Horn. In all cases, expanded conflict was accompanied by vast refugee flows. Conventional international wars, by contrast, were not a major reason for the rising refugee population in the developing world during the second half of the twentieth century.

While the Cold War tended to centralize and simultaneously simplify the patterns of violence in the developing world, these conflicts also reflected the nature and pace of social change locally. The processes were complex and varied, but two principal categories can be discerned, each having distinct regional variations.

Conflicts over state formation involved the definition of membership in the 'nation'. In the second half of the twentieth century, conflicts over state formation were a major cause of refugee flows from the predominantly multiethnic states of sub-Saharan Africa and South Asia. In parts of Africa, however, the profile was more complex. Ethnic divisions merged with social revolutionary struggles defined in the prevailing Marxist terms of that period to create a multidimensional conflict. The other main causes of large-scale refugee movements were social struggles of a revolutionary kind. In their clearest form, these unfolded in regions other than Africa.

The adverse external economic conditions which faced most developing states during the 1970s and the 1980s also shaped the pattern of conflict and associated refugee flows. While some states were able to overcome these restraints by means of their relative resource advantage and capacity to utilize it, others were constantly pressed against the floor of subsistence. The situation for sub-Saharan Africa was particularly difficult. In the 1970s, the continent's already marginal position within the international economy deteriorated as a result of the energy crisis, the mounting burden of debt, the corruption of economic managers as well as of their foreign patrons, and the disenchantment of investors. Several countries registered severe degradation of marginal agricultural areas as the result of overgrazing and overcultivation, expanded commodities production for export at the cost of subsistence farming, and catastrophic droughts. The adverse economic environment continued into the 1980s to make it a decade of economic decline for much of Africa. Amplifying the effects of these factors was rapid population growth. Overall, from 1960 to 1986 food production per capita decreased by nearly 20 per cent.

The consequences in terms of political economy were many and negative; most obviously, a weak economy allowed little room for negotiating political compromises to the many conflicts which arose in the process of social change.

The diversity of conditions encountered in contemporary Africa stems from a combination of varied cultural traditions with distinctive colonial experiences, together with differentiations arising from geopolitical and economic factors. From the perspective of refugee-producing conflicts, two distinctive regions can readily be identified: the Horn, marked both culturally and strategically by its relationship to the Red Sea and therefore the Arabian Peninsula, and southern Africa, whose recent history was shaped by the availability of precious minerals, the presence of white settlers, and the international role of the Republic of South Africa. These will be considered separately in the analysis below. In addition, a third analytical category emerges – the weak but predatory state, which is unevenly spread throughout the continent.

In the long shadow of South Africa

Major refugee flows first appeared in southern Africa in the mid-1960s and continued until the close of the 1980s. By that time, there were 700,000 refugees in Malawi (from Mozambique), another maybe 300,000 Mozambicans in South Africa, 200,000 in Zimbabwe and 50,000 in Swaziland. The other major refugee population was from Angola, of which an estimated 200,000 were in Zaire, 120,000 in Zambia and a smaller number in Congo and Namibia. Some 80,000 Zairians had taken refuge in five neighbouring countries (US Committee for Refugees 1994). Large but uncounted numbers were internally displaced.

Refugee-producing conflicts in southern Africa exhibit the characteristics of long independence struggles, whose conflictual legacy was nourished by foreign intervention. Initially, the refugee movements were linked to the struggles for national liberation, starting with Portuguese-ruled Angola and Mozambique, then extending to Rhodesia/Zimbabwe, and finally encompassing South-West Africa/Namibia, the UN trustee territory which South Africa effectively had annexed after World War II. At the root of the problem was the political economy of settler rule, characterized by a massive appropriation of land and its subsequent transformation into private property owned exclusively by whites. The condition foreclosed the sort of negotiated decolonization that had taken place in other parts of the continent. Another distinctive feature was the incorporation of all the countries in question in an emerging regional system dominated by South Africa. As a result, violent decolonization became an interactive process, in which international factors played an important role.

Given the entrenched position and coercive capacity of the settler governments, African protest was initially expressed through 'weapons of the weak', in the apt phrase of James Scott — non-confrontational forms such as withdrawal into subsistence production or emigration, interspersed with rare peasant insurrections, strikes, and boycotts which were ruthlessly repressed (Scott 1985). Settler governments were able to deter organized political protest until well after extensive nationalist movements emerged in the rest of the continent. However, as the pace of decolonization quickened, the balance of organizational costs and benefits shifted to favour the African side.

The region's earliest political stirrings produced a few activist exiles. As the struggles got under way, refugees became more numerous but mostly remained in the region, in liberated zones inside their own country or across the border of some newly independent neighbour. The growing availability of such havens helped turn the trickle into a flood, and the formation of large refugee pools further facilitated the recruitment of liberation fighters.

Fearing the victories of black nationalism throughout the continent, in the second half of the 1960s, South Africa started to assist beleaguered white regimes. Troops were sent to Rhodesia in 1967, where they helped delay independence for almost another decade; concurrently, Portuguese colonial governments received economic aid which enabled them to cover the escalating costs of warfare. The intricate and layered nature of external involvement, and its interaction with domestic sources of conflict, is clearly demonstrated in the case of Angola.

Angola

Angola's political movements initially reflected differences arising from the situation of various groups in relation to the colonial political economy, their geopolitical location, ethnic identity and religious denomination. The earliest one, which evolved into the Movement for the Liberation of Angola (MPLA), originated among the Mbundu population of Luanda — mostly Catholics or Methodists — who, by virtue of their proximity to the colonial centre, were incorporated into the margin of Portuguese life, giving rise to an intermediate stratum of *mestizos* and *assimilados*. While these Angolans gained access to education and the professions, they also experienced more intensely the frustrations of racial discrimination and declining opportunities, which resulted from the influx of Portuguese settlers in the post-World War II period. Like some of its French African counterparts, the MPLA had links with the Portuguese Communist Party, which was then an underground organization. The Union of the Populations of Northern Angola, which later evolved into the National Front for the Liberation of Angola (FNLA) was launched in 1957 among the Kongo in the districts adjoining Zaire in the course of a confrontation with the Portuguese over succession to the Kongo throne. Under the leadership of Holden Roberto, with a cadre of successful Baptist traders and coffee farmers, the movement spread rapidly among a population primed by the political ferment among their fellow Kongo in Zaire and the French Congo.

From the mid-1960s onward, Angola became an arena for competition between the two world camps. The Soviet Union gained entry early on by way of the MPLA's links with the Portuguese Communist Party. Despite its alliance with Portugal within the framework of NATO, the United States responded by providing covert support to Holden Roberto's FNLA. As part of the same operation, in 1965 the CIA installed Col. Mobutu as leader of Zaire, where Holden's FNLA movement had established a government-in-exile. Afterwards, the Zairian army undertook to organize, train and equip the FNLA armed forces (Kaplan 1983). The FNLA was also aided by the People's Republic of China, which likewise viewed it as a counterweight to the Soviet-backed MPLA. A third Angolan movement arose among the large Ovimbundu population in the south. Jonas Savimbi's National Union for Total Independence of Angola (UNITA) initially adopted a 'Maoist' ideology; but because it constituted a thorn in the side of the MPLA, it was tolerated, and perhaps also assisted, by the Portuguese (Heimer 1979).

The first phase of the war generated massive population displacement, most of it caused by Portuguese reliance on air power. In 1966, an estimated 400,000 of Angola's black population (about 8 per cent) had fled to the relative safety of neighbouring states, and many more had moved to Luanda and other towns.

After the Portuguese revolution, Angola moved rapidly towards independence, prompting a more intensive jockeying for power. Thanks to its Luanda base, the MPLA gained control of the government. In October 1975, a South African force crossed into Angola, citing the new Angolan government's support for the guerrilla movement in South-west Africa (Namibia); this in turn prompted the Soviet Union to accelerate the flow of military supplies to its MPLA client, including the dispatch of several thousand Cuban troops. Constrained by its recent Vietnam experience, the United States provided only limited covert support to the FNLA and UNITA. The latter welcomed South African intervention as a source of potential support and mutual aid. By training and equipping Savimbi's UNITA faction, South Africa sharpened the instrument most likely to unseat the pro-Soviet regime in Luanda; in return, Savimbi allowed the South African armed forces (SADF) to raid Namibian guerrilla bases located in southern Angola. Thus, at the dawn of independence, the hostile Angolan factions built up and armed by foreign patrons faced each other in a divided country. The refugees mostly did not return.

South Africa's 'rogue elephant' behaviour was part of a new 'total national strategy' which entailed systematic military intervention and economic intimidation to destabilize neighbours who did not acquiesce in Pretoria's white supremacist rule. The policy was directed most ruthlessly at Angola and Mozambique whose governments were both Marxist and black nationalist. The policy was abetted by the West (Callaghy 1983). Evident since the late 1960s, this point was openly demonstrated in the UN Security Council in August 1981, when the United States refused to condemn a large South African military raid into Angola. Driven by its struggle against 'the evil empire', the Reagan administration viewed Pretoria as a necessary, if distasteful, partner to counter Soviet presence in a resource-rich and strategically significant region.

US covert aid to Savimbi was, for a time, blocked by the US Congress but resumed in 1985. Over the years, US financing and South African training turned UNITA's soldiers into a regular army with some 5000 men and 20,000 followers who controlled a vastly expanded territory. In the logic of competitive intervention, Moscow increased its support to the Angolan government to keep pace. With the arrival of over 30,000 Cuban troops, 1200 Soviet advisers, and deliveries of an estimated US$2 billion worth of supplies, Luanda was able to affirm its control over the major towns in the south and to stage an annual summer offensive.

The finely tuned destructive balance of the Angolan civil war was peculiarly a product of the deepening Cold War during the 1980s. The mounting East–West tension during the Reagan–Brezhnev era made it possible for a poor African country of five million people and some oil reserves to become a principal battleground between the Superpowers. Admittedly, the Angolan parties were divided by their own ethnic and political animosities. But the international environment transformed a rag-tag band around Savimbi into a state within the state, while giving the Luanda government just enough destructive power to pursue the conflict in military terms. For Angola's society and economy, it was a disaster. By 1985, about 5 per cent of the population had registered as refugees in neighbouring countries, and the figure kept rising. Half a million were internally displaced by war, drought and hunger. Untold numbers were killed, millions of hidden land mines steadily claimed their victims,[8] and the legacy for the future was more violence.

The end of the Cold War also ended Soviet aid, and Cuban troops departed from Angola. This encouraged a similar South African withdrawal, thus bringing about the 'linkage' which US diplomats previously had formulated as a bargaining strategy (Crocker 1993). Simultaneously, South Africa terminated its interventions in Mozambique and finally gave up Namibia. The reversal of regional interventionist policies was part of a more fundamental reorientation in Pretoria that shortly thereafter led to the formal abrogation of the apartheid system.

In Namibia and Mozambique, the foundations for normalcy were gradually put in place, and refugees returned or were repatriated. In

Angola, relief was more uncertain. In this respect, the contrasting cases of Angola and Mozambique illustrate the role of foreign intervention in shaping the patterns of conflict in the region. The Mozambican rebellion was most clearly a foreign product. Initially sponsored by the white settler regime of Ian Smith in Rhodesia, RENAMO became South Africa's weapon against the Marxist-oriented government of Mozambique. As Pretoria moved in new directions in the early 1990s, RENAMO lost its patronage. A weakened RENAMO greatly facilitated concurrent efforts to end the war, and a peace agreement was signed in October 1992 (Sidaway and Simon 1993).

In Angola, however, the internal struggle had deeper local roots and stronger ethnic underpinning. The function of competitive foreign intervention was to transform these factions into opposing and formidable military forces. When foreign support ebbed, Angola's oil and diamonds made it possible to purchase arms on the international market to continue the fighting. Cease-fire agreements were concluded in 1991 and 1992, only to be broken. UNITA-leader Savimbi agreed to participate in internationally supervised elections in 1992, but withdrew from the political process when he lost the presidential contest. His army moved quickly to consolidate its hold over major parts of the Angolan territory, including the diamond fields, and a devastating round of renewed war followed. By late 1994, however, the balance of international support, including US recognition, had shifted further in favour of the Luanda government. South African 'advisers', apparently mercenaries, were now attached to the government forces rather than the rebels.[9] Savimbi's position appeared tenuous and a new cease-fire was concluded. This time, the prospects for a lasting agreement were so good that the UN Security Council in early February 1995 authorized a sizeable peace-keeping unit for the troubled country.

Competitive state formation and revolution in the Horn of Africa

Already bearing the sad distinction of ranking as the poorest country in the world, Ethiopia has in the past three decades been racked by interlocking conflicts which express the complexity of violence in the Horn. Much of the Ethiopian picture is captured by the concept of competitive state formation whereby rival 'nations' claim statehood (Eritrea vs. Ethiopia) or territorial adjustments to complete statehood (Somalia vs. Ethiopia). These conflicts were decisively shaped, and the total violence compounded, by the struggle over social order in Ethiopia and its revolutionary outcome in the early 1970s. Given the location of Ethiopia as a strategic bridge between Africa and the strategically vital Middle East, as well as the ideological context in which strife unfolded, the conflict was rapidly internationalized. This escalated the conflicts, increased the firepower and magnified the refugee flows. Since the conflicts unfolded in agrarian societies, located in a semi-arid zone where, even under the best of circumstances, the harvest was uncertain and the margin of survival narrow, the fighting had a devastating effect on local economies. In drought years, the flows increased sharply. In refugee terms, it was a classic case of flight from war, poverty and natural disaster combined.

Ethiopia

The first call of defiance came from Eritrea, where a separatist rebellion had gained ground in the early 1960s. By 1966, rebels had turned much of north-western Eritrea into a liberated zone with a thriving underground infrastructure. In response, the Ethiopian air force razed villages, whose inhabitants were moved to government-controlled settlements. Unable to drive the Ethiopian forces back, the Eritreans turned instead on each other. By 1970, the rival Muslim and Christian-socialist rebel movements – which reflected the almost even division of the Eritrean population between Muslims and Coptic Christians – were openly at war. A long, stalemated war ensued.

The escalating war in Eritrea was just one of several breaking points of an Ethiopian empire whose fragility was increasingly exposed. In contrast to sub-Saharan Africa as a whole, the traditional social order in Ethiopia was founded on control by an Amhara aristocracy over the land and the peasants who lived on it, with support from an established Christian church. Attempting haltingly to modernize from above, the emperor succeeded only in sharpening social contradictions. The younger military cadre and emerging professional middle classes resented Haile Selassie's archaic patrimonial rule and the obvious backwardness of the country. A severe drought and famine in the early 1970s destroyed the last vestiges of authority of the aging emperor. In September 1974, a military coup inaugurated the revolution.

Led by Major Mengistu Haile Mariam, the Derg ('committee') aimed for a total social transformation, starting with radical land reform and forced settlement of peasants to the southern region. The process brought the Derg into conflict with a wide range of social forces including defenders of the *ancien regime*, competing revolutionary factions, and non-Amhara populations that tried to take advantage of the collapse of imperial rule to achieve greater autonomy. The resulting wide swathe of violence cut through all sectors of Ethiopian society. Only in the large estates of central and southern Ethiopia, where the serf-like tenants were liberated by the land reform, did the peasants support the Derg. By 1977, there were uprisings in nine out of fourteen provinces besides Eritrea. The Somalis of the Ogaden – a region captured by Ethiopia in the late nineteenth century

– spearheaded a revival of Somalia's long-standing irredentist claim. This campaign led to regular war between the two states in 1977–8.

The international situation enabled the local protagonists to upgrade their arms, and probably prolonged the conflict by giving full play to the logic of competitive intervention, which required that a gain by one side be offset by a commensurate strengthening of the other. The strategic value of the Horn – originally derived from the completion of the Suez Canal in 1869 – was inflated after World War II by the extension of the East–West rivalry to the Middle East, in relation to which the Red Sea region constituted a major staging base. In the 1950s, the United States took up the British mantle as the dominant Western power in the area and backed Haile Selassie, who as an anti-Moslem also obtained substantial support from the Israelis. The Soviets lined up with Somalia. The rivalry fostered a decades-long arms race which resulted in the militarization of both states.

The Ethiopian revolution produced a realignment: the Soviet Union switched its support to the self-proclaimed Marxist Ethiopian Derg, while the United States took up Somalia's military dictator, General M. Siad Barre. In 1977, to help the Ethiopian government repel the Somali invasion and roll back the Eritrean uprising, the Soviet Union launched a massive airlift that within a few weeks brought in 11,000 Cuban troops alongside 1500 Soviet advisors. Concurrently, the United States supplied the Somalis as well the anti-Derg Tigray Liberation Movement in Ethiopia. The vastly increased stock of weapons amplified the destructive consequences of the Horn's internal and international wars. The proliferation of handguns was also a boost to bandits, who multiplied and preyed on refugees in the border region between Ethiopia and Sudan.

The combination of war, dislocation and recurring drought in 1984–6 brought on famine. The lines of refugees heading for relief camps in the Sudan or Somalia became longer. Estimates of the number of refugees vary greatly as a result of the shifting and complex patterns of conflict in the Horn, as well as propagandistic use of refugee statistics. At least half a million, and perhaps one million, persons were displaced from Ethiopia to Somalia as a result of the war and a local famine in 1981. Between the early 1960s and the late 1980s, about 1.5 million refugees from Ethiopia arrived in Sudan. Of these, about half a million came at the time of the famine (Jacobsen 1993).

The end of the Cold War had an immediate impact. Almost totally dependent on the Soviet Union and East Germany, the Ethiopian regime was doomed from the moment the Gorbachev government decided to reduce sharply its engagement. The war in Eritrea had reached a turning point in 1990 when, after nearly three decades of struggle, the Eritrean People's Liberation Front took Massawa, Ethiopia's major port. With control of the delivery point for relief food as well as military supplies, the rebels laid siege to the regional capital, Asmara. At that point, the government forces were fatally hampered by the Soviet Union's refusal to provide aircraft for transporting troops to the besieged city. Concurrently, the Tigrayan People's Liberation Front advanced southward towards Addis Ababa. With the treasury empty and a critical shortage of fuel, the Ethiopian army disintegrated in early 1991 and President Mengistu fled the country. The successor liberation movements formed a new government. In Eritrea, independence was celebrated with a formal referendum in 1993. Refugees started to return from neighbouring countries.

While Eritrea's nationhood had been forged through 30 years of warfare, divisions between Muslims and Christians ominously moved to the fore when the struggle with Ethiopia ended. If these divisions had developed into a confrontation, the confrontation most probably would be internationalized and linked to the conflictual international relations of the Middle East.

There were other signs that this part of the Horn might see renewed struggle and refugee flows. Ethiopia remained a fragile constellation of ethnic and regional groups. With Eritrea gone, the main challenge came from the Oromo, who constitute perhaps an entire 40 per cent of the total population. Mostly Muslims, they generally view themselves as an enslaved people and may exact retribution from their defeated Amhara masters. Also the role of the minority Tigrayans was uncertain. The Amharas, who make up some 25 per cent of the population, remained firmly committed to Ethiopian integrity but were themselves deeply divided by the conflicts of the past two decades. On the other hand, it should be emphasized that neither these divisions nor the sudden disappearance of the strong-man – who, as in Somalia, had done little to build stable structures of governance – produced an immediate implosion. By early 1995, at least, Ethiopia was weathering the succession crisis, whereas Somalia had failed.

The various outcomes and scenarios in the Horn indicate what applies to sub-Saharan Africa as a whole: despite structural uniformities which make it possible to speak of 'the African condition' and identify prototypical patterns of conflict – as we have done – the complexity and variations in national development are considerable. This makes projection of future conflicts and refugee flows hazardous. Yet, refugee policy is often and at least implicitly based on some assessment of past conflicts and likely future flows, whether this takes the form of efforts to deal with the flows or to modify the causes by developing root cause strategies.

In the next section of this chapter we shall consider some principal responses which seem relevant to contemporary South Africa. We shall not develop particular scenarios relating to conflict development in the region and beyond, but simply assume as a starting point that, given South Africa's proximity to states that fit the model of vulnerability delineated earlier, there is a fairly high probability of turbulence and consequent demand for assistance and protection. We assume further that South Africa will continue to play a leadership role in the regional international system, and hence that it will have to adopt responsible policies in this domain.

The weak, predatory state

In much of sub-Saharan Africa, conflicts that generate refugees are closely linked to the dynamic of 'the weak, predatory state'. This is tragically illustrated by disparate cases including at various times Zaire, Chad, Uganda, the Central African Republic (under Bokassa), Equatorial Guinea, Somalia, and – most recently – Liberia and Sierra Leone.

The underlying causes of such conflicts can be briefly sketched. At the dawn of independence, the extreme infrastructural weakness of the new states was hidden from view because they displayed a considerable capacity for engaging in repressive action (Mann 1984; Zolberg 1985, 1992). Although the African state looms powerful in relation to other organizations, it has a limited capacity for managing society and directing change – a paradox well expressed by Thomas Callaghy's term, 'lame Leviathan' (Callaghy 1986). Despite their extreme infrastructural deficiency, these weak states persisted because of support from a relatively benign international environment (Jackson 1990) – except in southern Africa, as indicated below.

Africa's condition stems from a combination of distinctive precolonial and colonial structures. In contrast with states in other parts of the developing world, which were often carved out of larger empires, most of the African ones are amalgams of small-scale societies that were bundled into entities designed by European colonial entrepreneurs in response to imperial rivalries of the late nineteenth century. These societies had a low ratio of population in relation to land and lived close to the level of subsistence; under conditions of slash-and-burn agriculture, their domain was not fixed. Chieftainship tended to be over people rather than over land, and political dynamics focused on competition among clientelist factions. The absence of political centralization and the low population density left open the possibility of 'exit', giving rise to a process of segmentation whereby new social clusters were constantly being established by emigrants on available land.

Consequently, precolonial political structures could offer relatively little resistance to the formation of a new system of domination, and the remnants of traditional societies were grouped for purposes of colonial administration into entities the Europeans termed 'tribes' or 'ethnic groups', which were sometimes altogether new. Governing their possessions with traditional imperial techniques, the Europeans exploited tensions among these groups to enhance their own power; existing differences were sharpened also by the uneven impact of social and economic change. Ethnic groups became 'advanced' or 'backward', rich or poor. Although African movements for self-determination were 'nationalist' in the sense that many of them sought to mobilize the entire population of a given colony, democratization also sparked ethnic solidarities in that competing leaders exploited particularistic identities as ready-made political resources.

The post-colonial elite's project has been aptly characterized by Frederick Cooper as 'self-aggrandisement combined with enough redistribution to maintain its tenuous and vital hold on the state' (Cooper 1981). However, Africa's predatory rulers are severely constrained by extreme poverty, and the prevalent structural weakness makes it as difficult to increase extraction by way of state action as by capitalist exploitation. Takeover of the apparatus of the colonial state provided resources for organizing the initial array of clientelist networks by which the state was managed. Additional aid came from the former colonial power, as well as in the form of grants and loans from outside powers seeking to establish a sphere of influence within the African arena. In a few instances the new elites had access to mineral royalties; more commonly, they could squeeze income only by fostering a shift from subsistence to export agriculture, while stepping up exactions from primary producers.

Some of the loot was redistributed to relieve pressures from the urban sector, to which rulers were most valuable; but much of it was appropriated. In the face of demands occasioned by broader mobilization and rising expectations, resources had to be expanded and demands managed. Beleaguered governments relied heavily on the police and military forces inherited from the colonial state. This strategy proved self-defeating, however, as the agents of repression quickly learned where true power lay. Within a few years, a majority of the new states experienced military coups. Because soldiers during the colonial period had frequently been recruited from minority groups in hinterland regions, 'unspoiled' by dawning political consciousness, they tended to be even more parochial than the civilians they replaced and quicker to fall back on brute force.

Weak predatory states with a large supply of firepower are subject to a distinctive form of deterioration. In the face of shrinking resources and an absence of institutional restraints, authoritarian rulers step up extractive pressure and abandon any pretence at redistribution. In the African context, this usually entails a narrowing down of the regime's ethnic or clan foundation. At its worst, 'ethnocracy' can trigger a violent implosion, a disaggregation of both rulers and ruled into primary solidarity groups vying with one another in a desperate search for security. Where the international configuration allows, this results in a massive exodus.

The central African states of Rwanda, and to some extent also Burundi, initially deviated somewhat from the model. An old state with an established monarchy rather than an amalgam of small-scale societies, Rwanda had some capacity for managing change, despite the 1959 revolution and its violent aftermath. Nevertheless, it exhibited some critical characteristics of the weak and predatory state: it did not have the reserves to manage a crisis when it occurred, and power was accumulated around a small elite which used the state to enrich and otherwise advance the interests of its own regional clan. While group boundaries in the political arena came to be determined increasingly by region rather than ethnic group (Hutu vs. Tutsi), when Rwanda did explode the violence followed predominantly ethnic lines.

Rwanda

The recurring conflict in Rwanda refects an unusual ethnic hierarchy that came into being in the pre-colonial period, establishing between the pastoralist Tutsi (who currently comprise about 15 per cent of the population in each of the two countries) and the agriculturalist Hutu. The unequal relationship between the two was exacerbated under colonial rule and extended to new domains in the course of modernization. Because the Tutsi were given preference in education and access to the colonial bureaucracy, they became over time more 'advanced'. At the same time, traditional mechanisms of interdependence that had promoted co-existence between the two groups disintegrated (Chretien 1985; Lemarchand and Martin 1974; Lemarchand 1970; Newbury 1983).

As the Belgians reluctantly prepared to leave in the late 1950s, the colonial legacy collided head-on with the formal democratic ideology of independence in a typical post-colonial struggle for power. With Belgian support, the Hutu succeeded in translating their demographic weight into political power by means of an anti-Tutsi social revolution that was confirmed by elections in 1961. The Tutsi were eliminated from all command posts and their numbers drastically reduced in every sphere of public life. Backed against the wall, the Tutsi attempted a *coup d'état*, but this backfired and provoked massive retaliation. As many as 15,000 members of the minority community were murdered. By 1966, 185,000 – or almost half of the entire Tutsi population – were registered as refugees in neighbouring states, with Uganda receiving the largest share.

The precarious status of those who remained rapidly worsened. Rwanda's population, already one of the densest in Africa, increased at an annual rate of 3.0–3.5 per cent, creating a crisis of subsistence which was further exacerbated by unfavourable market conditions for coffee, the main export commodity. Given the further shrinking of an already miserable pie, President Habyarimana consolidated his power around his clansmen and reduced the share allocated to other Hutu clans as well as to the Tutsi. Along with a rising climate of violence, this prompted an intermittent stream of exiles.

Meanwhile, Rwandan refugees had, with Uganda 'blessing', organized themselves into a fighting force, thus forming a 'refugee warrior' community. From late 1990 onwards, the Rwandan Patriotic Front (RPF) launched probes into north-eastern Rwanda. When Belgium refused to bolster the government's military capacity, Habyarimana turned to France, which stepped in, in keeping with its 1975 military assistance agreement (Isnard 1993; Human Rights Watch 1994). The fighting and renewed retaliatory crackdowns on Tutsi civilians occasioned additional refugee flows.

In the face of mounting opposition bolstered by the rising democratic tide that swept Africa at the beginning of the 1990s, in April 1992 the Habyarimana regime agreed to form a coalition government with several groups of the Hutu opposition; shortly afterwards, they signed a ceasefire with the RPF and agreed to expand the coalition to include representatives of the Tutsi minority as well. However, the negotiations dragged on and the cease-fire was violated, while inside Rwanda organized killings of members of the Tutsi minority took place. The Tutsi-based RPF responded with a major military offensive in February 1993, but France helped rescue the government forces from complete defeat by deploying an enlarged military contingent (680 men). A new cease-fire and final agreement was signed at Arusha in August 1993, to be enforced by UN peace-keepers. However, the Arusha Accords foundered when Habyarimana stalled on their implementation, thereby setting the stage for the final, confrontational phase. His death in the downing of his plane on 6 April 1994 became the opening phase of massive violence against Tutsi and moderate Hutu, led by the presidential guard and Hutu militia and triggered a resumption of the war (Prunier 1994).

As the UN peace-keeping force UNAMIR was sharply reduced, the killings developed into genocide of Tutsi and mass flight. The RPF took control over the capital and encouraged refugees to return, while Hutu leaders ensconced themselves in Zaire with the remnants of the army. Here they sought to prevent the more than a million Hutu refugees from returning, except under their leadership. Yet another refugee-warrior community was formed that seemed likely to continue the cycle of violence.

The unprecedented size of the Hutu outflow must be understood against the background of several distinct features of the country and the conflict. The small size of Rwanda makes foreign sanctuary critically important. Moreover, generalized Hutu participation in the genocide of Tutsi made many fear reprisals if they remained, and defeated Hutu leaders did the rest by engendering a mass hysteria so that people would leave and be regrouped in exile.

As the Rwanda case suggests, ethnically intermingled groups rarely express their conflicts in terms of competitive state-formation (secessionist or autonomy struggles, as in Sudan). When conditions turn violent, conflict among intermingled peoples typically take the form of riots and, in extreme cases, pogroms or even genocide. States that are unable or unwilling to prevent this become accomplices – proactively so in the Rwandan case. As noted above, even weak states can have a concentrated capacity for violence.

While not predominant in Rwanda, several weak states in Africa have another characteristic. In the tradition of the European absolutist kings, the state 'is' a strong-man; his position is based on narrowly circumscribed support, typically from clansmen, and is shored up by critical foreign assistance in the form of arms and sometimes presence. Not infrequently, foreign aid of this kind also has the effect of reducing incentives to build a broad internal constituency and establish legitimate political institutions. When the strong-man falls, there are no structures to secure civil order. Violent struggles, typically defined along ethnic or clan lines, fill the power vacuum. Such a conflict dynamic was observed in Somalia in 1992–3, and in the outbreak of civil war in Liberia after the fall of the old regime.

Given these characteristics of the weak state, the end of the Cold War had a severe impact on countries whose strong-men had been closely tied to the Superpower rivalry. Local clients whose principal strength had derived from external patrons found their power base eroded and internal challenges mounting. In some cases disintegration proceeded as if in slow-motion. Elsewhere, as in Somalia, the fall was swift. General Mohammed Siad Barre fought an uphill battle against northern insurgents in the 1980s, and his clannishness precipitated a rebellion in the central part of the country as well. In the south, disgruntled army commanders began to go into business for themselves. Abandoned by the United States, which had built up his regime with money and weapons since the mid-1970s – before which time the Soviet Union had done the same (see below) – Barre turned to Libya, but to little avail. When the dictator fled in 1991, the centre collapsed and anarchy descended on Somalia.

In this perspective, one can understand the ambivalent stance of the Western powers – notably France and the United States – on the issue of President Mobutu's continued rule in Zaire: on the one hand, his abusive exactions were a source of suffering for the Zairians and a scandal for his international supporters, as well as likely contributing factors to future conflict; but on the other hand, his sudden departure or removal might precipitate a catastrophic implosion.

Refugee policies and dilemmas

A 'comprehensive' refugee policy

In the United Nations in the early 1980s, attempts to link refugee policy with foreign policy generally took the form of the so-called root cause debate. Then, as now, there was a sense of an imminent refugee crisis – the number of actual and, especially, potential refugees in the world seemed to overwhelm conventional forms of protection and assistance. The solution, it seemed, was to focus on the causes of refugee flows so that the problems could be tackled at the root (Suhrke 1994b).

The 1980s' debate had sharp ideological undertones relating to East–West and North–South divisions. Anti-communist governments were accusing communist states of producing refugees by their very practices, while developing countries argued that structural international inequality, racism and colonialism were the main 'root causes' of refugees. These undertones are absent or have been muted in the present discourse. Instead, a more pragmatic notion has come to the fore: refugee problems can and should be modified through better conflict management.

Under High Commissioner Sadako Ogata, UNHCR has played a leading role in the international policy discourse on a 'comprehensive refugee policy'. By emphasizing that refugee problems are not simply humanitarian in nature but must be dealt with in a political process which considers the underlying causes of flows and addresses conflict management, the High Commissioner has undertaken a deconstruction of the political culture of the agency (UNHCR 1993b). Even the more limited concept of 'protection' has come to be interpreted in the context of conflict management, thus accentuating the links between refugee policy and foreign policy. As stated in the recent semi-official publication of the organization,

> Protecting people against forced displacement requires a comprehensive and integrated response that deals with such problems in their entirety. It is likely to begin by tackling the immediate humanitarian needs of the people affected, including the need for asylum, at least on a temporary basis. It continues with an array of actions designed to enhance respect for human rights and humanitarian law, to prevent further displacement, to resolve armed conflict and to create conditions conducive to voluntary repatriation
> . . .
> Implementation of a comprehensive response to a refugee problem requires the co-operation of a broad range of actors: the governments of the country of origin and the countries of asylum, donor states, international agencies, NGOs and opposition forces .... [This is] likely to include co-ordinated action in the fields of foreign policy, international law, economic co-operation, immigration and asylum policy, as well as official development assistance. This is obviously beyond the scope of humanitarian organisations alone. (UNHCR 1993b: 139–40).

The premise of a 'comprehensive' refugee policy is that foreign and refugee policies are deliberately and closely interrelated. As the history of African refugee movements demonstrates, foreign policies of states have, in the past, often exacerbated conflicts and the consequent refugee flows by such means as intervention to subvert unfriendly governments, support for rebellious factions and assorted 'refugee warriors', disregard for basic principles of human rights and participatory politics, and manipulation of ethnic divisions. All this was part of Pretoria's previous 'total national policy' designed to defend aggressively an apartheid state against black African nationalism. By contrast, a foreign policy that promoted regional co-operation in consonance with some principles of democracy and social justice and attuned to concerns of conflict management and human rights would be likely to produce less refugees.

Beyond this rather obvious point, some aspects pertaining to the limitations and possibilities associated with a 'comprehensive' refugee policy are evident.

First, on a conceptual level, the frequently used term 'comprehensive refugee policy' resembles that of 'sustainable development'. As a general notion based on a simple core principle, its particular form will vary according to the concrete situation. And while permitting various interpretations, arguably the core remains and must be seen as the integral linking of refugee policy with foreign policy.

Second, root causes of refugees that relate to structural conditions or historical legacies are not easily, if at all, subject to policy modification — certainly not in the short run. In this respect, the root cause debate in the 1980s and the accompanying social science literature concur. Hence, a 'comprehensive' refugee policy that tries to address root causes should not raise unrealistic expectations. It follows — as critics of the European Union initiatives have pointed out — that a declaratory 'root cause policy' cannot be substituted for asylum.

Other limitations of a 'comprehensive' refugee policy have been demonstrated in the region where it was first developed. As noted, the war in former Yugoslavia created fears in the rest of Europe not only of a widening war, but also, more immediately, of a deluge of refugees. It was hoped that the humanitarian operation under UN auspices would provide a 'comprehensive and integrated' protection so as to modify the conflict and reduce the outflow of refugees. A large humanitarian presence, operating under the over-all security of the UN peacekeeping force (UNPROFOR) was undertaken. Significantly, UNHCR was given an unprecedented lead role and launched among other things the concept of 'preventive protection'. It soon became evident, however, that in this conflict UNHCR could not even protect its own people. While the operation no doubt saved some lives and probably pre-empted some flight, the problems of mounting a large-scale humanitarian effort in the theatre of war were manifest (Mendiluce 1994). Critics argued it served mainly to prolong the conflict and the agony (Higgins 1993).

By contrast, at least one intervention in the post-Cold War period designed to pre-empt flight by restoring normalcy appeared to achieve its objectives. Undertaken with UN authorization and the reluctant co-operation of the Haitian military junta itself, and after an uncertain start, the US military intervention in Haiti in 1994 had by early 1995 restored the elected president Aristide. New elections were planned, and a UN peace-keeping force was preparing to replace the American units that had constituted the advance force. This successful intervention gave the US government a rationale for the interdiction of future flights, as well as for the termination of the temporary protection which had been given to several thousand Haitians in US-supervised 'safe havens' at the Guantanamo base in Cuba. Simultaneously, the intervention emphasized that temporary protection 'makes little sense as a strategy if ... divorced from efforts to address the causes and attain solution' (EXCOM 1994: 24). Addressing the causes of refugee flows, in other words, constitutes an integral part of a comprehensive refugee policy.

In a related development, efforts were underway in the United Nations in the early 1990s to strengthen the legal and institutional machinery for protecting internally displaced persons (Deng 1993; UNHCR 1994). While these efforts reflected varied motives and institutional interests, one concern was that internally displaced persons might spill across borders unless effectively aided and protected *in situ*. The same applied to refugees who might re-migrate if unsafe in the asylum area. While the UN-system emphasized that it was the responsibility of states to provide protection within their own borders, the corollary to this was that 'where Governments lack the means ... they need to receive the assistance of the international community to enable them to do so' (EXCOM 1994: 10). In contrast to conventional asylum which requires that the person(s) cross an international border, this innovation represents a form for internalization of asylum with far-reaching implications. In the early 1990s, this development of the asylum institution was receiving increasing attention.

Insofar as a comprehensive refugee policy includes elements of conflict management and internalization of protection, it connects to issues of national security and sovereignty that have traditionally constituted the sphere of 'high politics'. The same applies to an array of initiatives taken in the UN system in the post-Cold War world to strengthen preventive diplomacy, peacekeeping, human rights and 'humanitarian diplomacy' (see Boutros-Ghali 1992). How to co-ordinate refugee policy with developments in these areas, and hence to minimize the burden on the refugee, as well as on the receiving country, is a central but yet evolving discourse among actors concerned with refugees.

Dealing with the flows

Refugee law and practice in Africa have roots in the 'wars of national liberation' of the 1960s, which displaced hundreds of thousands of people. Because these struggles constituted the single most important element of pan-African consciousness, the African states collaborated in the elaboration of a formal support system for refugees. Accordingly, the Organisation for African Unity (OAU) formalized in 1969 a generous convention governing asylum and refugees in the region. Concurrently, under pressure from the African states in the General Assembly, the UNHCR steadily expanded its mandate to protect and aid displaced persons under a 'good offices' doctrine.

Compared to the UN Convention, the OAU code has stronger provisions for access to seek asylum and broader criteria for refugee status. Article 2 of the OAU code stresses the right of asylum, and Article 5 prohibits rejection at the frontier; neither has a counterpart in the UN Convention. Access to seek asylum is thus more strongly grounded in the OAU, and once inside a signatory country, the presumptive beneficiary enjoys a broad definition of eligibility for refugee status. These strong provisions reflect the political realities at the time: the OAU provisions were formulated after a decade of increasingly violent struggles for liberation in Angola, Mozambique, Rhodesia, and Southern Africa. For Africa's independent states, these were unquestionably just wars, hence the derivative need to extend maximum support to the victimized populations (Olaka-Onyango 1991).

The broad OAU definition was eminently suitable for a war situation that produced massive outflows of people necessitating collective determination of eligibility. Moreover, it was the only realistic determination procedure at the time, given the 'absence of decision-making infrastructure' in receiving states (Arboleda 1991: 195).

Two decades later, the African system of asylum regime remained generous in formal–legal terms, drawing continuous strength from its original legitimizing ideology of anti-colonialism and anti-racism. In practice, moreover, easy asylum conditions often prevailed. Cross-border ethnic ties facilitated hospitality, and the much-discussed weakness of African states made it difficult to impose rigorous border controls. In these situations, *de facto* asylum could be had by default.

Since the early 1960s, Africa has probably had the largest share of the world's refugees on a continuous basis. It also has highly developed migration systems, but these flows are self-evidently quite different from refugee flows. Claims for refugee assistance typically come from mass displacements of obviously miserable, often starving people who flee from very visible disasters and who are clearly in need of immediate relief. As a result, African states do not generally see abuse of the asylum system by non-refugees as a major problem in the region (Africa Group Geneva 1990). Arguably, this also constitutes the moral pillar of the protection system: an elementary sense of justice – as sociologist Barrington Moore has traced it through the ages and across continents – upholds the strong declaratory commitment to asylum in contemporary Africa.

Symmetry in vulnerability strengthens the institution. African states are typically both sending and receiving countries for refugees. If mass displacements are likely to occur in all populations and states at one time or another, a strong asylum institution is self-evidently a common good.

On the other hand, it is clear that practice has differed. Post-colonial African states have also emerged among the leading *producers* of refugees. As victims of anti-colonial struggles are followed by victims from despotism, civil wars, or ethnic violence in independent African states, both rejection at the border and mass expulsions have occurred (Zolberg 1989). Once inside a country, refugees can be subjected to abuse that renders asylum as a place of protection meaningless. In these cases, formal asylum is little better than rejection at the frontier. Few states have incorporated refugee law in national legislation, and administrative practices often fall far short of the law in those that have (Roxström 1995). Asylum is not infrequently endangered by attacks from or by neighbouring states, and security problems are aggravated by the development of refugee-warrior communities of various kinds.

African critics argue that the 'traditional, much-touted generosity of African states to refugees cannot be the fundamental basis of real and guaranteed security for the refugee' (Oloka-Onyango 1991: 460). Efforts to improve the legal framework have *inter alia* focused on the principle of non-refoulement (the 1981 Banjul Charter). More fundamentally, it is recognized that the primary weakness of the African refugee system reflects the very heavy burden it imposes on poor and often weak states.

Modifying the nature and process of asylum

The two basic ways to deal with refugee flows are to grant or deny asylum. In contemporary European and North American experience, asylum had come to be understood as a gateway to refugee status and permanent resettlement, in contrast to Africa and Latin America, where return was considered the norm even after years of exile, especially with respect to mass flows. Irreversibility was not prescribed by international refugee law, and refugees in Europe had indeed returned in large numbers to their own countries after World War I. Yet, asylum after 1945 came to be identified almost exclusively with irreversible flows.[10] One reason for this was that the 1951 Convention was developed not in reference to mass outflows from wars, but to select groups or individuals who were persecuted. With the memory of the fate of the Jews under Nazi rule still fresh, and the appearance of new refugees from Stalinist regimes in the Eastern Bloc, the notion of return naturally seemed alien. Moreover, relatively few refugees managed to escape the Iron Curtain; those who did were therefore easily absorbed in the West. Apart from the Cubans, Vietnamese and various *pieds noirs*, the refugee consequences of upheavals outside the industrialized states were largely confined to the region of origin.

When these conditions changed, so did the concept of asylum. The new and complex situation led to generalized fears of hordes arriving and to exclusionary reflexes, but also to legitimate concerns that the very institution of asylum was endangered.

Already in the 1960s, some Northern European states had recognized the diversity of movements from Eastern Europe and introduced so-called B-status, or permit to remain on humanitarian grounds. With an increase of asylum-seekers from the Third World, and the collapse of the Cold War order — especially the subsequent war in former Yugoslavia — virtually all Western European states moved to adopt some form of protection in addition to Convention status (Eurostat 1994). While 'B-status' in practice differed little from Convention status, both it and the specifically temporary permit gave receiving states some flexibility, and Convention status was less commonly granted.[11] More admissions categories made it easier to manipulate statistics to show that states took in few or many 'refugees' as the occasion warranted. With *de facto* status, moreover, the permit to stay could be terminated without the constraint of refugee law and associated institutions (including UNHCR) leaving advocacy groups to fight such terminations only on the more diffuse grounds of human rights law or, when applicable, national aliens laws. In the United States, temporary protection was given through administrative discretion to particular refugee populations until 1990, when temporary protection was formalized through legislation to accommodate several hundred thousands of *de facto* war refugees from El Salvador.

Despite the introduction of new admissions categories, the temporary is likely to become permanent when — as in the El Salvadoran case described above — refugees move between countries of greatly unequal wealth and security, and when the democratic institutions and processes which contribute to societal security also confer considerable rights upon individuals. The principal scenario for temporary protection when it was first granted was mass inflows from wars, but unless conflicts were speedily terminated and peace restored, the beneficiaries soon developed claims on the receiving country. In some European states (e.g. Scandinavia), aliens laws conferred permanent residence permits after a few years of residence, whether as a *de facto* refugee or as an immigrant, on the basis of an implied theory of social contract. Where this legal reference was lacking, political and moral pressure made it difficult to terminate the 'temporary' protection — particularly given the practical problems of rounding up the target group. For instance, even three years after the December 1991 peace agreement was signed in El Salvador, the United States was not formally returning *de facto* Salvadoran refugees.

European states encountered similar problems of return with asylum-seekers whose applications had been rejected. Often these cases were even more complicated because many had arrived undocumented, making it uncertain to which country they could be deported. A 1992 sample study estimated that 80 per cent of all asylum-seekers stayed on even though only 25 per cent were formally accepted (Widgren 1992). This figure was widely cited in the informal consultation process among industrial states, and the concern resurfaced in later studies (IGC 1993).

To reduce the intake, European states had also pursued a separate strategy of tightening up the asylum process itself. This included speeding up the determination process (often instituting a fast and slow 'track'), reducing the benefits accorded asylum-seekers while their application was pending, and narrowing the grounds for application of Convention status (IGC 1994a). However, when it was realized that a significant proportion of applicants stayed on even though they were formally rejected, the more exclusionary strategy of preventing access to seek asylum was emphasized.

Limiting access

A strategy of limiting access can take many forms. Most direct, and probably most questionable from the perspective of international law and ethics, is interdiction in neutral territory or at the border and subsequent return without adequate hearings. From 1981 to 1994, the United States basically adopted this policy towards Haiti by interdicting Haitian 'boat-people' on the high seas. Prolonged legal battles ended in the US Supreme Court, where UNHCR, among others, presented *amicus curie* briefs arguing that the practice violated the principle of *non-refoulement*, but to no avail.[12] Other publicized cases of interdiction have occurred in South-east Asia (push-back of Vietnamese boat-people in the early 1980s and Khmer 'land-people'), and Europe (in the form of border closings and visa restrictions to prevent entry of war refugees from the 1991–2 war in Croatia, and, subsequently, in Bosnia-Herzegovina).

Less direct forms of interdiction designed to restrict access to asylum procedures have been institutionalized in Western Europe and are, in whole or part, practised by many states. Most commonly, this takes the form of visa restrictions on countries likely to produce refugees and sanctions on carriers that bring in undocumented travellers. Other restrictions lay down criteria for *bona fide* asylum-*seekers*, so to speak, by designating 'safe countries' of origin that are presumed not to produce refugees, with the result that persons from these states are denied access to the asylum process or, at least, to a complete hearing. A similar restrictive concept is 'third host country' (i.e. an applicant can be denied if he or she already has been granted protection or 'has had an opportunity to seek ... protection' in another country) which was adopted by the Immigration Ministers of the European Community in a December 1992 resolution (Hailbronner 1993; Joly 1994). Both concepts were, by early 1992, commonly used in Western European states to restrict access to national asylum procedures. Also (West) Germany, which had written Europe's most liberal asylum guarantee into its post-war Constitution, amended this clause in May 1993 to permit exclusion of persons coming from either a 'safe country of origin' or a 'third host country'. The consequences of applying these procedures depended upon how 'safe' countries and 'third' countries were identified, a process that varied considerably over time and place within Europe. Certain aspects of the practice were found by national institutions of law to be contrary to international refugee law.[13] Liberal advocacy groups also denounced the practices as creating a 'Fortress Europe'.

The collectively restrictive accent in European asylum policies never-theless had become firmly implanted by early 1995. The results were soon evident: a dramatic decline in asylum applications was registered from 1992 and onwards, with a year-end total in 1994 estimated at about half of the 1992 level of 666,000. The other side of the coin was also visible. Illegal entries seemed to be on the upswing, generating a new round of international consultations to stem the flows.[14]

In a seemingly never-ending dialectic of moves and counter-moves, European states reached for the solution of setting up safe havens with processing centres in the region of origin, a practice already used by the United States in the Caribbean area. The basic idea of this approach was to move the asylum process closer to the country of origin and outside of the Northern industrialized states where, as we have seen, authorities found it difficult to control the asylum process. A European initiative was floated in late 1993, leading to an officially sponsored study which outlined the pros and cons of such practices (IGC 1994c). In theory, such schemes could be designed to enhance the welfare of all parties concerned, including *de facto* refugees. How the costs and the benefits in practice would be distributed would depend on a number of issues, including, above all, the norms laid to grounds for the screening process itself and the mechanisms for 'off-loading' those accepted or rejected by the process. In general, this form of 'forward asylum' gave the processing authorities and the country of final destination enhanced control over the asylum process. In the US case, the aim and, indeed, the result of this practice has been to reduce sharply the in-take of refugees. This has also been the initial European experience. At the same time, this does not necessarily solve the problem if the concurrent result is merely to shift the refugee burden onto other countries (as in the European case), or to delay its solution (as in the US case).[15]

Regional co-operation

A striking aspect of the efforts to exercise firmer control over asylum in Europe and North America was the growth in initiatives towards greater international co-operation. At a basic level, this meant co-operation among actual or potential receiving countries for an elementary reason: given a certain level of emigration pressure towards an area, successful unilateral measures by one state to reduce the entry will constitute a form of 'beggar-thy-neighbour' policy by merely shifting the burden onto others. As in the case of competitive protectionism within a trade system, the disruptive efforts of such policies are self-evident. Co-operation is therefore a better approach to addressing regional migration pressures. Indeed, the main impetus to the harmonization of asylum processes in Western Europe was the progressive integration of the European Community members, as marked in 1986. Partly codified in the 1990 Dublin Convention and the 1985 Schengen Accord (which became a Convention in 1990, scheduled into effect in 1995), these harmonization measures were developed at a fairly restrictive level, yet this does not necessarily have to be the case. Thus, European liberal advocacy groups have responded with a plea for harmonization at a more refugee-friendly level, but a harmonization nevertheless.

The tendency towards harmonization appears to have an inherent expansionary dynamic which has important implications. The harmonization in Western Europe, for example, was not confined to European Community members. The walls of 'Fortress Europe' were steadily moved outwards as neighbouring states in Central and Eastern Europe joined in a system of consultations and streamlining of policies, thereby preventing themselves from becoming places where problematic asylum-seekers would linger, and concurrently giving the 'core' states — particularly the most exposed of them, Germany — a buffer of sorts. Other industrialized states in North America and Canada were brought into a system of semi-institutionalized consultation with a secretariat in Geneva (IGC).

However, regional co-operation can also be used as the instrument of a more generous policy and a means of fostering genuine burden-sharing arrangements. This is, understandably, difficult to achieve. One form of burden-sharing, which may be of particular interest to South Africa is where a relatively rich and stable state that attracts spontaneous asylum-seekers, tries to 'share' by off-loading refugees onto smaller and poorer regional neighbours — as the United States tried to do in 1994 with Haitians and Cubans. However, the neighbours are unlikely to co-operate unless they are also receiving refugees of their own, or unless there are other strong incentives to co-operate. If all states in the region receive *some* refugees, co-operation becomes a matter of *redistribution*; otherwise, it is a trickier matter of distribution.

Regional co-operation which takes a regionally exclusionary form must be considered. While seemingly attractive to rich and stable states, it should be noted that there are trade-offs here as well. A principal one is the nature of 'minimum winning coalitions': 'core' states want to expand membership so as to create a buffer or a forward asylum 'defence' — this is why EU states have been eager to bring Eastern and Central European neighbours into the common consultation process and the like. But the more states that are brought in, the greater the likelihood that refugee flows will arise within the group itself.

A trade-off of a different kind is that if only potential receiving states join together, without any action on the originating side, the asylum burden will be effectively shifted onto other areas and regions. Typically these will be the poorest and most unstable of nations, since they are least likely to be included in the co-operating group. We would then get a sharp division in the favoured group: the A-team, which includes rich, stable, receiving states that are not producing refugees, vs. the B-team, which includes poorer, less stable states that both produce and receive refugees. This configuration has been termed 'international apartheid' (Richmond 1994) because it reflects some of the unsavoury and counterproductive aspects of that system.

Most importantly, burden-sharing in this fashion is likely to enhance instability and hostility among the 'B team'. Although assistance and development funds may be provided to alleviate this, such programmes are characteristically insufficiently comprehensive to modify refugee-producing conditions significantly. Hence the result may be that the 'A Team' will face more refugees. Beyond this, the more affluent states must also consider how regional confrontations over refugees would affect their more general foreign policy interests. Conversely, if regional co-operation across stratification lines is desirable for economic and political reasons, then co-operation in the matter of refugees might serve as a useful meeting ground. Although precisely how such co-operation might be worked cannot be discussed here, the issue brings us back to the imperative of casting refugee policy in a comprehensive framework, which recognizes its inherent links with foreign policy.

Notes

1. The term normally refers to a set of norms, structures and functions that make up the collective international capacity to regulate problems arising from involuntary migration across state borders and, occasionally and pre-emptively, to regulate internal movement.

2. The South-east Asian states in question were not party to the 1951 UN Convention on refugees or equivalent international legal instruments, and were thus in a narrow legal sense entitled to refuse asylum.
3. In 1979, the ASEAN countries (Association of South-east Asian nations) succeeded in obtaining a commitment from Western states to the effect that Indochinese refugees seeking asylum in South-east Asia would be processed for resettlement elsewhere; asylum was thus made contingent upon rapid resettlement. At the same time, the main source country (Vietnam) was brought into the conference and agreed to restrict illegal emigration. The political importance of the Indochinese refugees to the United States was a major reason for this unusual arrangement. Ten years later, a second Geneva conference to deal with the Indochinese refugees was called by the receiving states, this time to fashion what came to be known as a 'Comprehensive Plan of Acton' (CPA) for the Indochinese. As the limits of resettlement in the West had been reached, a new approach was devised which linked temporary first asylum to a careful screening process and return of those found not to be refugees. Simultaneously, arrangements were made to strengthen so-called 'Orderly Departures' in what had become an established migration stream from Vietnam to the US and, to a lesser extent, Western European states.
4. For an analytical framework which elaborates the variables in a refugee system, see Richmond (1993).
5. By early 1994, it was estimated that the number of *de facto* and recognized refugees from former Yugoslavia in Central and Western Europe had risen to perhaps 600,000 (Suhrke 1994a).
6. Recent estimates suggest that the proportion of intake of Convention refugees to regular in-migration is about 1:3, but this does not tell us much since there are few Convention refugees in the EU.
7. The following section is partly based on Zolberg (1995).
8. After the November 1994 ceasefire it was estimated that Angola had some ten million unexploded land mines scattered throughout the country. Land mine clearing would be a principal issue in the reconstruction and repatriation process. *Washington Post*, 13 February 1995.
9. *Washington Post*, 7 February 1995.
10. The 1951 Convention defines asylum with respect to a situation (persecution) that by its nature is variable and has historically been proven so. The cessation clauses in the 1951 Convention permit states to terminate refugee status *inter alia* when 'the circumstances in connection with which he has been recognised as a refugee have ceased to exist'. In other words 'international protection is meant to be an interim measure', as UNHCR clearly affirms (UNHCR, 1993a: 44).
11. The precise figures are difficult to determine, since receiving states provide selective and often non-comparable statistics, particularly as regards *de facto* (i.e. non-Convention) status. As a result, neither Eurostat (the statistical office of the European Union) nor the broader semi-institutionalized consultation form of European and North American states plus Australia (IGC) publish aggregate statistics on acceptance rates. There seems no doubt about the trend, however; Widgren (1992) estimated that by 1991 about one-third of

those accepted in Western Europe received Convention status. Later, influxes of *de facto* refugees from former Yugoslavia, who were mostly not allowed into the formal asylum stream, brought the proportion down further, as indicated by partial country statistics published by Eurostat (Eurostat, 1994).

12. The US Supreme Court upheld in June 1993 a ruling that interdiction of Haitians did not violate the principle of *non-refoulement* and hence was permissible (*Sale vs. Haitian Centers Council, Inc.*).

13. The Belgian State Council declared that a formal list of safe countries would be incompatible with the Geneva Convention (Art. 3) and the German Constitutional Court ruled in December 1993 that 'Germany cannot deny an application merely because the applicant comes from a safe country' (Blay and Zimmerman, 1994: 376–7). Objections of these kinds can, of course, be overcome by not having a list and by permitting access only to a 'fast track' application procedure.

14. It is indicative that the secretariat of the IGC shifted its focus back to illegal migration, producing an initial report on 'trafficking of aliens' and control measures in member states in 1994 (IGC, 1994b). IOM (the Geneva-based International Organisation of Migration) took up the issue as well.

15. The United States' experience in Guantanamo has already been mentioned. On the European side, faced with a large inflow of spontaneous asylum-seekers from Bosnia in the autumn of 1993, the Danish government decided to impose visa requirements on all travellers from Bosnia and instead opened a refugee processing centre in neighbouring Croatia. The immediate result was a sharp reduction in the processing rate, ostensibly due to shortage of processing personnel (Suhrke, interviews in Zagreb, 1993).

Part Two

A proposed policy framework for controlling cross-border migration to South Africa

Ann Bernstein, Lawrence Schlemmer and Charles Simkins

Introduction

In South Africa, migration is an emotive and complex topic. For 50 years, apartheid governments tried to control and prevent internal rural–urban migration within South Africa's borders. The result of this ill-conceived policy was not to stop migration but, among other things, to create a society which is struggling to this day to meet the challenges of internal migration.

The long-delayed onset of democracy seemed to lead to an influx of migrants of a different kind. One of the defining features of transitional and now democratic South Africa has been the much more visible presence of 'foreigners' in different parts of the country. Traders from West Africa, poor peasants from Mozambique, sharp operators from Nigeria and Zaire – these are the images that fill the popular imagination.

Foreigners are not new to South Africa. The country was initially built by immigrants, from Africa as well as Europe. There have been 'foreign' workers in the country for many decades: contract workers on the mines, Zimbabweans in Johannesburg's northern suburbs, Mozambicans deep in the heart of Soweto or Mpumalanga, Chinese entrepreneurs in Port Elizabeth or Johannesburg. And yet in the 1990s it seemed as though a large number of people, mainly from Africa but from elsewhere as well – Taiwan, China, India – had suddenly arrived here. In the absence of hard numerical data – about either South African internal migration or cross-border immigration – all kinds of wild guesses about numbers and trends gained credence.

Isolated incidents of tension between South Africans and migrants received prominent coverage in the media. Links were made between the government's commitment to reconstruction and development for South Africa's citizens and the reputedly enormous influx of foreigners denuding the country's resources. 'Illegal immigrants' became the new scapegoats for anything from an increase in crime to the government's problems with delivery (see box below). The whole question of immigration into South Africa — by both skilled and unskilled people — has emerged as one of the most important areas of controversy in the 'new' South Africa.

The 'new' scapegoats

The minister of housing said yesterday that when she took over her portfolio the housing backlog was estimated at 1.5 million, but in a second assessment it now stood somewhere between that figure and 3 million homes. The reason? 'We can't keep immigrants out. Somehow our borders are porous' (Sankie Mthembu-Mahanyele, minister of housing, quoted in *Business Report* 31 January 1997).

The government, struggling with its inheritance of people, policies and institutions, felt pressurized to react to 'illegal immigration'. Existing legislation was amended; an amnesty was declared first for mineworkers and then for other foreigners. Simultaneously, promises were made to tighten up on restrictions on foreigners entering or staying illegally in the country. Evidence emerged of problems in South Africa's system of border controls, of injustices in the attempts to arrest and deport people who had no legal papers, and of the costs and unintended consequences of deportations and other control measures. Negotiations with the other countries in the SADC region produced in first one and then an altered (more restrictive) approach to subregional movement. All these pressures resulted in the establishment, in 1996, of a task team by the department of home affairs to develop a Green Paper on migration policy. As its work has progressed, the minister of home affairs has issued strongly worded statements of intent on toughening up on 'illegals'.

It is in this context that the Centre for Development and Enterprise has formulated its proposals on how to approach this complex area of national policy. Besides the international research, its work is also based on considerable local research as well as intensive discussions with a diverse range of South Africans.

CDE's approach tackles migration from the perspective of South Africa's national interests, and aims to strengthen the legitimate authority of the South African state, its laws and officials. The proposed policy complements and supports the government's macro-economic strategy, and aims to harness the economic benefits of migration for South Africa while limiting any additional new burdens on state resources. The policy is built on a realistic assessment of the country's limited institutional capacity, and is therefore reasonably simple to implement and easy to communicate. It provides a channel for law-abiding, work-seeking and enterprising, if unskilled, migrants to register with the South African authorities and enter our economy. It is only once they are full tax-paying, continuously working residents that migrants will qualify for permanent residence and the right to join South Africans in the queues for services. On the control side of the policy, CDE proposes a mechanism which switches the main focus of attention away from mass deportations or street raids inside South Africa towards a focus on individuals who have contravened the terms of their probationary entrance into the South African economy.

In a country as complex as South Africa, no policy on migration issues will be perfect. The CDE proposal tries to put together an optimal approach on what is a multifaceted and potentially beneficial phenomenon. Its proposal should therefore be seen as a contribution to what it hopes will be an open and vigorous debate on the direction of national policy in an area of great importance for many years to come.

Key issues arising from migration policies

At the outset, it is important to isolate key issues which arise from South Africa's migration policy. In dealing with what is a very complex and difficult area of policy for many societies, not only ours, we believe the following are the issues most relevant to developing a new approach to migration in South Africa.

National interest

In an increasingly global world, it is tempting to downplay the importance of nations and their domestic political concerns. This temptation should be resisted. While recognizing the realities of 'a shrinking globe', we strongly support the view that a government's first duty is to the citizens of the country it governs: to protect and advance their security, well-being, rights, freedoms and economic prosperity. This is not to say that governments should ignore the claims of neighbouring states, regional welfare, international obligations and other humanitarian considerations, but that they should do so in the framework of their own national interests. Thus, in thinking about migration policy for South Africa, the government should be guided first and foremost by issues of national interest. It is from this perspective that government should assess and respond to the many and complex issues of fact and philosophy involved in the migration debate.

Understanding the migration process

In the course of the heated and sometimes fractious debate on issues surrounding migration, various assumptions are made about the migration process that are integral to different policy positions. Many claims are made on how this process works, why people migrate, and what they do when they get there. Migration is in fact a very complex process, and one about which people in southern Africa are rather ignorant. If one thinks about the enormous disparities in wealth and opportunity within South Africa itself and between South Africa and the other countries on the subcontinent, the really intriguing question is why so many people stay where they are — in rural South Africa or in the countries surrounding South Africa.

If migration were — as it seems at first sight — driven solely by poverty, economic hardship and a lack of opportunity, then far more people would be camped in the middle of Johannesburg, Durban or Cape Town than there are. The truth is that the vast majority of people in poorer countries do not move, and do not try to move. A critical building block for any migration policy, then, is a sound understanding of the phenomenon at work, the many different forms of migration, and its real causes and nature.

The financial and institutional capacity of the state

In an ideal world, one can formulate an ideal migration policy. The political miracle of 1994 notwithstanding, South Africa today is not an ideal world. Fiscal and institutional realities have to be an essential component of any migration policy. The government's macro-economic strategy spells out the stringent fiscal constraints facing the South African exchequer for the foreseeable future. Any single budget item will probably be cut in real terms over the next five years, thus making any policy built on the assumption of greater financial resources a non-starter. In similar vein, the realities of state capacity need to be understood and integrated into any policy proposals. South Africa is large, diverse, and a complex society to govern. The realities of apartheid, democratization, state transformation and affirmative action mean that the instruments of government — the institutions, procedures, personnel and output — are extremely weak. The prospect of the civil service being able to effectively perform even its most basic functions is in doubt for at least the next five to ten years. To suggest that the government can undertake additional tasks with a modicum of effectiveness in this context is unrealistic. These two realities, then, of fiscal and institutional limits on policy implementation need to be factored into the discussion of migration policy in South and southern Africa.

Domestic policy concerns

Migration policy needs to be consistent with a government's core economic and political philosophies. First, if South Africa — as was clearly stated in the government's macro-economic strategy — wants to become a competitive economy in the global system, consideration must be given to the relationship between opening its borders to trade, industry, culture, communications and capital, and the movement of people which must inevitably follow. Second, if the government is committed to establishing a human rights culture in South Africa, the interaction between this and policies to deal with the inevitabilities of migration into the country must be considered. Third, government needs to consider how its attempts to provide certain basic social needs inside the country (employment, education, health care, housing, welfare) are affected by its approach to migrants. Conversely, its approach to these issues could also be a factor in promoting greater migration, and this too needs to be borne in mind.

International policy concerns

By its very nature, cross-border migration has foreign policy implications. These naturally involve economics and politics. The content and implementation of South Africa's migration policy will affect its relations with neighbouring states.

Sustainability

In designing a migration policy, attention must be given to its long-term implications as well as the ability of the state to sustain such a policy over time. This does not mean that a country's migration policy should never change — far from it. Migration policy must be sensitive to a range of factors, such as the rate of economic growth, the need for skilled migrants, the capacity of the state, or actual migration pressures. It is perfectly sensible to adopt a policy for a period of time, evaluate its impact, and then adapt or even change it.

Implementation considerations

Migration policy and its implementation affect many departments of state. It is important, therefore, to establish an effective, ongoing policy-making process, a framework for interdepartmental co-operation and co-ordination, and an ongoing process for evaluating the impact of policy. Of course, the production of information and analysis on important migration questions is essential. All these concerns apply at the interstate level as well.

These are the broad considerations which have shaped CDE's approach to migration.

The government's current approach

At present, the entry of non-nationals into South Africa is governed by what has been called a dual system of control. This takes the form of immigration and work permits under the Aliens Control Act 96 of 1991 (as amended in 1995), and bilateral treaties between South Africa and the governments of Botswana, Lesotho, Swaziland and Mozambique. (According to the Commission to Investigate the Development of a Comprehensive Labour Market Policy (1996), the treaty with Malawi seems to be non-functional.) This 'two gates' system is an inequitable one, as those people entering the country in terms of the Aliens Control Act may gain permanent rights to work and residence whereas those whose status is governed by the bilateral treaties remain perpetual contract workers:

> The perpetual temporary status of contract migrants reflects government's concern to limit the number of foreign workers to whom permanent status is granted as well as concern for the impact that a drastic change in the pattern of labour supply would have on the sending countries and on South African employers. (ibid. 172)

Control over migration in terms of the Aliens Control Act is enforced via a system of immigration, work, work-seeking, study, business, visiting and medical permits (see box below).

Whom does the department of home affairs let into South Africa?

Applicants wishing to emigrate permanently to South Africa have to meet certain requirements. These are:

- the applicant must be of good character;
- he or she must be a desirable inhabitant;

- he or she must not be likely to be harmful to the welfare of the Republic of South Africa; and most important
- he or she must not follow an occupation for which there already are enough persons available to meet the requirements of the country.

There are a number of categories of immigration procedure, for example workers; family reunion schemes (for persons who are economically active but unable to submit a firm offer of employment); spouses and children; persons who are sponsored (such as an infirm, aged or destitute member of the family); fiancées; financially independent persons that is, investors; and those who own a business.

Investors are required to:

- transfer a guideline amount of not less than R1,500,000[1] to the Republic, of which R700,000 must be invested in the South African economy for a period of three years, either as a deposit with a financial institution or by any other means, such as the acquisition of immovable property. After three years the applicants must show proof that this requirement has been complied with, failing which their immigration permits may be withdrawn;

- refrain from engaging in employment or establishing own businesses without the approval of the department; and
- notify the department of any change of address during the period under review.

Those in the *own business* category must, besides providing sufficient funds for their maintenance and that of their families:

- transfer such minimum amounts as may be determined by the Immigrants Selection Board, with or without consultation of other bodies or instances, as being sufficient to establish such businesses, taking due consideration of their nature and extent; and
- submit to the department after twelve months of the establishment of the business:
  - audited financial statements in order for the viability of the business to be assessed;
  - documentary evidence that, since the establishment of the business, at least two South African citizens or permanent residents excluding family members have been appointed and are still in service; and
  - documentary evidence that the amounts, as determined by the abovementioned board have been utilized for the intended purposes.

A fee of R5580 is payable in respect of a formal application for an

immigration permit/s, per individual or per family. However, the fee is
not payable by a spouse, a dependent child, a destitute, aged or infirm
member of the family, or a person permanently or lawfully resident in
the Republic.
(Extracted from *Permanent Residence, Republic of South Africa,*
Department of Home Affairs Policy Document 7 January 1997.)

Following the deliberations of a government interdepartmental committee
on the problem of illegal entry into the country, the Aliens Control Act
was amended in 1995 in order to tighten controls over entry and broaden
the scope of sanctions on offenders. The amended act is intended to
express the two pillars of the government's migration policy: non-
racialism, and job preference for local South Africans. And yet in many
respects the bulk of the act is built on South Africa's past.

For the previous 50 years of apartheid rule, South Africa's approach to
migration was a racial one. It could be summarized simply as 'whites in,
blacks out'. This principle is evident from European immigrants' easy
access to South Africa (notwithstanding the attempts to curb Jewish
migration in the 1930s and Catholic migration in the 1950s), and the harsh
domestic controls on black migration within the country, controlling
access to the 'white' cities and towns and trying to encourage black people
to stay in the rural reserves (see box below).

It didn't work before

South Africa is no stranger to the desire to control movement. Influx
control in South Africa was intended to limit, indeed eliminate, all
African workers with a permanent residential base in the urban areas.
Under this system, employers in the cities were supposed to rely on a
stream of short-term migrant workers. By the 1970s there were signs
that the system was costly and ineffective; it simply didn't work. Each
year the government spent money on apprehending, prosecuting,
imprisoning and rusticating pass law offenders, and still the black population in urban areas grew. The pass laws could not halt black
urbanization. Successive governments arrested people under the pass
laws in their millions — no fewer than 17.12 million between 1916 and
1981 (an average of 721 every day non-stop for 65 years) 'according to
their own figures' (*Weekly Mail* and *Guardian* 4 March 1994). The pass
laws were rendered unworkable through the efforts of ordinary folk
who, despite unjust laws, went to town to find jobs, better health
services, more opportunities and, in most cases, a better life.
(Extracted from Bernstein 1985; statistics from Kane-Berman 1990.)

It is also evident from the extensive and long-standing system of bringing foreign black workers to South Africa for highly controlled participation in the mining industry and commercial agriculture. Thus, the new government inherited a migration policy package inappropriate for a non-racial country committed to opening its borders to trade and investment and, inevitably, acting as a magnet for people from all over the continent. And, simultaneously with democratization, access to South Africa was suddenly made easier with the reduction of border controls after the end of the 'liberation struggle'.

The current 'two gates' approach to migration is inadequate. The policy context in South Africa has changed dramatically. A new vision is needed, together with an understanding of the policy options available to facilitate the formulation of effective policy in this complicated area. In short, we need to 'shift gear'.

Government action, 1994–7

Since the democratic elections of 1994, numerous developments in the area of migration policy have occurred. In 1995 the new government amended the Aliens Control Act of 1991 by means of which South Africa deals with the admission, control and expulsion of foreigners. According to the department of home affairs, this amended act 'underscores the government's policy to *inter alia* prevent foreigners who do not qualify to immigrate or to work in South Africa from entering the country under false pretences, or to take up employment' (media release, Department of Home Affairs 23 July 1996). Aliens who enter South Africa for holiday purposes may no longer change the purpose of their visit as in the past, where 'many holiday visitors, once inside the country, applied for work permits or permanent residence'. Comments the department: 'The true intention of the visit was more often than not "work" rather than a holiday visit.' A foreigner now has to apply for the correct visa or permit before entry, and must await the result of his or her application outside the country. Conveyors such as airlines are subject to fines being imposed if they 'convey persons' to the Republic of South Africa without the necessary visa or permits. The department of home affairs has also introduced fees for a vast range of immigration services. The principle involved will be one of reciprocity in that countries which exempt South African citizens from visa requirements and/or fees will likewise be exempted by South Africa. However, reciprocity will not apply in respect of fees for work, study and immigration permits, as these are aimed at compensating the state for the cost of the services rendered to such foreigners (ibid).

The Aliens Control Amendment Act increased the powers of officials to act as immigration officials. The act removes certain unconstitutional powers previously possessed, and regulates the handling of different categories of illegal aliens; those suspected, those found and those detained, pending removal. It requires officers to have warrants before entering properties to search and seize. However, it allows search and seizure without a warrant if a warrant is expected to be forthcoming and it is believed that valuable evidence may be destroyed. Commenting during the Aliens Control Amendment Bill debate, Dene Smuts, Democratic Party MP, charged that 'The bill simply tinkers here and there with a subsection of the principal act, leaving gapingly wide powers of arrest without a warrant, of arrest and deportation, whether or not a person had been found guilty, of presumption of guilt and the like, untouched' (Hansard no. 15, 12 September–11 October 1995, col. 4238).

Also in 1995 the South African Citizenship Act, Act 44 of 1949, was repealed. The present South African Citizenship Act, Act 88 of 1995, details the acquisition of citizenship by birth, descent (which also applies to adoption), and naturalization. No person born in the Republic shall be a South African citizen if, at the time of his or her birth, one of his or her parents had not been lawfully admitted to the Republic as a permanent resident. The conditions for citizenship by naturalization include that:

- the person has been admitted to the republic for permanent residence;
- has lived in the country for not less than a year preceding the application and for a further period of not less than four years during the eight years preceding the application;
- is of good character;
- intends to continue residence;
- is able to communicate in any one of the official languages to the satisfaction of the minister; and
- has an adequate knowledge of the responsibilities and privileges of South African citizenship.

In June 1996 the Department of Home Affairs announced an amnesty for people illegally in the country. It applied to citizens from other SADC member states – Angola, Botswana, Lesotho, Malawi, Mauritius, Mozambique, Namibia, Swaziland, Tanzania, Zambia and Zimbabwe – and applicants were required to prove:

(1) continuous residence in the Republic for five years before 1 July 1996;
(2) engagement in productive economic activity in the country (either formal or informal sector); or
(3) a relationship with a South African partner or spouse (customary marriages included); or
(4) existence of dependent children born in or residing lawfully in South Africa; and
(5) that they had not committed a criminal offence listed in Schedules I and II of the Aliens Control Act, 1991.[2]

The residential status of people who obtain exemption are similar to those with permanent residence in South Africa, namely they may 'sojourn' legally and may ultimately obtain South African citizenship on application. Where an application is rejected due to an inability to comply with the criteria, or where the illegal person failed to submit an application timeously, the person may be deported/repatriated. The spouse(s) and children of a principal applicant whose names were listed on his or her application form had to lodge applications individually whether they were resident in South Africa or in their country of origin. The family of an SADC applicant may only consist of a spouse (customary marriages included), stay-together partners (only if the partner also resides in South Africa), and dependent children under the age of 18 years. Parents and family of the principal applicant and spouses who have been approved may apply for immigration permits under the family reunion category.[3]

SADC citizens were initially invited to apply for this amnesty up to 30 September 1996. However, the department was apparently 'inundated' with applications, and as a result the cabinet extended the date to 30 November 1996. A total of 50,692 mineworkers and 199,254 people from SADC countries applied for the amnesty.[4] As at 23 April 1997, 102,541 applications had been approved (see Table 16). The majority of the applications (61 per cent) were lodged in Gauteng.

In 1996 the Department of Home Affairs announced a further measure to combat the influx of illegal immigrants: a 'forge-proof' passport and identity document. This was to coincide with the implementation of an Automated Fingerprint Identification System (AFIS). The expected capital expenditure to implement this new system is estimated at R407 million during the first eight years.[5]

Table 16   SADC amnesty approvals

Applicant's country of origin	Number of approved applications	Percentage of total
Mozambique	70 350	68.84
Zimbabwe	16 727	16.37
Lesotho	7 194	7.04
Malawi	5 389	5.27
Swaziland	1 271	1.24
Botswana	908	0.89
Mauritius	108	0.11
Tanzania	96	0.09
Namibia	77	0.08
Angola	73	0.07
Total	102 193	100.00

Source: Faxed letter from the Director-General, Department of Home Affairs, 5 May 1997. The percentages were calculated by CDE

Table 17 Repatriations and deportations from South Africa, 1990–6

Year	Repatriations	Deportations (convicted criminals)	Total
1990	53 418	293	53 711
1991	61 345	204	61 549
1992	82 575	531	83 106
1993	96 600	633	97 233
1994	90 692	208	90 900
1995	157 084	611	157 695
1996	180 714	517	181 231
Jan–Mar 1997	41 466	173	41 639
Total	763 894	3 170	767 064

Source: Faxed letter from the Director-General, Department of Home Affairs, 5 May 1997

More and more illegal immigrants have been deported. For example, 181,231 people were removed in 1996, about 100 per cent more than in 1994 (see Table 17). The department of Home Affairs has reported that removals cost R7,571,680 during the financial year 1 April 1996 to 31 March 1997.[6]

During 1996 and 1997 the South African government negotiated with SADC countries on the subject of free movement within the region. In January 1997 the SADC's Draft Protocol on the Free Movement of Persons in the SADC region (1995) was retracted. According to Article 3 of this protocol, its ultimate objective was to eliminate progressively all controls on SADC citizens so that people in the region could move around freely in ten years after its adoption, thus promoting the region's interdependence and integration. Article 2 granted the following rights to citizens of member states:

- to enter freely and without a visa the territory of another member state for a short visit;
- to reside in the territory of another member state; and
- to establish oneself and work in the territory of another member state.

During the negotiations it emerged that some governments believed the free movement of people would not benefit the more developed or least developed states of southern Africa. It was felt that the free movement of people would place a large burden on states such as South Africa, Namibia and Botswana, and intensify the brain drain from states such as Lesotho, Malawi and Mozambique. Hussein Solomon (1997) has argued that the 1995 protocol did not sufficiently recognize the discrepancies between various countries in the region. Moreover, as Zimbabwe's Minister of Home Affairs has declared, 'We are not ready to sign the protocol on the free movement of people. Doing it at the moment would be like opening the floodgates to criminals.'[7] Eventually the 1995 protocol was replaced by the Draft Protocol on the Facilitation of Movement of Persons in the SADC region of 1997, which is currently being discussed. The document has more modest objectives, and aims, *inter alia*, to:

- gradually remove barriers to movement of citizens of member states within the region;
- expand the network of bilateral agreements among member states in this regard as a step towards a multilateral regional agreement;
- reduce red tape for those interested in investment in countries;
- secure co-operation in preventing the illegal movement of citizens of member states and the illegal movement of nationals of third states within and into the region;
- co-operate in improving control over external borders of the SADC community; and
- promote common policies in regard to immigration matters where necessary and feasible.

It also redefines a 'short visit' as a period not exceeding 30 days as opposed to the 1995 protocol's six months.

However, the 1997 proposals for easing visa requirements have since been changed, following objections by South Africa, Namibia and Botswana, which are reportedly alarmed about the flood of illegal immigrants into their countries. The charge is being led by the South African government, which has suggested that the entry of immigrants at border posts should be more tightly controlled. This proposal will be discussed when the home affairs ministers of SADC states meet towards the end of 1997. South Africa is proposing a SADC desk at all entry points to member states. A spokesperson for the department of foreign affairs has stated: 'The new draft is being circulated among the SADC members as the original agreement was not acceptable to South Africa ... This is done to alleviate pressure on our resources. We are at the service of SADC, and we will not do anything provocative' (*Sunday Independent* 4 May 1997).

In May 1997, the South African Minister of Home Affairs advocated a more stringent approach to illegal immigrants, arguing for a new identification system that would discourage illegals from fraudulently using ID documents, and ensuring that social services are inaccessible to them. He also said his department would clamp down on those who assisted illegal immigrants (ibid). Concomitantly, the Ministry of Defence has warned that the electrified fence on South Africa's northern and eastern borders could soon be switched to 'lethal mode' to stop cross-border violations. The minister of defence cited immigrant criminal activity as a primary motivating factor: 'we are facing an internal crime threat which is threatening to destabilise the country. Crime is a definite deterrent to investment, and not only that, but people are being held up, tortured and shot ... if we are not coping with the influx of illegal immigrants, and our people are being threatened, there will come a time when we will switch on the fence to lethal mode' (*The Star* 6 May 1997). The minister later modified his position, stating that 'lethal mode' would only be used in a worst case scenario, which might include a war situation (*The Star* 7 May 1997).

The South African government has also accepted the United Nations Convention Relating to the Status of Refugees of 1951, and the 1969 Convention Governing the Specific Aspects of Refugee Problems in Africa of the Organisation of African Unity. South Africa does not have a refugee act, and it is being debated whether or not separate legislation for refugees is required or whether this should form part of immigration policy.

Towards the end of 1996 the Department of Home Affairs appointed a task group to prepare a Green Paper on migration policy to be completed and presented by the end of May 1997. The task group's mandate stated: 'The parameters of the brief have been defined broadly to include all areas of migration. Current legislation relating to migration is governed by the Aliens Control Act. Any new migration policy or legislation derived from the Green Paper process will have to be premised on the Rule of Law; a Bill of Rights culture and established international norms.'[8]

Evaluation

The government's current approach is unclear

The establishment of this task group is to be welcomed, as government's current approach to migration appears to be *ad hoc* and rather confused. Statements by leading government spokespersons indicate an uncertainty on how to proceed in respect of overall migration policy, and many of the fundamental problems remain. It appears as if the government has no coherent grasp of the migrant question, as is evidenced by its divergent perspectives on the scale and impact of migration. It has offered no clear assessment of the impact of amnesties, and has not indicated how it intends to determine the real number of migrants.

The development and implementation of migration policy require numerous government departments to work together. For example, the Aliens Control Act is administered by the Department of Home Affairs, whose overall emphasis is on the national interest as opposed to integration with the region. But interaction at the political level with neighbouring states is undertaken by the Department of Foreign Affairs. The two departments seem to be coming at the issue in different ways.

As expressed in the Aliens Control Act, South Africa's migration policy is based on strict entry criteria for foreigners, especially for work and permanent residence purposes. This is in contradistinction to South Africa's emerging policies *vis-à-vis* the southern African region. South Africa became a member of the SADC in August 1994, and committed itself to the aims of the SADC treaty of 1992. This calls for greater and more equitable economic integration in the region, facilitated by a freer movement of goods and services. This greater acceptance of the need for greater economic and financial co-ordination and integration in the region is not reflected in policy relating to the movement of people (Solomon 1997).

Conflict over the 1996 cabinet decision to declare an amnesty and allow illegals from neighbouring countries to take up residence in South Africa, subject to certain conditions, revealed that there are differences between departments on the issue of policy. The Minister of Home Affairs, Dr Mangosuthu Buthelezi, objected to the amnesty, warning that this decision could cost the economy 'billions of rands ... Calculations done in 1993 showed that accommodating 250,000 aliens would cost the economy R1 billion a year by the year 2000.' He added that the real figure was closer to 600,000 people, and that his department had worked out that this could lead to as many as six million new citizens, with each legalized alien bringing dependants from his home country into South Africa to settle. 'According to our custom as black people, polygamy is allowed. It's common for people to have three wives; now can you imagine if they bring them?' (*Sunday Times* 3 March 1996). Commenting on the cabinet's decision to declare an amnesty, he added: 'Decisions are taken on the basis of majoritarianism. I must say that I'm very unhappy' (ibid).

Commenting on the amnesty in the national assembly, the chairperson of the Home Affairs Portfolio Committee, Desmond Lockey, noted:

> I want to commend the minister for his vision in implementing this amnesty. This will bring about an end to the racist policies of the past government in dealing with migrants from our neighbouring states. For decades, South Africa had an immigration policy that allowed whites in and kept Africans out. Migrant labour from southern Africa contributed generously in building the South African economy to what it is today. The proposed amnesty will regularise the position of those migrants who have helped to build up our country, and they richly deserve this.

He added that

> most of the applicants would already have been assimilated into our society. It will also provide us with the moral highground to deal firmly with those illegal immigrants who are involved in criminal activities in South Africa. (Hansard no. 6, 3–7 June 1996, col. 2127)

When CDE asked the Department of Home Affairs what had persuaded the cabinet to grant amnesty to certain categories of illegal immigrants, the Director-General replied that it had 'only received the instruction to execute the decision', and could not answer. He added it could 'speculatively be mentioned that certain neighbouring states requested that a moratorium on the repatriation of a large number of their illegal citizens in South Africa be considered as a gesture of goodwill. It was decided to grant exemption to the SADC member states.' Asked what facts had formed the basis for this decision, he replied: 'As the facts are not known, it is not possible to reply to this question.' When asked what the expected impact of this decision might be, he replied: 'A large number of illegal persons will probably eventually be exempted and obtain the rights and privileges of a person with permanent residence status in the Republic. They will sojourn legally in the country, and may ultimately obtain citizenship on application.'[9] It therefore appears as if the impact – socio-economic and otherwise – of this far-reaching decision has not yet been properly analysed; surely the first step to take before such a significant policy innovation is embarked upon. The figures and calculations about costs being thrown around by commentators are totally speculative. Little mention is made of the possible benefits of immigration.

Policy in the midst of ignorance

One of the major problems in dealing with the migration issue in South Africa is the absence of accurate information. Cabinet ministers, senior officials, citizens and the media have been talking since 1993–4 of anything between 2.5 and 8 million illegal immigrants. The reality is that we do not know what the scale and nature of clandestine movement from other countries really are. Therefore, all the current figures are highly speculative. It is likely that a number of people are being counted twice or even more than that (see box below). Figures on emigration are also totally unreliable (see box below). The 1996 census will provide no solid information on this topic. The census co-ordinator and head of Central Statistical Services' demographic surveys, Pali Lehohla, has stated that the census questionnaire would not enquire about the legality of any individual's residential status (*Business Day* 7 June 1996). The Statistics Act forbids Central Statistical Services from determining which individuals are in the country illegally.

Nobody knows the real numbers – so take your pick

How many illegal immigrants are there in South Africa?

- According to the Public Relations Department of the South African Police Service, there were 2 million illegal immigrants in South Africa in 1994 (quoted in Toolo and Bethlehem 1994: 7).
- During the same month a police estimate of 8 million illegal immigrants was reported (*Mail and Guardian* 1 January 1996).
- In 1995 the Department of Home Affairs estimated that there were about 3.5 million illegal aliens in South Africa (*The Star* 15 September 1995).
- A study commissioned by Eskom in 1995 and released in April 1996 found that there were at least 2 million illegal immigrants in South Africa (*The Argus* 16 April 1996).
- According to a study by the Human Sciences Research Council published in 1996 – at the request of the Department of Home Affairs – there were as many as 2.5–4.1 million illegal aliens in the country (Hansard no. 3, 3–7 June 1996, col. 2108).

Various political agendas may have an effect on the way in which the figures are massaged. For example, at a time when the defence budget is being slashed, various security agencies are using the 'threat' illegal immigrants pose to the South African state to justify their continued existence.

The result of this is that policy decisions are being taken in the absence of solid empirical information about numbers and trends. In this climate, the attitudes and outlook of policy makers and others on migration questions are influenced by their own prejudices, anecdotes or a current favourite set of numbers. Is it really possible that South Africa's illegal population is as high as 5 million, or even 8 million? This would mean that about one-eighth, or even one-fifth, of the population is illegal. If the higher estimates are even vaguely correct, this would mean that illegal immigrants comprise between one-third and one-half of the economically active population of the entire country, estimated at just less than 15 million. We concur with the view of the Commission to Investigate the Development of a Comprehensive Labour Market Policy (1996) on this topic:

> In the commission's view, it is highly unlikely that the country has absorbed 5 to 8 million foreigners, documented and undocumented, in this short space of time. If this had been the case, the effect of undocumented people on the labour market and social services would have been far more startling than it appears to be. These estimates have nevertheless influenced the policy debate and public perceptions.

Policy is also being made in a context of ignorance on other important issues, such as the real economic or other impact of migrants on the country (positive or negative) and what kind of people (level or nature of skills) move to South Africa. We also have no real idea of trends of movement. For example, was there a sudden rush to South Africa from about 1990 onwards, which has now stabilized? Was this mainly skilled or unskilled migrants? Or is there a steady (or growing) stream of newcomers coming across our borders?

Critical questions need to be asked before major policy decisions are made. We need to know numbers; trends; the impact on different cities and regions of South Africa; costs and benefits to the country; the nature of migration to South Africa — i.e., who comes from where and why; what migrants do once they arrive here; what kind of work they perform, how many are self-employed, etc; and the impact of this on the economy, on other citizens and so on (see box below). This information will not emerge instantly or on command, as much of it is hard to come by and will require detailed research on the ground. Policy will have to start by pointing roughly in the right direction, with the capacity for fine-tuning over time being built in.

Needed urgently: reliable information

*1996 Labour market commission:

A major survey should be undertaken into immigration and the labour market, since the absence of reasonable estimates of this phenomenon and its labour market implications makes much labour market analysis rather speculative.

*1996 Draft White Paper for Population Policy:

There are no reliable estimates of illegal immigrants, though their number is thought to be high. The number of refugees in the country is estimated to be high, though again no reliable estimates are available ... No comprehensive review of the impact of immigration on the population structure, economy and demand for services has been undertaken ... The population concerns include the absence of adequate analysis of the nature and impact of international immigration for policy development purposes.

Since 1994 the South African government has wrestled with the many and complex issues involved in dealing with migration. It is a confused story, reflecting the many pressures on the government from all the different issues and interests that influence and are affected by migration.

The appointment in late 1996 of a task team to review and assess migration policy is an important and welcome opportunity.

What the task team does, and how the minister and then the cabinet will respond to the issues on the table, is critically important. What is required is a thorough review of South Africa's policy options in this area; an informed and constructive airing of the costs and benefits of the different policy options in public; and then a decisive choice on how to deal with migration – a difficult phenomenon with numerous policy implications, that will not go away. The worst response to the situation will be for government not to make a decisive choice on where it stands on the process of migration and its management. The country and the region need firm leadership on this question, sound information and a policy choice that harnesses the benefits of an inevitable migration process into South Africa, while minimizing any possible costs.

Notes

1. Shirley Smit, Assistant Director, Department of Home Affairs, affirmed during a telephone conversation with CDE on 28 May 1997 that the guideline amount of R1,500,000 would take effect on 1 July 1997. Prior to this date, the amount had increased incrementally every year from an amount of R50,000 in 1992.
2. Faxed letter from the Director-General, Department of Home Affairs, in response to a CDE query, Ref 21/3/3/4, 31 January 1997.
3. Faxed letter from the Director-General, Department of Home Affairs, in response to a CDE query, Ref 21/3/3/4, 19 February 1997.
4. Faxed letter from the Director-General, Department of Home Affairs, in response to a CDE query, Ref 21/3/3/4, 31 January 1997.
5. Minister of Home Affairs, introductory speech, policy debate, national assembly, 4 June 1996.
6. Faxed letter from the Director-General, Department of Home Affairs, in response to a CDE query, Ref 22/2/13/3/4 v9, 6 May 1997.
7. Nipping drug trafficking in the bud, *Southern African Political and Economic Monthly*, 9(12), September 1996, 21. Quoted in Solomon (1997: 5).
8. Mandate of the International Migration Green Paper Government Task Team, 1997, as published on the internet: www.polity.org.za/govdocs/green_papers/migration/. The members of the task team are: Dr Wilmot James (convenor), Prof M. Hough, Prof K. Oosthuizen, Z. Mbeki, S. Molefe, J. E. Pokroy, Dr G. Sibiya, J. Sindane and Dr E. Kornegay.
9. Faxed letter from the Director-General, Department of Home Affairs, in response to a CDE query, Ref 21/3/3/4, 31 January 1997.

A spectrum of voices

It is very easy to whip up anti-foreigner sentiments in the short term, but the long-term consequences would be disastrous. Home affairs has been running a consistent scare campaign ever since the elections ... a new form of apartheid, we feel, is very dangerous. The demon is not illegal immigration, it is xenophobia and racism. Home Affairs persists in the use of the term 'aliens' to describe people from our neighbouring states, people intricately bound with the destiny of South Africa, people who are, if anything, owed reparation for apartheid crimes.

Neil Coleman, Cosatu, 1996 (*The Argus* 16 January 1996; *Mail and Guardian* 23 September 1996)

The view is that because many of our people were in exile in many countries in Africa, my department ought to be lenient in handling the issue of African illegal immigrants. I want to state that none of us can forget the way African heads of state throughout the continent gave sanctuary to many of our people fleeing apartheid South Africa. I, however, do not believe that this gives us a pretext to close our eyes to the influx of illegal immigrants to further compound the problem of joblessness.

Mangosuthu Buthelezi, Minister of Home Affairs, 1994 (*The Star* 3 December 1994)

Only people without morals would ignore the contribution that has been made by neighbouring countries. We, the majority party in government, are taking the view that a sensitive and appreciative approach should be adopted. It looks insensitive to say, now that we are in power, 'Go back to your countries, we don't want you here.' It is our duty to address the problems of our own people, but we have to take into account the background from which we came.

President Nelson Mandela, 1995 (*The Citizen* 8 September 1995)

South Africa has no moral obligation to accommodate the citizens of neighbouring states. [It] only has a moral obligation to accommodate refugees. Destabilisation has been a contributing factor to migration, but there are other more substantive reasons, such as economic decline.

David Laubscher, Department of Foreign Affairs, 1995 (Quoted in Reitzes 1995: 14)

Yes, certainly, this country owes a moral debt – but how do you compute this? What do we do to atone?
> Penuel Maduna, former Deputy Minister of Home Affairs, 1995 (Quoted in Reitzes and De Villiers 1995: 80)

We try to deal with them in as humane a way as possible. We regard them as human beings in dire straits. It's the police that said that illegal aliens are criminals.
> Piet Colyn, Director-General of Home Affairs, 1995 (*Mail and Guardian* 7 June 1996)

The repatriation of illegal aliens is a waste of resources.
> Deputy President Thabo Mbeki, 1995 (*Financial Mail* 12 May 1995)

Illegal immigrants are not wanted, and they have no friends here.
> Inspector Andy Pieke, police spokesman, 1996 (*Sowetan* 11 March 1996)

We are losing the battle to keep illegals out. So now we plan to crack down on employers who are hiring them, because they can get away with paying them lower wages.
> George Orr, Department of Home Affairs, 1994 (*Business Day* 7 October 1994)

Another big rush of people we don't want in the country.
> Attie Tredoux, Department of Home Affairs, 1995 (*The Daily Dispatch* 24 August 1995)

We are sick of the foreigners. They must be sent back home.
> Tim Singiswa, Hillbrow resident, 1994 (*Sowetan* 5 September 1994)

Let them go home. They do a lot of horrible things, and have no respect for the laws of this country.
> Walters Mojapelo, a returnee who led an organized campaign against foreigners in Alexandra, 1995 (*Mail and Guardian* 3 February 1995)

In a way those countries have been our home for decades. We regard those illegal immigrants as our brothers and sisters. We attach importance to people who have helped us in the difficult years of the struggle.
> President Nelson Mandela, 1996 (*Sowetan* 24 May 1996)

Our citizens know no boundaries. They regard themselves as an integral part of each of our countries. Therefore they do not feel like aliens.
> President Joaquim Chissano, 1996 (*City Press* 4 February 1996)

People here ask me why am I here, why do I take their jobs. I would like to tell them they are cowards. I remember just a few years ago when South Africans were refugees.
> Jean-Claude Rutausere, refugee from Burundi, 1996 (*The Argus* 18 March 1996)

We are here to remind South Africans that they live in Africa, not America; although if this place wasn't a lot like America, I doubt many of us would be here.'

Zairois resident, 1994 ('Trans-urban migration – South Africa as a test bed', *The Urban Age* Spring 1994, 14)

We are Africans, and should be allowed to live here also. We were allowed to stay in the era of political violence when some of our compatriots lost their lives. We also contributed towards the struggle against apartheid. Now the ANC-led government is turning its back on us. They [ANC] are treating us shoddily. They forget that some of their members were given refuge by Mozambique. They did not treat white foreigners in the same way.

Frans Maphosa, Mozambican, 1995 (*The Star* 28 January 1995)

Why should we throw in the towel? We love this country, we want to put down our roots, we could create jobs for South African nationals and we are not a burden on anybody.

David Foulds, British-born entrepreneur seeking permanent residence, 1996 (*Mail and Guardian* 19 April 1996)

Roughly one out of five squatters in South Africa is illegal. Many of these people have acquired false passports and identity documents placing them in line for RDP assistance. If they continue to elbow out needy South Africans, ethnic antagonism, conflict and a violent backlash could be spawned. The high rate of crime and violence in South Africa – mainly drug trafficking, car theft, gun-running and armed robbery – is directly related to the rising numbers of illegals.

Colonel Brian van Niekerk, police spokesman, 1995 (*Financial Mail* 9 September 1995)

We have to start looking at these millions of people as a vast regional asset. We need to start exploiting their skills and entrepreneurial spirit in much the same way the United States did when it welcomed with open arms all immigrants that could help the country grow. The nation has to treat foreigners as valuable visitors, whose determination to succeed could do more to uplift the economy of southern Africa than any government policy. The trained artisans among these people should be utilised to combat the current shortage of skilled workers in the building industry, which will go a long way to boost the delivery of homes.

Ravi Moodley, president of the Institute of Artisans, 1996 (*Business Day* 16 May 1996)

We know that 14 per cent of white adults were born outside the country, and we have welcomed them because immigrants tend to be determined, enterprising people who often make it on their own resources. We don't have to grow the economy by 6 per cent a year to provide for the 2 million or more illegals; they are busy looking after themselves.

> Teddy Langschmidt, Integrated Marketing Research, 1996 (*Natal Mercury* 9 April 1996)

At the moment government sees illegal immigration primarily as a security issue. It's a lot more than that: it's a human rights issue and a development issue. While Buthelezi is jumping up and down about immigrants threatening the RDP, the constitution, through socio-economic rights, actually extends the RDP to that group of people.

> Maxine Reitzes, Centre for Policy Studies, 1996 (*Mail and Guardian* 7 June 1996)

Illegal immigrants are deprived of any basic right under South African law. It is not even legal to give them food or water and they are constantly exploited ... Immigrants create economic opportunities. They usually work harder and bring skills and efficiency with them.

> Paul Pereira, South African Institute of Race Relations, 1995 (*The Star* 30 January 1995)

We want to be treated with dignity. Human rights do not exist for foreigners ... It is not right to call us enemies. I am disappointed with our brothers. A black foreigner is an enemy while whites are called tourists. There is a notion that black foreigners are all illegal aliens and whites are visitors or investors.

> George Hamilton Watson, refugee from Sierra Leone, 1996 (*Sunday Independent* 30 June 1996)

Locals have been turned away when there has been no space available [at Green Point flea market]. I do not see why illegal immigrants should work at the expense of residents.

> Gerald Blaber, spokesman for Green Point traders, 1996 (*Cape Times* 30 April 1996)

I have been here since 1989, and go home to collect items myself. Other traders and the police hate us, but there is nothing we can do. It is their country. We make money but we also spend a lot of money here. We also employ people to sell the goods for us so that we do not get caught by the police.

> A Swazi trader at Green Point flea market in South Africa illegally, 1996 (*Cape Times* 30 April 1996)

We want the government to intervene before we decide to physically chase these people away from our city ... We are greatly distressed with the Immigration Department, as these immigrants are so clearly recognisable and yet nothing gets done.

> Redman Kandanisa, East London Vendors' Association, 1996 (*Daily Dispatch* 11 June 1996)

Gauteng could be spending up to R208 million a year subsidising the schooling of about 80,000 illegal immigrants at a cost of about R2600 per child.

Annelize van Wyk, National Party MP, 1996 (*The Star* 12 June 1996)

In response to this:

Last year's increase in the Gauteng school-going population does not bear this out, as it was a 32,000 increase which is accounted for by natural population increases; inter-provincial movement; and the fact that a number of children who left school for various reasons are now returning.

Mary Metcalfe, Gauteng MEC for Education and Culture, 1996 (*The Star* 12 June 1996)

Many of my neighbours will go out of business if they cannot employ the Zimbabweans who are prepared to work for R250 a month ... We don't want to appear to be opposing the principles of the RDP, and we will gladly employ South Africans, but then we need help in recruiting and transporting them, which we simply cannot afford ourselves ... and a crackdown on farmers will merely force illegals to go elsewhere in search of work.

Philip Nel, Limpopo farmer, 1994 (*Financial Mail* 9 September 1994)

Mozambicans working on commercial farms receive between R60 and R150 per month over and above board and keep. Some black farmers also allocate small vegetable plots to their workers, in a form of labour tenancy. These are the lucky ones; a common ploy is for farmers to engage Mozambicans at the beginning of the month and then to call the Prohibited Immigration Unit just before pay day; the police then arrest and deport the labourers and the farmer has enjoyed another month of free labour.

Chris Dolan and Vusi Nkuna, Witwatersrand Rural Facility (Dolan and Nkuna 1995)

We are not here because we have a disease called xenophobia. We are here to eliminate opportunists and greedy people who waited for us to kick the white government from power to move in for the fruits. These are the sort of people who sit on the fence always waiting to claim victory with the winning side.

Mthuthuzeli Madalani, South African Council of Hawkers and Informal Businesses, 1994 (*Mail and Guardian* 23 September 1994)

Those who illegally evict immigrants from their areas should suffer the wrath of the law. Some of them are said to be arresting (foreigners) at gunpoint.

Nkele Tingane, Alexandra Civic Organisation, 1995 (*The Star* 28 January 1995)

We are not assaulting or threatening these people [illegals]. We are mainly doing the job for the police by handing them over and asking for them to be deported to their own countries.

Anonymous, Alexandra Property Owners Association, 1995 (*The Star* 25 January 1995)

We do not wish to do what was done to immigrants in Alexandra by the community, where some were stabbed and burned to death. We want them to go home alive.

Memorandum presented to Etwatwa police station commander by residents living near Daveyton, 1995 (*Sowetan* 7 August 1996)

The government [needs] to crack down on illegal immigrants living in Alexandra ... charity begins at home.

Tony Leon, Democratic Party, 1995 (*The Citizen* 18 October 1995)

(Government departments should) request the identity documents or passports of all foreigners requesting services subsidised by the government and in this way ensure that they do not gain access to services in short supply to our own people.

Mangosuthu Buthelezi, Minister of Home Affairs, 1997 (*Sunday Independent* 4 May 1997)

[I]f we are not coping with the influx of illegal immigrants and our people are being threatened, there will come a time when we will switch on the [border] fence to lethal mode.

Joe Modise, Minister of Defence, 1997 (*The Star* May 6 1997)

Lessons from international policy experience

Democratic South Africa is not alone in having to cope with multiple migration challenges simultaneously. Many developed and developing countries around the globe provide useful information and experiments from which South Africa can learn and which it can adapt to its own circumstances.

Relevant international experience can be briefly summarized as follows:

- Migration policy in any country is an interacting set of tools and instruments, none of which works perfectly.
- Policy must distinguish between the different types of migration affecting a particular country, and devise appropriate policies for each type.
- States have a right to defend their borders and protect their citizens against undesirable elements. It is necessary to decide whether controls should take the form of border or internal controls or both.
- Only in very rare cases is it possible to prevent illegal immigration completely. Co-operative arrangements with neighbouring countries and bilateral return agreements are useful.
- Employer sanctions are difficult to enforce in countries with a large informal sector, and might exacerbate discrimination against certain groups within a country. Corruption militates against effective enforcement of employer sanctions.
- As governments become more restrictive on legal migration, illegal migration and claims for asylum increase (Weiner 1995: 5).
- The politics of migration policy is very important.
- Governments must assure their own populations that some control policies are in place, even though there may be a considerable amount of leakage. Unless citizens are reassured that borders are controlled, xenophobic attacks against foreigners are likely to increase, since the smooth integration of legal migrants depends upon public assessment that their number is finite.

- Guest worker programmes are second-best solutions that everywhere produce at least some distortion and dependence. These programmes are easier to start than to stop.
- Guest worker programmes come closest to their aim of adding workers to the labour force and not residents to the population if three conditions can be satisfied: (1) there is little illegal immigration and there are strong labour market institutions; (2) employer taxes or levies minimize the distortions due to the presence and availability of foreign workers; and (3) economic incentives promote the return of guest workers to the country of origin (for example, forced savings schemes).
- With respect to skills migration, governments need to consider whether they are doing enough to keep skills within the country.
- To be successful, targeted skills migration programmes must determine need, select and recruit appropriately qualified workers, integrate them into the national economy, and conduct subsequent evaluations of effectiveness.
- Trade, investment and development assistance are weak instruments in terms of changing employment opportunities in poor countries and thus in affecting migration outflows from neighbouring countries.
- In the short term, development spurred by freer trade results in more rather than less migration.
- Refugees have normally been driven from their countries of origin by a national crisis, whereas illegal immigrants make a primarily individual decision to cross borders. Countries need to reconcile their national interest with their international obligations towards refugees.
- Distinguishing between people who qualify as refugees under international norms and illegitimate asylum-seekers could be seen as an administrative rather than a moral problem. However, states cannot escape the moral obligation of devising ways of deterring false claimants without deterring genuine refugees.
- In most countries migration and refugee policies are not the responsibility of any single government department. Fragmentation of decision making is typical of migration policy making in most countries, since the issues intersect with the concerns of so many ministries.
- In the absence of a co-ordinating mechanism for settling migration policies, special interests – certain employers in most countries, and ethnic minorities in some – exercise a major influence.
- In many countries, when migration has moved to the top of the political agenda in response to an immediate crisis or an awareness of growing public anxieties, national leaders have often responded in an *ad hoc* fashion.
- Few governments have sought to develop more coherent policies through the establishment of an immigration and refugee commission, made up of government and party officials and representatives of the

business community, trade unions, ethnic groups and academics or by turning responsibility over to a lead department.
- Whether a special commission is the best mechanism or a lead ministry should be given primary responsibility for reforming policy is less important than the broader questions of how a policy process can be created that is informed by research, that considers public opinion, but is not wholly guided by it and takes into account a country's diverse interests and objectives.

These are among the insights garnered from international experience that should inform South Africa's approach to migration policy.

Different views on how to deal with migration to South Africa

There are a number of different views on how policy makers should respond to migration questions in South Africa. In this section we will describe these different positions. In doing so we will divide immigrants into two broad categories: skilled migrants, and unskilled or semi-skilled migrants.

Skilled migration

With respect to skilled migration, there are only two really different views. On the one hand there is the current government position which involves strict controls over the entry of skilled people into South Africa. The view is that skilled people should only be allowed into the country in professions or technical areas where a shortage of such people can be demonstrated. The way such a shortage is identified is through government statistics and through consultation with the professional or technical bodies representing that group of skilled people already within South Africa. Besides potential migrants with these formal skills, individuals with money to invest in the country (see box, pages 188–90) are also eligible for immigration.

A number of different reasons are given to support this position, which severely limits the entry of skilled migrants into the country. There are people who advocate restrictions on skilled migrants on the basis that there are many black South Africans who can either do the job required or who should be trained to do it. It is argued that the importation of foreign skills would hamper this process of affirmative action. It sometimes appears as if those holding this position would prefer not to have any skilled migration into South Africa at all. Other people argue that South Africa should only allow skilled people into the country in those categories 'where there is an identified shortage, and we need those skills'. There is not much discussion around how this shortage will be identified, as it seems to be assumed that this is a simple, self-evident process easily handled through bureaucratic channels. Lastly, there is what might be called a region-specific variant of the control argument. Some people – including some southern African governments – argue that South Africa should not denude its neighbouring countries of their skilled people, and should therefore not recruit with SADC countries for any of the skills South Africa needs.

The contrary position is that the country's doors should be opened to all the skilled people who would like to come here, irrespective of where they come from. Also, many arguing this position believe that 'skilled' should be broadly defined, and include informal entrepreneurial skills.

Unskilled migration

With respect to unskilled migration into South Africa, a number of different views can be identified which essentially cluster around two basic positions. We have termed these positions 'fortress South Africa' and 'the open door'.

Fortress South Africa: maximum control and exclusion

The most central position, and the one that initially elicits our sympathy, is based on the notion that 'charity begins at home'. Mindful of the resource constraints in South Africa and the existence of backlogs and shortages of employment opportunity, school classrooms, teachers, hospital beds, adequate shelter, welfare funds, land close to employment and a host of other necessities which many South Africans do not have, a strong view is taken that the country cannot afford to be lenient. Illegal migration, particularly of unskilled migrants whose contribution to the economy will be limited, simply has to be tightly controlled.

A variation on this position – although not presented as such – involves a two-step approach. People holding this view argue that what the country should do is to offer permanent residence and rights to anyone in South Africa now, and having done that, apply all its resources to stemming the flow of new migrants into the country. This is also an initially appealing position, and in many respects a clearer and more consistent version of the government's current approach.

The open door: accommodation and free movement

There are two positions in this 'open door' category. The first may be described as one of 'humane accommodation'. Its proponents argue that the migrants coming to South Africa are largely refugees from strife and great privation in their countries of origin, and that a humanitarian response to their plight should be the fundamental policy consideration for South Africa. This empathy is strengthened by the consideration that the peoples and governments of the countries of origin – at least in Africa – supported South African exiles and refugees both directly and indirectly in the bitter years of the struggle against apartheid. Both these sources of sympathy for migrants help to establish a case for a lenient and accepting response by the authorities to the presence of illegal immigrants. Some people even go further than this and argue that national borders, an artificial construct, are no longer very important anyway, and that individuals should have equivalent rights wherever they happen to be and whether they are citizens of that particular country or not.

The second strong position in the 'open door' category is what might be called the economic argument for free movement. Its proponents hold that the best policy for economic growth in South Africa and the broader region is to lift all restrictions on the movement of labour, capital and goods. They also believe it is a waste of time, money and effort to try to police South Africa's long and porous borders.

Points of departure for CDE's analysis

In this chapter we will put forward ten analytical points of departure. These build on considerable research on migration, South African policy generally, and on the country's governance and development capacity. On the basis of this analysis we will then return to comment on the different points of view on migration policy discussed in the previous section.

South Africa's national interests must come first

The globalization of the world economy and the inevitable spread of markets, transportation, communication, capital and skills has challenged the geographic hegemony of national governments. By implication, this process of internationalization is at least qualifying established notions of the jurisdictional authority of nation states. We believe this weakening of the state should not be allowed to go too far. National interests are important, even, and perhaps especially, in a globalizing world.

A perception of uncontrolled migration across borders could lead people to question the state's ability to carry out its fundamental responsibility of guaranteeing the rights of citizens. Hence a country's approach to migration must be seen to be part of an ordered policy. An approach which simply throws open the country's borders could lead to a breakdown of the authority (and even legitimacy) of the state, or to perceptions that this is happening. In South Africa, as precedents in the field of safety and security have shown, this could be an invitation to groups to take the law into their own hands. As Myron Weiner puts it, 'No country has given up control over entry, nor is there any reason to do so' (1995: 205).

It is for this reason that CDE is opposed to expanding the definition of 'refugee' to include not only groups of people who respond collectively (most often) to extreme situations of peril in their country of origin (civil war, natural disaster, persecution of a racial or ethnic group), but also all those individuals or families who want to leave one country in order to seek improved economic and other opportunities in another. This is much too broad a notion of 'refugee'. It confuses two different processes taking place within and among countries. It is also an extremely dangerous and loose definition which could impose totally unmanageable obligations on South Africa as the most developed country in sub-Saharan Africa. Furthermore, it undermines the narrow and legitimate definition of refugees and how states should respond to such people in their hour of need. Notes Weiner:

> The definition of refugee need not be expanded to include all whose human rights are violated or who are in economic distress, for that would result in a massive increase in claimants beyond what states can reasonably be expected to accept, and hence would undermine the asylum and refugee regime. (ibid: 219)

Similarly, it is our concern with South Africa's national interest that leads us to reject the 'globalist' position which in effect argues against the very concept of nation states, and, with respect to migration, holds that there ought to be a presumption in favour of a supposed right to free movement, with the burden of proof on the advocates of restrictions. As Weiner points out, 'globalists pay little attention to whether the adoption of their principles in a world comprising sovereign states would lead to an improvement or a worsening of the human condition in any specific country' (ibid: 180). For example, the adoption of a globalist position on migration by a single country puts that country at risk when other countries choose not to open their borders. Migration can then be used as an act of aggression against the country with open borders as one country passes its unwanted people on to another. Under such circumstances, an open door to migrants might well do many people more harm than good. Moreover, if a state chooses not to give preference to the well-being of its own citizens over the well-being of citizens of other countries, then local communities and regions within the country might protect themselves by imposing restrictions on entry or discriminating against foreign residents, generating the very opposite result from that intended by the globalists.

It is convincingly argued that people who belong to a community will defend their local politics and culture against strangers, and that if the state did not take on this responsibility one would not end up with a 'world without walls', but would rather 'create a thousand petty fortresses ...' Weiner (and CDE) therefore finds value in the sovereign state, not because it is exclusive but because it provides for greater inclusiveness than would be possible if it did not exist (ibid: 178–80).

There is another argument which, to our minds, effectively undermines and downplays the national interests of South Africans. This view suggests that South Africa's policy on migration should be determined by the needs of other countries in the southern African region. It is argued that these states suffered during the years of apartheid, that some of them actively assisted the ANC or South Africans in exile, and that South Africa should therefore open its doors to their citizens. There are many problems with this point of view. For example, since these states responded in different ways to apartheid, should our migration policy not do likewise? Given that some governments in the region do not want South Africa to recruit skilled people in their countries, should we therefore be generous only to their unskilled citizens? And is the presumption correct that South Africa's interests and those of the region are identical? But let us leave aside problems such as these.

We would argue that South Africa's migration policy (like any other area of national policy) must in the first instance be considered and assessed in the light of our national interests, and that there are often differences between South Africa's interests and those of particular states in the broader region beyond our borders.

Hard-nosed questions about migration policy and its implications are therefore legitimate issues of national politics. How many migrants are entering the country, or can be expected to do so during the next few years? What will they do once they get here? Will they be an economic asset to the country, or a drain on its already strained resources? Is it possible to prevent migration into a country such as South Africa? What will it cost to do so at some meaningful level of prevention? Will 'foreigners in our midst' heighten tensions and social conflicts inside South Africa? What are the political, social and human rights consequences of internal policing to get rid of illegal migrants? Do migrants come to South Africa to find employment or to benefit from our 'state entitlements'? How does migration policy support and interact with other national objectives and policies?

Policy implication: South Africans must debate and then decide on a migration policy that promotes this country's national interests.

Migration policy must support and complement government's macro-economic strategy

The government's Growth, Employment and Redistribution strategy (GEAR) is courageous because it puts medium- and longer-term benefits before short-term palliatives. It commits the government to exchange control liberalization on the assumption that capital which flows out in the early stages will return in due course, along with additional capital. It commits the government to creating conditions for greater labour market flexibility on the assumption that wage levels which drop initially will rise later with improved productivity. In order to support these principles in the field of cross-border labour flows, migration policy should sacrifice the semblance of short-run controls on inward migration on the assumption that the fiscal resources saved, the new skills and human capital acquired and the willingness of migrants to work for lower wages will all help to stimulate growth. GEAR also commits the government and the economy to improved competitiveness. By protecting uncompetitive local labour, migration controls are not helping that labour in the long run. The answer to labour vulnerability, which is compatible with economic growth, is to train local workers and job-seekers, rather than keeping out competition, which is only a short-term palliative in any case.

GEAR is based on the now global consensus on and understanding of modern economies which denies the zero-sum approach. There is not a finite pool of opportunities where one person's employment means that there is one less opportunity for someone else. We see South Africa as an expanding market of infinite opportunities where people can create their own jobs, run their own businesses, find employment with someone else, and so on. The very act of participating in the economy in this way, if well managed, helps to grow many more opportunities for employment. Thus the more skilled, energetic and entrepreneurial people we have in the country the better.

Policy implication: migration policy must be consistent with a more open economy and support maximum economic growth and job creation.

South Africa needs all the skilled people it can attract

GEAR aims to position South Africa's monetary, fiscal and exchange rate policy in such a way as to achieve a 6 per cent growth rate by the turn of the century. The modest growth of the past three years has already seen the re-emergence of a skills shortage (see box below).

Skilled emigration undercounts disguise crisis

- The magnitude of South Africa's 'brain drain' is disguised by serious data deficiencies. According to official South African data, in the period 1984–93 some 28,965 emigrants left for the United Kingdom, while 33,640 British immigrants arrived. For the same period, British data give the total number of immigrants from South Africa as 100,700, and emigrants to South Africa of 52,600. Overall the South African data record a net gain for South Africa of 4675, while British data record a net loss for South Africa of more than 48,000. In the year ending June 1996, Australia received 59 per cent more immigrants from South Africa than we recorded emigrating to Australia (Lewis and Kaplan 1997).

This means:

- our data is near-worthless; and
- South Africa has seen a significant exit of people, principally skilled people, over a long period of time.

'Brain drain' statistics should be treated with caution. They cannot take into account what has been termed 'grey' emigration, whereby people leave on holiday and simply do not return, or return as occasional visitors, thereby cutting out the red tape involved in emigration. A spokesperson for the Central Statistical Services has stated: 'We can't tell — we can only tell people who go formally' (*Finance Week* 18–24 July 1996: 31).

- Statistics reflect a substantial net loss of skilled professionals. CSS figures for the first three quarters of 1995 show that 6665 South Africans left the country permanently in that period while 3695 foreigners settled in South Africa, representing a net loss of 2970 persons. The net loss of persons in professional, semi-professional and technical occupations during this period was 680, with a net loss of 738 during the same period in 1994. In the first quarter of 1996, 3083 emigrants left South Africa, compared with 1118 immigrants who entered. The number of emigrants who left South Africa in this time increased by 27 per cent compared with the previous year, while the number of immigrants decreased by 21.1 per cent. Education-related occupations lost 132 people, with only 27 new arrivals to fill these positions. Likewise, 39 medical and dental professionals left, with only 18 new arrivals (*The Citizen* 4 July 1996).
- An increasing number of Afrikaans-speaking professionals are leaving South Africa. The director of an emigration agency has noted: 'We have many more Afrikaners than before; they make up about 50 per cent of our applicants' (*Sunday Independent* 31 March 1996).
- South Africa has a low and declining rate of formal (legal) immigration, the decline being most significant in the last two years. We have never attracted so few immigrants.

Number of immigrants admitted into South Africa, 1992–6

Year	Number
1992	8 686
1993	9 824
1994	6 398
1995	5 064
1996	5 407

Source: (Lewis and Kaplan 1997)

The expansion of opportunities for education and training will increase the supply of skilled labour, but it will take time. In some fields where training and education is expensive, it will be optimal for South Africa to import skills rather than to try and produce them locally. Moreover, studies of South African development and competitiveness all stress our weakness in respect of human capital. A greater supply of human resources would raise returns to other factors of production, such as capital, land and unskilled labour.

South Africa is perennially short of skilled and entrepreneurial people. Economic growth requires as many skills as we can grow, hire or import. It is a fallacy to think that there is a contradiction between equal opportunities for all South Africans irrespective of colour, and the active participation of employers (companies, universities, government and other institutions) in the global marketplace for skilled personnel. Therefore, it is essential that companies, universities, government departments and any other employers are free to buy in talent as and when they deem fit. The economic expansion that this talent will help South Africa to create and sustain will in turn help to create the resources necessary to train and educate more and more South Africans.

Race has been a key factor in South Africa's approach to skilled migration. Under apartheid only white people qualified. Under the democratic regime a new racial qualification has emerged. Some take affirmative action within South Africa to mean that we do not want skilled people who are not black South Africans to fill vacant positions. This has also been coupled with an idea (and policy in some neighbouring states) that South Africa should not 'steal' qualified black people who are citizens of neighbouring states. The consequence of these two positions is that people with skills throughout the subcontinent who are seeking greater opportunity are encouraged to leave Africa rather than come to South Africa, and that the skills shortage inside South Africa remains (see box below).

Africanize or indigenize?

The 'University of Ghanaphuthatswana'

South African universities, under pressure to reflect the demographic and social structure of the country more closely, often find Africanization a more viable option than indigenizing or applying affirmative action. This trend has emerged at the University of the North West (formerly the University of Bophuthatswana) — which some have dubbed the 'University of Ghanaphuthatswana' because of the number of Ghanaians allegedly employed there. This case highlights one of South Africa's major challenges: how rapidly can skilled black technicians, managers, entrepreneurs and, in this case, academics, be trained? And what is our attitude to skilled foreigners overall?

The number of academics employed at the University of the North West swelled from 32 in 1981 to about 200 in 1986. After remaining fairly constant until 1991, the numbers grew further to approximately 250 in 1992 and have since maintained that level.

There have been significant changes in the racial composition of the staff, and in the ratios of expatriates to South Africans.

Percentages of white and black staff

	White	Black
1981	56%	44%
1995	24%	76%

Composition of expatriate staff

	Europe	Africa	Asia	America
1981	86%	14%	0%	0%
1995	19%	56%	21%	4%

Percentages of South African and expatriate staff

	South African	Expatriate
1981	81%	19%
1995	68%	32%

(Extracted from Drummond *et al.* 1995)

We can understand the fears of countries in southern Africa who are worried about losing skilled people. But they are deluding themselves if they think that tougher restrictions on getting into South Africa will solve their problems. Skilled people will move in response to greater opportunities. South Africa's neighbouring states must make themselves more attractive to their citizens – which will require domestic political and economic reforms. If denied the opportunity to move to South Africa when and if they want, many skilled people will leave the continent – surely a consequence of policy which is not in the interests of anyone in southern Africa.

Any system of restricting the movement of skills into a country will inevitably be subject to the influence of interest groups. In this respect it is interesting to note the view of the labour market commission (1996): 'The commission is particularly concerned at the role played by local professional associations in the evaluation of an application for work status in this country. It appears that these organisations adopt a highly protectionist stance to the entry of foreigners into their ranks.'

How we define a 'skilled' person in the context of a developing country is important. In South Africa the term has been taken to refer to people who bring into the country their own formal technical, professional or educational skills. This has generally been coupled with the notion that people who can bring money into the country are also welcome – so investors bring a 'skill' in the form of resources into South Africa too. CDE would argue that we need to expand this definition of 'skilled' to include small-scale entrepreneurs, both formal and informal. We should be generous and in effect much more realistic about our definition of skills. South Africa is short of all types of professional and entrepreneurial skills, so we should welcome anyone who can add to the country's pool of talent, energy and expertise in these areas.

Policy implication: migration policy must aim to provide the country with an abundance of skilled people (with both formal and informal skills).

South Africa is a nation with many cross-border links – these create immigration pressures

The peopling and geographical definition of South Africa has created a multitude of cross-border links. Sotho, Swazi, Tswana and Shangaan people are to be found on both sides of South Africa's borders; Zulu offshoots are found in more than one neighbouring country. Other parts of the South African population have links with Asian, European and Middle Eastern countries. The development of South Africa's mines has, at one time or another, pulled in workers from most SADC countries. Through legal or clandestine immigration many people have joined the South African nation; migration is central to its character. Current international studies on migration point to the importance of social networks in the migration process. In other words, once a foreign community, village, country or area has established a beachhead in a new country, the process of migration for other people from that same original base becomes easier and more likely. Policy must recognize that many networks cross South African borders.

As Weiner notes:

> If there is a single 'law' in migration, it is that a migration flow, once begun, induces its own flow. Migrants enable their friends and relatives back home to migrate by providing them with information about how to migrate, resources to facilitate movement, and assistance in finding jobs and housing. (1995, see box below)

Networks into Africa

In February 1996 CDE conducted interviews with 30 taxi drivers and 20 flea market traders based in Gauteng. The following emerged:

- At the moment the South African taxi transport network does not extend beyond Harare. The areas catered for in the region include Lesotho, Swaziland, Zimbabwe, Botswana and Mozambique. Passengers who want to venture as far north as Zambia, for instance, take a taxi from Johannesburg to Harare, and then take another taxi there for the next leg of their journey.
- Job-hunters, migrant workers and petty traders replenishing their stock — of perfumes, spices, second-hand clothing, and electrical appliances, especially refrigerators — make up the bulk of the passengers on taxis.
- The load to South Africa is lighter with taxis ferrying only people; from South Africa, furniture and goods load taxis as well.
- Products sold in South Africa include wooden and wire products (such as toys, household accessories), cotton and wool, beads, sculptures, clay and pottery products, baskets, and leather products such as bags and watch straps.
- Preliminary findings of the SADC/South African Traffic Control Council cross-border traffic survey show that although Lebombo is one of three border posts between South Africa and Mozambique, there is a significantly higher flow of taxis (twice as many) through there than at Beit Bridge, the only border post between South Africa and Zimbabwe.

Increased migration into South Africa is inevitable; the only question is how to manage this phenomenon in the best possible way so as to capture the most benefits for South Africa and the people who live here.

Policy implication: increased economic integration with southern Africa will multiply migration pressures.

Increased development in southern Africa will not stop migration to South Africa

Many people suggest that a key policy measure in stopping migration into South Africa should be increased aid by the South African government to uplift the economies of neighbouring states.

This sounds like a plausible strategy; yet international experience clearly point to the contrary. The 1992 United States Commission for the Study of International Migration and Cooperative Economic Development put it this way:

> While job-creating economic growth is the ultimate solution to reducing these migratory pressures, the economic development process itself tends in the short to medium term to stimulate immigration by raising expectations and enhancing people's ability to migrate. (quoted in Harris 1996: 192)

This view is corroborated by Weiner (CDE 1997a), and Harris and Sassen (Harris 1996: 191). In any event, it is extremely doubtful whether South Africa has the resources to become involved in massive development aid to neighbouring states or the capacity to invest in them *for anything other than economic reasons*. Difficulties in implementing the RDP inside South Africa point to the need to be realistic about capacity and speed.

This does not mean that South African migration policy should work against the development of our neighbouring states. Far from it — South Africa should encourage and promote viable economic growth and socio-infrastructural development throughout the region. But to think that this will reduce the migration pressures to South Africa in the short to medium-term is an illusion. Economic growth in South Africa and the southern African region will increase the pressures for migration into South Africa. The results of better infrastructure, education, communications and other opportunities will be to facilitate greater mobility. For the vast majority of potential migrants in the region, greater mobility will mean moving to South Africa. If anything, increased development of southern Africa will heighten the demand for migration to South Africa.

It is generally assumed that if there were free movement into South Africa, all migrants would migrate permanently and they would be lost to their society in all respects. This ignores the role of migrant remittances (see box below).

Some migrants are itinerant traders

Maxine Reitzes, a prominent South African migration researcher, argues that the catch-all category of 'illegal immigrant' is inappropriately applied to undocumented migrants, principally traders, who sojourn temporarily in South Africa. Many migrants in South Africa regard themselves as migrants *per se*, rather than as immigrants. They do not desire permanent residence in South Africa. They are here for specific purposes, and expect to return to the country of their birth; or they wish to maintain a home base in their country of origin, and continually commute across South Africa's borders. Many are transient, trading artefacts which they bring from other African countries. They exit with the proceeds and South African consumer goods, procure more goods, and return to sell again. Similarly, many enter to find work, take goods and remittances back to dependants, and then re-enter.

Such migrants have no option but to remain undocumented, and therefore 'illegal', as there is no policy that adequately addresses their requirements. It is expensive and time-consuming for them to re-apply continually for temporary permits each time they wish to re-enter the country. Applicants for temporary work and work-seeker permits have to pay R360 each time they apply for permits or seek extensions. Tariffs are non-refundable, regardless of the outcome of the application. The SADC amnesty of 1996 was inappropriate for such migrants, since they do not desire permanent residence. Had migrants wanted to secure permanent residence, they would have been precluded from doing so by virtue of the imposed condition that applicants had to provide evidence of continuous residence in South Africa from 1 July 1991.

A unique policy response to this category of migrants is required; thus a long-term, multiple entry, temporary work or residence permit may be one way of regularizing and legalizing their status.

(Extracted from Reitzes 1997)

According to Harris (1996: 191), in the late 1970s it was estimated that illegal Mexican immigrants to the United States remitted or carried back more than $2 billion annually (or four times the earnings of the Mexican tourist industry), and this directly affected about 21 per cent of the population of the country. The size of the flow does not indicate the degree of impact on the country receiving remittances (ibid: 143–4). Their expenditure creates employment for many others in the making of goods and supply of services; therefore, migration is not necessarily a net loss to the 'sending' country. In many cases, the 'sending' country benefits as it receives inflows of foreign currency.

Policy implication: regional development is important in its own right. It is not an effective short-term instrument to control migration.

We know very little about the scale, nature and possible future trends with respect to immigration into South Africa

One difficult factor in the discussion about migration to South Africa is the paucity of information.

Most of the proponents of the 'fortress South Africa' position base their argument on a number of assumptions that are empirically dubious. We do not know how many people there are in the country illegally. We do not know how many people presently living in other countries would like to come here, or are planning to come. We do not know what migrants contribute to the South African economy, nor what they cost the society. There is no hard data on the overall impact migrants have on the social, political and economic life of South Africa, and those who claim to know exactly what this impact is should not be believed. And yet proponents of the 'tighten up' position make only negative assumptions about all these issues.

A new migration policy will need to be carefully evaluated, and this means that considerably more and better information is required. Sound empirical data are needed on:

- the pressures for migration into South Africa from the different SADC countries;
- the impact of new migrants on different communities (urban and rural), economic trends and services inside South Africa;
- the way in which the new policy is being implemented, and adjustments that might need to be made;
- the budget allocations needed to enable the implementation of migration policy, and the efficiency of such implementation.

The consequence of this lack of information requires honesty from policy makers on what they do not know, the introduction of a reliable, objective and ongoing source of information on international migration trends and impact, a degree of caution as to the knowledge of the real demand for migration into South Africa, and thus a need to monitor and review policy instruments annually with care (see box below).

Not everyone wants to become a South African!

Mineworkers, amnesty and permanent residence

In October 1995 the South African cabinet offered permanent South African residence to mineworkers from outside the country who had been working on the mines since 1986 and who had voted in the 1994 election. A survey of mineworkers in Lesotho provided some interesting preliminary answers to the question of the likely implications of the amnesty. As Jonathan Crush notes:

These findings are highly significant, for they contest the assumption that all Lesotho citizens cannot wait to move permanently to South Africa and abandon their home country. The vast majority see a permanent move as undesirable. Those with resources and assets in Lesotho are even less likely [to move]. Of those who move, most would continue contact with Lesotho, and would aim to retire there. (1997)

The findings showed that:

- only 18.7 per cent of respondents said they wanted to take up permanent residence in South Africa;
- only 6.1 per cent would take up South African citizenship;
- 68.3 per cent of those who said they would move to South Africa also indicated that they would keep a home in Lesotho.

As at 1 December 1996, 51,504 miners had successfully applied for amnesty out of an eligible population estimated at around 130,000 by the recruiting agency TEBA.[1]

(Extracted from Crush 1996)

Policy implication: South Africa urgently requires a thorough and objective process to obtain essential information on migration. In the meantime, some caution is needed in the policy field.

The economic contribution of migrants must be recognized by policy makers

Do illegal migrants really steal jobs from locals?

Many local people are fearful that they will lose their jobs to migrants who are prepared to accept work at a lower rate. By keeping wages down, illegals might displace some local workers, but the magnitude of the displacement is not clear. In a recent study on unemployment, Schlemmer and Worthington (1996) found that South Africans blamed illegals for unemployment more than they blamed anything else. No fewer than 79 per cent of all South Africans believed that competition for jobs from illegals was a major cause of unemployment, with all other explanations endorsed by lower proportions of people. But the study strongly suggested that unemployed South Africans, on average, would not accept work at the rates foreign migrants are happy with. On average South Africans claiming unemployment would not, by their own admission, accept formal work at much less than the going rates in formal, large-scale industry and commerce for unskilled labour.

The charge that illegal immigrants take work away from South Africans, at wage levels which South Africans would generally be willing to accept, has yet to be proved. Some evidence is surfacing on the positive socio-economic impact of some illegal immigrants (see box below). There are also reports of foreign traders who regularly travel to South Africa, sell their goods, and then use the money acquired to buy South African goods before returning to their country of origin. Such people contribute to the economy as a whole, and to local job creation.

Ghanaians in Durban – surprising findings

Interviews conducted in 1996 with 50 self-employed Ghanaian immigrants in the Durban metropolitan area cast doubt on a number of common misconceptions about such people, namely:

- that immigrants take more jobs than they create
  - 78 per cent of respondents believed that South Africans do not have adequate skills in the areas in which they were engaged;
  - 68 per cent felt that they had special skills to contribute to the Durban metropolitan area;
  - 52 per cent of respondents had trained locals in the skills that they are engaged in: shoe repairs, barbering, hairdressing and dressmaking. Some of the locals had set up their own small businesses in the Durban area, while others had been employed by the immigrants who trained them. Most South Africans working in hair salons were apparently trained by the Ghanaian owners of those salons;
- that xenophobic attitudes prevent immigrants being integrated into communities
  - only 16 per cent of respondents indicated that their hosts had hostile attitudes to them. Some 36 per cent indicated indifferent attitudes, and 48 per cent said their hosts had warm attitudes towards them;
  - as many as 90 per cent indicated that they did not feel threatened by South Africans engaged in the same economic activity. This might of course be because not too many South Africans are involved in the same economic activity;
  - 92 per cent did not have any difficulty communicating with people of the host area, with English being the common medium of communication.

(Extracted from Geyevu 1997)

The international evidence is interesting in this regard. Most work done concerns the United States. According to Borjas in a 1993 study for the OECD: 'The methodological arsenal of modern econometrics cannot find a single shred of evidence that immigrants have a major adverse impact on the earnings and job opportunities of natives of the United States' (quoted in Harris 1996: 194). In an earlier study, concluded in 1990, Borjas concluded that 'despite all of the concern about the displacement effects of illegal immigration, the available evidence suggests that illegal aliens ... have a minor impact on the earnings and employment opportunities of the natives.' According to Harris, other studies reach the same conclusions: 'Black unemployment rates are not increased – if anything, they are lowered – by a rise in the proportion of Mexican immigrants in the local labour market' (ibid).

According to Harris, some studies suggest that immigrants have a positive effect on native employment by saving industries that would otherwise either close or relocate – for example, the shoe, vehicle, garment and fruit-processing industries in California. In the case of Los Angeles, McCarthy and Valdez (cited in Harris 1986) found that when in the 1970s national employment contracted by a total of 5 per cent in the leather goods, textile, garments and furniture industries, employment in the city in these industries expanded by 50 per cent, largely, they argued, as a result of the availability of immigrant workers, legal and illegal, which increased the demand for native-born workers as owners, managers, supervisors, technicians in the input and machine supplying industries and in transport. If these industries in Los Angeles had contracted at the national rate, its labour market would have had 83,000 fewer jobs. Portes came to similar conclusions for the OECD in 1993. Harris goes on to argue that these calculations omit to include the increase in native employment as a result of immigrants (including illegals) spending the incomes they earn – on housing, foodstuffs, furnishings, journeys to work, and so forth (Harris 1996: 194–5).

Are migrants parasites on the host society?

The foreign migrant makes his or her contribution to the economy with rather lower levels of demand for state resources than local participants in the economy.

Again, the international evidence is instructive. North and Houstoun (1976) found that, in the case of illegal immigrants to the United States, a majority paid direct taxes to finance public support programmes but were rare users of tax-supported programmes. In the case of Caribbean migrants to Britain, it was found that in the 1960s few immigrants drew retirement pensions (one of the largest items in the national insurance and benefit systems), and their use of other provisions was slightly lower than that of the native-born. In California, McCarthy and Valdez found that less than 5 per cent of Mexican immigrants received any assistance from public welfare services – well below all other low income groups (cited in Harris 1996: 205–6).

South Africa benefits from migration

For decades, South Africa has relied heavily on the contribution of skilled immigrants. Nevertheless, the low quality of South African mass education results in South Africa's Human Development Index (as calculated by the United Nations) remaining low in relation to our general level of development, so that skilled immigrants will continue to play a role in the softening of a major constraint on economic growth. Formal managerial and professional qualifications are not the only index of skill: our underdeveloped small and medium enterprise sector will also benefit from the importation of proven but informally acquired entrepreneurial skills. Even immigrants with limited skills are generally risk-takers in their communities of origin, and are people with the drive to work hard and succeed in their new settings.

CDE believes it is important to see immigration as a valuable additional source of human capital which creates opportunities for more rapid growth, rather than as a source of competition for a fixed number of jobs. In this respect South Africa has more to learn from the immigration history and policies of the United States than from European history and practice, even though some of our current immigration law and policy follow British practice for historical reasons. Indeed, Europe taken as a whole is in serious demographic and labour market disequilibrium at present, a fact Europeans will have to struggle with for decades. It is possible to avoid the emergence of this problem in southern Africa if migration policy is appropriately formulated now.

Policy implication: the benefits of migration outweigh the costs of extraordinary border controls and internal policing measures.

Popular fears and misconceptions about migration must be dealt with. Leadership is required

It is very important that the authorities should be fully acquainted with the attitudes of citizens on an issue such as illegal immigration and migration generally. Weiner (1995) documents instances in the United States, Europe and Asia where political leaders have been out of touch with and underestimated the reaction of citizens to influxes of foreign immigrants, and have suffered political setbacks as a result.

An issue of very great concern is the evidence from numerous surveys that the vast majority of the South African population are antagonistic to the voluntary in-migration of people from across the borders. In a survey conducted for the Human Sciences Research Council in February 1995, Minnaar and Hough (1996) found that 72 per cent of respondents felt the government should act more strictly against illegal immigrants, and that the proportion had risen from 56 per cent in a 1994 survey. This evidence was interpreted to mean that xenophobic attitudes were increasing sharply. The evidence was also interpreted to mean that there is a perception that foreign migrants compete unfairly for scarce resources and employment opportunities.

Associated with these perceptions is the danger of hostilities developing which could lead to reactions of protest or violence against foreign migrants. There are instances where this has already occurred.

One very understandable reaction to this type of evidence is that the authorities should heed the prevailing sentiment (the 'voice of the people' as it were) and clamp down on foreign migration. Obviously, as a democracy, South Africa has to be responsive to the perceptions of the mass of its citizens. At the same time, however, politicians have an educational role and a duty to lead public opinion where issues are more complex than the rank and file citizenry might realize. The argument that the government has to follow the sentiments of the majority of people was made in respect of the abolition of the death penalty and abortion on demand, and even to major aspects of GEAR, but the government was clearly convinced by a range of other important factors and chose not to respond to 'populist' perceptions in these cases. Governments need to consider many factors in making policy, and popular sentiment is only one of these. There is thus no reason why the initial wishes of the population at large should define government policy on migration – popular views are important, and the government should attempt to understand such views fully. But it should balance them against other considerations which are in the longer-term interests of the population.

It is important to realize that the attitudes expressed in opinion surveys, while valid reflections of broad sentiments and of a typical inclination to respond according to perceived self-interest, do not necessarily mean that a majority of people feel so strongly about the issue that they would reject a more balanced policy towards migrants if they were to be presented with all the facts and the policy fully communicated and explained.

There is also a wider consideration at play in this regard. While there have been popular reactions against foreign migrants, the most serious instances of conflict over jobs and resources have occurred and still occur between interest groups within the South African population. One need only think of the ethnic clashes on the mines, and faction fights between rural communities. Hence the potential for conflict over resources is much wider than that which relates only to foreign migrants, who in any event, precisely because of their foreign status, tend to avoid conflict as much as possible. They also seldom present themselves as factions or groups, tending rather to operate within the system as individuals, adapting to the constraints and opportunities presented to them.

This wider consideration should focus attention on the critical need for the economy to grow, and for fiscal and infrastructural resources to expand more rapidly than they are at the moment. To the extent that an expensive and probably ineffective attempt to clamp down on illegal foreign migration will consume scarce resources, and perhaps even constrain the contributions that foreign migrants make to wealth creation and cross-border trade, an attempt to 'get tough' on foreign migration will hinder rather than help to address the wider and more urgent challenge of growth. Controls have costs, and ineffective controls simply waste money, becoming a tax on growth.

Policy implication: South African public opinion needs information on the realities of migration. New migration policy must give a lead and make a clear choice on the realities and benefits of migration for South Africa.

Crime and conflict must be tackled directly, not through migration policy. Illegal immigrants are not a primary cause of social tensions and conflict

Negative assumptions are often made about the behaviour of all illegal immigrants. Illegals are supposedly responsible for stealing jobs from locals, for crime, drug trafficking, arms proliferation and spreading diseases. Consider the following press report:

> Certain nationalities had been identified by the police as being associated with specific crimes. Nigerians had been linked with drug smuggling, particularly cocaine, Zairians with diamond smuggling, Taiwanese and Chinese with the smuggling of perlemoen and crayfish, Thai girls with prostitution, and Mozambicans and Angolans with arms smuggling. (*The Citizen* 29 June 1995).

The police estimated in 1994 that some 14 per cent of crimes, aside from illegal migration itself, are committed by illegal immigrants.

There is no doubt that some illegals are exploiting opportunities for crime. This is not so much a problem of migration but an example of a much wider problem in our society, namely the breakdown of law and order and of social discipline.

One cannot address this problem from the 'edges' as it were, one edge being illegal migration. It has to be addressed at its core, and for what it is. Laws of supply and demand require basic law and order in which to operate effectively and without distortion. Crime can be regarded as a case of some participants in the marketplace taking unfair advantage of others by using coercion, violence and fraud in order to obtain resources. The scope for this kind of distortion of all markets has to be reduced to something approximating that of a normal society before we will be able to understand the issue of illegal migration in its proper perspective.

It is often suggested that tight border controls are necessary in order to prevent the entry of criminal elements, smugglers and the passage of stolen goods into South Africa. But it is obvious that criminals are the type of person most likely to take the risks of crossing tightly controlled borders, because their entire mission is the rejection of law and order. This would be like using a very large net which catches thousands of little fishes in order to catch fewer big fishes with the agility to jump out of the net before they are landed. The damage to the interests of the non-criminals would be disproportionately greater than to the real criminals. This simply cannot be an efficient basis for an anti-crime drive. The principle should be to use a special net to catch the fishes that need to be caught, as it were. A crime strategy must be focused on criminals, and not hope to catch offenders by chance.

Policy implication: do not put more resources into migration policy in order to deal with crime. Target cross-border crime directly, and put more resources there.

Immigration policy must be humane and avoid unnecessary criminalization

For decades, South Africa's influx control system made criminals out of ordinary people who did not break other laws in pursuit of their interests. The system eventually collapsed under its own weight, but not before it had fined or jailed millions of people with scant respect for due process, separated families, and eroded respect for the rule of law. Under current immigration policies there remains the need for indiscriminate mass raids on the streets, illegal immigrant detention camps, and deportation trains. These institutions are not easily reconciled with a human rights culture, and can be the means by which burdens are imposed on many thousands of people (not all of them foreign).

On the streets of South Africa it is often difficult to distinguish between local and foreign people. In 1994, a black reporter wrote:

> [Al]though pass laws requiring every black person to carry identity documents were abolished in 1985, blacks would still be wise to carry their IDs when in Johannesburg. A stroll in Hillbrow or a shopping trip at the Smal Street Mall in the city centre without your ID could get you arrested if you are mistaken for an illegal immigrant and you are black. (*The Star* 27 November 1994)

Some already acknowledge that these burdens are often pointless (see box, page 203). There are costs in imposing them, and they do not stop clandestine immigration. Such a situation points to the defects in current immigration policy. These defects are systemic; they will not be removed by a once-off amnesty, unless it is followed by a more realistic accommodation of demographic and labour market pressures.

The removal of unnecessary criminalization will also pave the way for immigrants to meet their tax liabilities more fully.

Policy implication: South Africa has enough real criminals. Migration policy should not condemn (potentially) millions of otherwise law-abiding people as criminals. This will be costly, and undermine attempts to build a new human rights culture in the country.

Migration policy must be realistic about South Africa's limited institutional capacity

Does the state have the capacity and resources to stop illegal migration?

Many who argue for a 'get tough' approach to manage illegal immigration do so on the basis of certain assumptions. Speaking in the national assembly in June 1996, the Minister of Home Affairs said:

> The department [of home affairs] is confident that the influx of illegal immigrants who pose a threat to the reconstruction and development programme and the prosperity of citizens can be stemmed, but only if the central and regional governments, as well as all political parties, are willing to support the department in its application of strict control measures and intensified law enforcement action. (Hansard no. 8, 3–7/6/96, col. 2110)

The Institute for Security Studies has suggested that South Africa can do more to control the influx of illegal immigrants through tighter border controls (floodlights, motor detectors, etc.) and internal controls such as tamper-proof identity cards, a comprehensive national registration system with built-in punitive measures against employment, and 'a system to ensure that illegals are not employed in the underground economy' (Solomon and Cilliers 1996).

Is it practical to suggest that a country which cannot even measure its underground economy, collect rates and service charges from residents who live at listed addresses, enforce television-licence requirements, collect parking tickets or register voters without duplications and omissions could actually implement these measures? More stringent internal regulation of migrants is not feasible, given the financial and administrative demands, the state's weak institutional capacity, the political consequences, and difficulties of enforcing employer sanctions in a country with a large informal sector such as South Africa. This suggestion also mistakenly assumes that one can ignore South Africa's failed history of influx control and impose it all over again. Those advocating such an approach need to explain how exactly this might be done, and at what cost.

The former Deputy Minister of Home Affairs, Penuel Maduna, has underscored the country's limited resources as follows:

> It can be mentioned that England, as an island, has a total of in excess of 5000 immigration officers, while South Africa, with its vast borders, has

fewer than 1000 officers to fulfil the same task. The allocated funds for 1996/97 unfortunately do not allow the enlargement of the department's establishment in regard to immigration officers. The service simply cannot be rendered at the required level' (Hansard no. 8, 3–7/6/96, col. 2119)

It is dangerous to adopt unimplementable laws and policies

The 'get tough' position on cross-border migration raises the danger of the legitimate authority of the state being undermined. First, this could happen as a result of adopting unimplementable laws – and the experience of the United States government in trying to patrol the border with Mexico must surely be instructive here. Second, it needs to be appreciated that peoples in southern Africa do not necessarily regard an official border as sacrosanct, unlike the case in countries where borders have been established for centuries and more or less coincide with the territories of defined national communities. The notion of border sanctity must not be pushed too far when Changana-Tsonga, Tembe-Tonga, Ndebele, Swazi, South Sotho and Western Sotho or Tswana people have for centuries lived astride the modern South African boundary. Chiefs with subjects on the other side, or families with relatives, would soon come to regard 'the wall' as a target for legitimate protest.

Immigration policy must be consistent with the modest resources South Africa can afford to devote to its administration and policing. These resources should be applied in such a way as to yield the maximum useful effect, rather than being squandered in pursuit of unachievable goals.

South Africa has long borders, and limited resources with which to police them. The decriminalization associated with a more liberal immigration policy would free up policing resources to deal with a real social problem in the form of cross-border crime. Rational administration of a realistic immigration policy requires only modest human resources.

Above all, South African immigration policy should not make implicit promises on which it cannot deliver. An immigration policy which is beyond the state's capacity to enforce it will lead to trouble, not only in the form of official self-delusion but also in the form of stress at the popular level when developments do not meet expectations, and the state yet again is seen to be failing to deal with society's needs.

Policy implication: migration policy should not assume the country has the capacity for elaborate, sophisticated and comprehensive migration control policies modelled on the richest industrial democracies. We do not.

Note

1. Updated figures acquired during a telephone conversation with Roger Rowett, managing director, TEBA, on 22 May 1997.

The implications of CDE's analysis, values and orientation

Now we can briefly consider how the CDE's analytical points of departure relate to the different views about international migration.

With respect to skilled migration into South Africa, it is clear that the CDE analysis points strongly in the direction of opening the country's doors to all the skilled people who want to come here, irrespective of which country they come from. At present the country is losing skilled people, all of whom are desperately needed if we are to achieve our growth and development goals. There are now more opportunities for skilled black South Africans than the education system can meet – this mismatch will expand with increased economic growth. Attempts to restrict immigration from SADC countries seems to be a self-defeating proposition. Skilled people are mobile – they will seek out opportunities wherever they can find them. We need to attract them to stay in southern Africa, not 'imprison' them where they do not want to be, with the effect of encouraging individuals to leave the region. And finally, our analysis points strongly in the direction of reassessing the conventional and formal definition of 'skills' to include people with established informal entrepreneurial skills, appropriate for a developing country.

Turning to unskilled migration, we will comment on the various positions separately. We are uncomfortable with the 'fortress South Africa' position in either of its two variations. At first blush the 'get tough' position seems the obvious approach to adopt. And yet the CDE analysis reveals many considerations that make this a problematic approach: it is unworkable, requires considerably more resources to be devoted to policing and controls, makes many wrong assumptions about the process of migration (its nature, causes and consequences), does not complement but goes against the thrust of the government's macro-economic strategy, focuses official resources and attention on a negative rather than a positive dynamic, criminalizes whole classes of people inside the country, and will probably increase bribery and corruption in the South African system.

The second variant on 'fortress South Africa' argues for an amnesty for everyone inside the country, and then 'getting tough' on any newcomers. This seems at first to be a neat, manageable and fair approach. On reflection, however, it has less appeal as a long-term government policy. This is a stop-gap policy: it makes no headway in sorting out the society's and government's approach to migration generally, and what impact migration has on the economy and other aspects of our society. It provides a mixed message: anyone who has got in up to now can stay, but we do not want any more people. Why?

This approach also assumes South Africa can be effective at stopping more people from coming into the country, and that it is worth spending real and additional resources on attempting to do that. It also ignores the nature of the migration process and the fact that networks develop between the migrants who are here already and their connections back home. Once these kind of networks are established, it is very difficult to prevent additional new migrants from entering the country. To our mind, although we sympathize with the intention behind this approach, we would rather see the country start developing a policy that establishes a clear attitude to migration and its costs and benefits for South Africa; start the process of informing and educating South African society about the nature, reality and contribution that migrants can make; and also start the process of developing a decent information base of the real pressures for migration to South Africa from neighbouring countries.

In summary, then, we would argue against the two variants of the 'fortress South Africa' position. If either is implemented, they would at best fail because of the sheer impossibility of policing South Africa's extensive and remote borders, and at worst will undermine sensible budgetary policy by requiring more and more state finances to be devoted to border controls and the tracking of illegals. Worse still, to the extent that a policy of tight control is successful, it could lead to a ballooning of bribery and corruption on both sides of the border which would further strain South Africa's resources for the maintenance of national safety and security. The spectre of South Africa returning to an era of mass 'pass raids' with all the negative consequences for human rights, relations between police and citizens, and injustices where innocent citizens are mistaken for 'illegals' would be a real threat to the democratic, open, 'good neighbour' nation that the government is trying to build.

'Fortress South Africa' is incompatible with the key components of the government's macro-economic strategy, with its commitment to expanded trade, tourism and general openness to economic forces.

If we now examine the 'open door' positions on migration policy, CDE's analytical conclusions are revealing. Our analysis leads us to oppose the 'humane accommodationist' view that national borders are not really all that important, and that migrants should have the same rights whatever country they come from or were born in. It is not in South Africa's interests (or any other nation's for that matter) to give up on the idea of nation states and the responsibilities of government for promoting the interests of the country's citizens and permanent residents. National interest requires a distinction between citizens, permanent residents and others. These distinctions help countries to define their own interests, their own national policies, and their work to promote them. Trying to do that is not inexorably an attack on the human rights of migrants in the country. We should restrict the word 'refugee' to its original meaning. Trying to stretch this concept too far obscures the real and material difference between a migrant and a refugee, and doing that could have negative consequences for 'real' refugees.

The economic case for free movement is an appealing one, albeit in isolation from other considerations. Our differences with this position concern strategy and not principle. The considerations that have influenced our analysis of this position are political and practical. States should not give up the right to control their own borders, so how movement into the country is regulated or channelled is important. In addition, we would argue that the country has an interest in ensuring that once migrants are in the country they are not a new burden on the state and its limited resources. So conditional or probationary access seems to us to be a preferable approach. No migration policy will be able to work perfectly — there will always be ways in which people can slip through the system. However, it seems essential for citizens of a country to believe that the government is controlling the process of migration, and to have some confidence in how the authorities are managing this phenomenon. This requires a more subtle strategy and leadership from the politicians.

Simply stated, a policy which, for whatever good reason, creates the impression of a total 'open door' to foreigners with no conditions at all, and allows people to play on the spectre of 'millions of foreign people' coming into South Africa and immeasurably adding to the burdens of the state, could produce reactions among the populace which at best will vindicate the tough 'charity begins at home' viewpoint, and at worst will lead to punitive popular reactions against all foreigners and possibly violence. The too hasty introduction of unconditional free movement could result in a situation that sets back mobility and openness in and into South Africa for a long time to come.

A carefully modulated policy mix with the emphasis on the 'open door', but retaining some instruments for control as the first phase of a broader liberalization, is what is most likely to contain optimal benefits for the South African economy and social structure, local citizens, and the surrounding countries of southern and central Africa (see Figure 3).

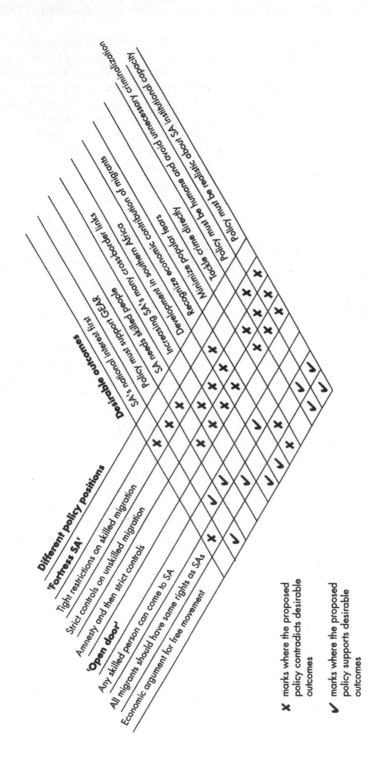

Figure 3 South African migration policy: options and outcomes

CDE's analysis and orientation is clear. We are in favour of migration as a phenomenon. We see many migrants as the risk-takers of their communities, and as people with the drive and need to work hard. This philosophy should apply to rural–urban migration within South Africa and to migration across our borders. South Africa will not become a successful world competitor as a closed, nationalistic, narrow society. Diversity, an openness of spirit and the opportunity to maximize the energy and unforeseen talents of people are required to build a great society and to encourage entrepreneurial growth and development.

This does not mean that an open invitation should be issued to everyone in Africa to migrate to the southern tip. States have a right to secure their borders and keep out undesirables – criminals, vagrants, drug traffickers, gun-runners, cross-border cattle rustlers and so on – and to do this effectively. Security agencies should be doing more to combat the entry of these people in any event. A clear distinction needs to be made between crime control and migration issues. The two overlap, but they are not the same issue. Strict and tough crime control measures should not be mistakenly used as tools of immigration controls. It is important to distinguish between South Africa's national interests and the interests of the region. These are not always synonymous, and it is our view that national interests should predominate in this and other policy areas.

What the analysis does mean is that CDE's approach to migration policy and the individuals whom it most affects is a positive one. In most cases, migrants do not take jobs of local workers (see box, on 'Ghanaians in Durban', page 227). Many migrants will establish small enterprises, and can add to the skills and economic base of our society. We are also short of small-scale entrepreneurs who can create one to two- or ten-person enterprises.

Regional development throughout southern Africa is an important objective in itself. However, we arc dcluding ourselves if we believe that such development will in any way diminish the pressures for migration into South Africa for a very long time to come. Convincing evidence is available of the positive migratory impact of development – it acts as a spur, and provides new opportunities for groups of people to migrate to areas of new opportunities. Thus developments such as the Maputo Corridor are more than likely to increase the flow of migrants into South Africa (particularly Mpumalanga and Gauteng) for the foreseeable future.

The development of a human rights culture is long overdue in South Africa, but it must be remembered that the rights of citizens and of foreigners in a given country are different. A very important ingredient in the development of a South African migration policy has to be firm realism as to the limited institutional capacity and resources of the South African government. The failure of the most powerful government in the world – that of the United States – to halt illegal immigration should be borne in mind. CDE shares deputy president Thabo Mbeki's view (see 'A spectrum of voices', page 203) that deportations as a key instrument of policy are futile. We would go further to argue that they are probably counter-productive, as research shows that they often lead to extended family migration so that someone is always left behind in South Africa to look after the deported person's dwelling and possessions (Reitzes *et al.* 1996).

With respect to the issue of skilled migrants, we are convinced that economic growth in South Africa will require a much greater supply of skilled people than is now available or even on the horizon. In the words of the 1996 report by the National Commission on Higher Education, '[there is a] chronic mismatch between higher education's output and the needs of a modernising economy' (quoted in Cohen, 1997).

Having said all of this, CDE is mindful that the politics of migration policy need to be carefully thought through, and that firm political leadership is required. The politics and perceptions about migration need to be carefully considered and managed. This requires leadership, the integration of migration policy into other facets of government policy, and factual information.

Summary

CDE's analytical points of departure

- South Africa's national interests must come first.
- Migration policy must support and complement the government's macro-economic strategy.
- South Africa needs all the skilled people it can attract.
- South Africa is a nation with many cross-border links, and these create migration pressures.
- Increased development in southern Africa will not stop migration to South Africa.
- We know very little about the scale, nature and possible future trends with respect to immigration to South Africa.
- The economic contribution of migrants must be recognized.
- Migration policy is not just about economics. Political leadership is required to deal with popular fears and misconceptions.
- Crime must be tackled directly, not through migration policy. Illegal immigrants are not a primary cause of social tensions and conflict.
- Immigration policy must be humane and avoid unnecessary criminalization.
- Migration policy must be realistic about South Africa's limited institutional capacity.

Policy implications of CDE's analysis

- South Africans must debate and then decide on a migration policy that promotes this country's national interests.
- Migration policy must be consistent with a more open, trading economy and support maximum economic growth and job creation.
- Migration policy must aim to provide the country with an abundance of skilled people (formal and informal skills).
- Increased economic integration with southern Africa will increase migration pressures.

- Regional development is essential for itself. It is not an effective short-term instrument for controlling migration.
- South Africa urgently requires a thorough and objective process to obtain essential information on migration. Some caution in the policy field is needed in the meanwhile.
- Benefits of migration can outweigh the costs of claims on social services.
- South African public opinion needs educating on the realities of migration. New migration policy must give a lead and make clear choice on the realities and benefits of migration.
- Do not put more resources into migration policy. Target crime (cross-border and domestic crime) directly and put more resources there.
- South Africa has enough real criminals. Migration policy should not condemn − potentially − millions of otherwise law-abiding people as criminals. This will be costly and will undermine attempts to build a new human rights culture in the country.
- Migration policy should not assume the country has the capacity for elaborate, sophisticated and comprehensive migration control policies. We do not.

CDE's proposals[1]

The goal of South Africa's migration policy should be to free up controls on movement in ways that are most consonant with our national interest. South Africa needs high and sustained economic growth, skilled people and entrepreneurs, and a more efficient labour market. Our migration policy must be generous and humane, while strengthening the South African economy rather than being a drain on our resources. It must accommodate regional pressures for migration, while enabling the state to re-establish its control over the process, and enhance its legitimate authority by introducing an effective management system. The policy must be simple, straightforward, easy to communicate and easy to understand.

Circumspection is required for a number of reasons. South Africa lacks reliable data at present about migration pressures and trends from each state in the region. Nobody can say with any precision how large the demand for migration to South Africa actually is. We must also recognize that the country's domestic labour market is characterized by high levels of unemployment, a degree of rigidity with respect to wages in the unionized sector, and the political reality of a relatively strong unionized labour voice. Furthermore, there is a certain fragility to the politics of our new democracy. South Africa in transition suffers from institutional weaknesses. The state is struggling to perform some of its most basic functions, with limited human and material resources. The government's macro-economic strategy must not be undermined by uncontrolled increases in levels of demand for benefits and services.

These considerations lead CDE to advocate the introduction of a two-tiered migration policy. While supporting the goal of free movement in principle, we advocate a more nuanced approach to liberalization for at least the next five years. This involves a differentiated strategy for skilled and unskilled migrants. We support the immediate lifting of all restrictions on skilled migration. Unskilled migrants, on the other hand, should be accepted only from SADC countries, and in order to remain in South Africa must demonstrate that they are able to become economically active, tax-paying and law-abiding residents.

CDE's proposals set out a broad strategic position. Within this framework, the legislative and regulatory details will need to be developed more fully.

This new policy will apply to:

- all potential immigrants from outside the country; and
- all foreigners illegally in South Africa at the time that the policy comes into effect, who will have to apply to the Department of Home Affairs for permission to remain here in terms of conditions applicable to all potential immigrants.
- CDE's proposals do not cover all the different categories of migration. For example, we do not deal with the question of refugees, itinerant traders or oscillating migrant workers. These are important issues which need specific policy attention. CDE's proposals address the central problem of migrants seeking medium- to long-term work and residence in South Africa.

Skilled people

There should be free movement of skilled people from anywhere in the world into South Africa. Skills must be defined broadly, as a combination of qualifications and experience. Opening the doors to skilled migrants immediately removes a major barrier to faster economic growth.

The definition of 'skilled persons' should be expanded to include not only the traditional professional, technical, managerial and investor categories, but also entrepreneurs of all kinds who have some demonstrated skills in the creation and management of either formal or informal enterprises. This approach is appropriate to the circumstances of a developing country, as it recognizes skills in the informal as well as the formal sector. A schedule defining acceptable levels of skill should be established. This can be revised from time to time.

Restrictions on the immigration of skilled people should be lifted with immediate effect. All skilled persons applying to immigrate:

- will be granted permanent residence rights; and
- will qualify for citizenship rights after five years.

Skilled immigrants must become citizens, however, to qualify for any one-off lump sum subsidies from the state, e.g. for land and housing.

Skilled immigrants should be allowed to bring members of their nuclear families (i.e. one spouse, and their children) into the country. If they want to bring in any additional members of their family, they will have to apply for special permission and prove that they have the means to support them.

All applicants and their families will need to provide recent medical certificates indicating their good health.

No one convicted of a serious crime in South Africa or elsewhere will be granted either permanent residence rights or citizenship.

Unskilled people from SADC countries

All unskilled people from SADC countries who apply to migrate to South Africa will be permitted into the country, provided that they register with the Department of Home Affairs and can furnish an address in South Africa. Thereafter, in order to qualify for permanent residence and citizenship they must satisfy a number of requirements at different stages, with different levels of rights.

Level one: trial entry

Two categories of applicants must be distinguished initially, namely persons applying from outside South Africa and illegal aliens inside South Africa at the time when the new policy is implemented.

Applications from outside South Africa

All applicants will be granted temporary work and residence permits for an initial period of six months. This permission will be granted to individuals only, and not to members of their families.

As a condition of entry, applicants must provide the South African authorities with their residential address in South Africa. The authorities must be informed immediately of any change of address, failing which the permit will be withdrawn and the person repatriated.

Applicants must pay a modest fee. The revenue raised will be used to defray part of the costs in cases where repatriation is necessary.

At the end of the six-month period they must provide proof that:

- they are able to support themselves. This will require proof of employment (e.g. an employment contract, a verifiable address for a business, or a savings book) or of their having established a business which is registered with the Inland Revenue Service, to which all tax returns are submitted; and that
- they have a fixed abode.

Persons unable to provide such proof must leave South Africa. They may not apply for re-entry until at least one year has elapsed after they leave the country. Persons who leave South Africa before the six months are up must wait for one year after their departure before applying for re-entry.

All applicants will need to provide recent medical certificates indicating their good health. While in South Africa they will be eligible for basic health care but for no other social services until they qualify for permanent residence.

Persons who falsely declare that they are able to support themselves must be deported, and must wait for two years before applying for re-entry.

No applicant with a criminal record should be granted entry. Persons charged and convicted of serious crimes in South Africa at any time before acquiring citizenship must be deported and prohibited altogether from re-entering the country.

Applications from inside South Africa

Unskilled persons who are illegally inside South Africa at the time when the new policy is introduced must apply to remain here legally. Such permission will be granted on the same terms as for applications from outside the country. Persons who would qualify to enter the country will be granted level one rights, and all subsequent provisions must apply to them.

We assume that many such people will have taken advantage of the amnesty granted in 1996. However, it is important to encourage any people who are inside the country but still outside the legal system to acquire legal status and become part of the official records.

The trial entry period provides powerful incentives for would-be immigrants to follow the legal channels. Once inside the country they have to prove their potential to become productive and support themselves, and they must abide by the law. If they complete this trial period successfully, they are duly rewarded.

Level two: two-year probation

Persons who have provided proof at the end of the initial six-month period that they are able to support themselves and have a fixed abode will be granted permission to remain in South Africa for a further period of two years. In effect, this is a probationary period.

They must provide the South African authorities with their residential address in South Africa. The authorities must be informed of any change of address, failing which the permit will be withdrawn. During this period they will continue to be eligible for basic health care but for no other social services. Persons charged and convicted of serious crimes during this probationary period must be deported and prohibited altogether from re-entering the country.

At the end of the two years, they must again provide proof that they are able to support themselves. This will require proof of employment (i.e.

an employment contract) or of their having established a business which is registered with the South African Revenue Service, to which all tax returns are submitted. Persons who prove that they are able to support themselves will be granted permanent residence rights. Persons unable to provide such proof must leave South Africa. They may not apply for re-entry until at least one year has elapsed after they leave the country. Persons who leave South Africa before the two years are up must wait for one year after their departure before applying for re-entry. Persons who falsely declare that they are able to support themselves must be deported, and must wait for two years before applying for re-entry.

The two-year probationary period requires immigrants to confirm their potential as productive, law-abiding people. They pay taxes, but make minimal claims on the state's social services. If they are successful, they receive the substantial reward of permanent work and residence rights.

Level three: permanent work and residence rights

Persons who have provided proof at the end of the two years that they are able to support themselves, and who have then been granted permanent residence rights, will be allowed to bring members of their nuclear family (i.e. one spouse and their children) into the country. If they want to bring in any additional members of their family, they will have to apply for special permission and prove that they have the means to support them. Members of their families will need to provide recent medical certificates indicating their good health, and must not have a criminal record.

Persons who qualify for permanent residence will have a right to join the queues for all social services, as they are taxpayers and have demonstrated that they are not parasitic on the state. Persons convicted of serious crimes after acquiring permanent residence rights must be deported and prohibited altogether from re-entering the country.

Unskilled immigrants who are granted permanent residence rights will qualify for citizenship rights after three more years, i.e. after five years including the two-year 'probationary' period.

People who have passed their two-year probationary period are contributing to the economy. As law-abiding taxpayers they are entitled to social services. They are an asset to the country and are welcome as immigrants who can duly qualify for citizenship (see box below). They must become citizens, however, in order to qualify for any one-off lump sum subsidies from the state, e.g. for land or housing.

From alien to law-abiding worker and resident

Skilled migrant

Applies for entry

Provides proof of skills
Provides proof of good health
Pays application fee

Permanent residence

Permanent residence granted
Can bring spouse and children

Pays taxes
Must not commit a crime
Eligible for social services

Citizenship

Qualifies after five years

Eligible for one-off lump sum
state subsidies

Unskilled migrant

Applies for entry

Pays application fee
Provides address in SA
Provides proof of good health

Level one – trial entry

Has six months to find work
and accommodation

Provides address in SA
Starts to pay taxes
Eligible for health care only
Must not commit a crime

Level two – two-year probation

Has work and accommodation

Provides address in SA and
pays taxes
Eligible for health care only
Must not commit a crime

Level three – permanent work and residence rights

Has work and accommodation

Provides address in SA and
pays taxes

Permanent residence granted
Can bring spouse and children

Must not commit a crime
Eligible for social services

Citizenship

Qualifies after five years, including
the two-year probationary period

Eligible for one-off lump sum
state subsidies

Illegal aliens

After the introduction of the approach advocated above, anyone within the borders of South Africa:

- who is not a citizen, or
- who does not have a temporary, probationary, or permanent work and residence permit,

will be deemed an illegal alien and thus subject to deportation. Such aliens must be humanely treated, and should have the right of appeal to South African courts. Deportation will disqualify individuals from applying for re-entry to South Africa for a period of two years from the date of their deportation.

The CDE policy is designed to accommodate law-abiding newcomers who can support themselves and become taxpayers. It is a generous policy, but in those cases where people do not qualify to remain in South Africa the state would be justified in taking stern action on economic grounds and to ensure that the law is observed.

Policing and control

Policing and control of South Africa's borders and all entry points into the country must be:

- in line with the principles outlined in this approach; and
- as efficient as possible, subject to available resources.

Controls within South Africa would involve officials of the Department of Home Affairs as well as the police.

One great advantage of the approach we are advocating is that it offers positive incentives for would-be immigrants to follow legal channels and, once they are in South Africa, to operate within the law.

Another advantage is that the system of control within the country then becomes focused primarily on specific individuals, with names and addresses, rather than a mass of nameless and faceless people whose existence can only be guessed at. Under the new system it will be easier to track down defaulters who fail to report back as required. This is very different from unacceptable mass 'pass raids'.

National database

A national computerized database on all matters relating to immigrants, their applications, status, and personal records is essential to this policy. An appropriate system will have to be designed and set up before the new immigration policy is implemented.

In the ordinary course of their operation, the procedures required by the new policy would feed reliable information into the national database, covering the vast majority of people intent on migrating to South Africa. The policy is designed to:

- encourage potential migrants to apply for legal entry into South Africa; and to
- establish a process to monitor and keep track of them once they are in the country.

Monitoring and evaluating immigration policy

CDE's proposals establish procedures which would go a long way towards remedying the grave lack of information about migration patterns which we have noted.

The data collected in this way will:

- determine the scale of the demand to migrate to South Africa in general, and from particular countries;
- track migrants' performance in the labour market, and the broader economy; and
- provide a reliable basis for a thorough review of the migration policy package which should be undertaken after five years, to evaluate and assess its results.

The process of data collection must be amplified by additional research on:

- the social and economic impact of migrants on South Africa's regions, cities and towns; and
- the numbers of people estimated still to be bypassing this system for channelling legal migrants into South Africa.

Communication and training

An effective and sustained campaign must be mounted to communicate the nature and purpose of this policy to:

- the media;
- neighbouring countries and potential migrants;
- the people of South Africa; and
- officials and police who will be involved in administering the policy.

Before the new policy is implemented, the police and all officials concerned must be given appropriate training in its administration.

Leadership

Political leadership is crucial to this policy's success. Political leaders must:

- inform the public about how the country can benefit from newcomers;
- stress the need for migration to stimulate economic growth;
- communicate the difficulty and costs of trying to stop migration;
- explain that migrants will have to obey the laws, support themselves and pay taxes;
- educate South Africans about the inevitability of increased migration;
- ensure that the public debate is about facts rather than speculation unsupported by evidence, or rumours and myths.

The politics of migration revolves around an exceptionally sensitive set of issues. We have set out a straightforward policy, which can be supported with strongly reasoned arguments. Its essential features are simple and easy to understand. Political leaders will be able to put forward this policy with confidence, knowing that they can make a sound and coherent case.

Summary of proposals

The policy proposed by CDE:

- is simple, easy to understand and easy to communicate;
- involves a two-tier approach, distinguishing between skilled and unskilled migrants;
- welcomes all skilled migrants for the economic contribution they can make immediately;
- gives unskilled migrants six months to prove that they can find or make work to support themselves;
- requires those who succeed in doing so to serve a further two-year probationary period;
- rewards them with permanent work and residence rights when they complete the probation successfully;
- provides powerful incentives for all migrants to go through the legal channels;
- requires them to abide by the laws of the land;
- ensures that they are contributing to the economy and paying taxes before they qualify for social services; and
- provides a coherent and consistent route for acquiring citizenship.

The policy provides real incentives for migrants to enter the country legally, register with the authorities, become economically productive, and observe the laws. It establishes a framework which offers the best prospects for the effective management and control of immigration.

CDE's policy package is designed to stimulate economic growth and strengthen the economy by enlarging the pool of skilled people and entrepreneurs, and by promoting a more efficient labour market. Our proposals accommodate regional pressures for migration while limiting claims on public resources until immigrants have demonstrated their capacity to make a contribution to the country. The proposed system encourages people to register as taxpayers, and rewards those who observe the laws of the land. It enhances the state's authority by introducing a manageable system of controls, which are also in accordance with democratic values.

This policy is based upon the recognition of real interests. It is also generous and humane. No doubt some will criticize CDE's proposals as being altogether too lenient. But if those critics object to the presence in this country of people who bring skills with them, who are able to support themselves, who pay their taxes and who abide by our laws, then they object to them simply because they are foreigners. We do not believe that such objections are valid.

Others again might think that CDE's proposals still entail too many controls and restrictions. To this we would say that if we open the door to all who believe they can find or create work in this country, it is surely reasonable to require them to show that they can do so.

The policy proposed by CDE builds on international experience and on South Africa's own experience. We believe it is in South Africa's best interests. We also believe it is a policy which South Africa has the capacity to implement.

Institutional capacity and CDE's proposals

Does South Africa have the administrative capacity to implement even CDE's modest approach to migration policy?

The CDE proposals will require:

- a significant initial investment in a national and international system of computerized record-keeping;
- thorough training of personnel;
- proper communication of the new policy in all its dimensions;
- an effective link-up between the registration and monitoring of the policy and the policing of individuals who do not report to the authorities when required;
- efforts by national political leaders to explain and sell the new policy to citizens;
- monitoring and evaluating the impact of the new policy;
- a process of accumulating reliable and comprehensive national data on migration processes.

We believe it is possible for South Africa to implement such a policy, current constraints notwithstanding. In order to do so, the government should enlist the co-operation of the private sector and civil society to establish the necessary capacity. The redeployment of civil servants will be required, and the policy will have to be phased in.

Note

1. The assistance of Professor Douglas Irvine, senior associate at CDE, in drafting these proposals is acknowledged.

Draft Green Paper on international migration: executive summary

On 30 May 1997, the South African Department of Home Affairs published a draft Green Paper on international migration in the *Government Gazette*. The document was prepared by a task team consisting of Dr Wilmot James (chair), Prof M. Hough, Dr E. Kornegay, Prof K. Oosthuizen, Z. Mbeki, Molefe S. Molefe, J. Sindane, Dr G.S. Sibiya, and J.E. Pokroy. An executive summary was provided, which read as follows:

There are three streams of people crossing our borders. The first are immigrants, individuals who would like to settle here permanently. We recommend the introduction of a labour market-based point system by which South Africa can pro-actively recruit immigrants with the skills, expertise and resources to make a contribution to the development of our country. The point system will replace the current apparatus, including the Immigrants Selection Board.

The second stream are refugees, people who flee persecution in their own country and seek asylum here. Presently, South Africa is not a recipient of large numbers of refugees. We recommend a system of refugee protection that is simple, practical and manageable. We also believe that the burden of refugee protection in South Africa should be shared with other SADC member states, and should therefore not be our responsibility alone.

The third and most controversial stream of people are migrants, many of whom are not authorised to be here. We believe that the problem of un-authorised migration should in part be dealt with by giving bona fide economic migrants from other SADC countries, who have no intention of settling here permanently, increased opportunities for legal participation in our labour market.

The other side to the solution is to introduce more effective but rights-based enforcement of new immigration policy. Based on the constitution and the bill of rights, we believe that government action should be restrained in favour of the rights of unauthorised migrants. This includes due process, administration review, and the right to information. Enforcement should be made effective within this framework, requiring a transformed Department of Home Affairs.

We recommend that the management of a point-based immigration system, the development of a plan for temporary SADC migrant access to South Africa's labour market and for rights-based enforcement should reside within the Department of Home Affairs. We further believe that the department should undertake a transformation process, such that it has the proper staffing levels, expertise and professionalism to deliver citizenship, migration, refugee and immigration services to the public.

It should be pointed out that until there is greater economic parity in the SADC region, we believe it is premature to agree to any proposal to open up our borders, i.e. to have a free movement of persons. We do believe that migration and immigration can be managed and regulated properly but flexibly, in the interests firstly of South Africa but also in the interests of our partner states in the SADC region.

Response to the draft Green Paper on international migration

Centre for Development and Enterprise, June 1997

The draft Green Paper on international migration was published by the Department of Home Affairs for information and comment on 30 May 1997. An invitation was extended to interested parties to submit comments by 30 June 1997.

CDE has just completed a major study of cross-border migration, both internationally and in South Africa, with a view to contributing to the debate on an appropriate international migration policy for South Africa. As an interested party, in the sense of having investigated the phenomenon at issue in considerable depth, we wish to submit the comments that follow, as well as the more detailed reports on the study on which they were based, for consideration during further development of policy in this vital field.

These comments are in effect a summary of CDE's major reactions to the draft Green Paper, and if it is considered appropriate, CDE would be happy to make a verbal presentation in support of this response.

Note: the comments that follow deal only with migration policy and not with refugee policy. Refugee policy is a special field, and CDE has not considered this aspect of policy on cross-border movement as deeply as the more general aspects of formal and informal migration across South Africa's borders.

1. The general approach to cross-border migration in the draft Green Paper

CDE fully endorses the implicit point of departure of the draft Green Paper that the interests of South Africa and of South Africans should be paramount in any policy approach to cross-border migration. As will be pointed out below, however, the interests of South Africa are not necessarily well served by policies which take a short-term view of the impact and consequences of migration, and propose measures which will cost more than the beneficial effects which can realistically be achieved.

If it were possible, on a sustainable basis, to exclude illegal cross-border migrants within the fiscal constraints imposed by the macro-economic policy (GEAR), and by competing priorities of utmost urgency, such as strengthening the safety and security agencies, there might be some justification for a policy of tough deterrence and tight controls, such as that recently proposed by the Department of Home Affairs and also implied in some respects in the draft Green Paper. However, as we explain in due course, the effective implementation of a restrictive policy or a policy which assumes a significant expansion of administrative capacity does not seem possible with current resource constraints and the likelihood of mounting pressure on our long and porous borders.

CDE welcomes other aspects of the general orientation to cross-border migration as contained in the draft Green Paper, and the following in particular:

- It correctly rejects an approach to the protection of work opportunities for South African citizens which views the labour market as a cake of fixed size, in which the acquisition of work by foreigners would amount to a net loss of opportunity to local job-seekers. CDE welcomes the fact that the draft sees the potential for migrants to help in expanding the cake and in making a contribution to the growth of opportunity for all.
- In a similar vein, it recognizes the salience of the shortage of skills in South Africa and the fact that appropriate migration policies, by alleviating certain of the skills deficits, can contribute to more dynamic growth in the country.
- It accepts in principle the fact that the economic prosperity of the SADC region will ultimately be promoted by the free movement of capital, goods and labour across the borders.
- The draft makes a convincing case for the official treatment of migrants within the limitations and prescriptions of the South African bill of rights and subject to the requirements of due process. It correctly identifies many current aspects of the treatment of migrants as lacking in transparency and accountability and as allowing too much ministerial and departmental discretion in the way individuals are dealt with.

Because of the prominence of these essential principles and points of departure in the draft Green Paper, one might have expected concrete policy proposals consistent with them. This, however, is not always the case. While the draft takes us part of the way to a resolution of current policy dilemmas, it falls short of satisfactory guidelines in certain critical respects.

CDE believes that certain central proposals in the draft will result in policies and regulations which will be counter-productive, impossible to implement, which will perpetuate costs and penalties for the economy and which will negate some of the very principles on which the draft green paper is based.

The points of comment below identify some of the major disadvantages of the proposals as CDE assesses the situation on the basis of its own research.

2. Problematic aspects of the proposals in the draft Green Paper

2.1   In the draft, it is argued that the current disparities in wealth between countries in southern Africa make a liberalization of migration policy which would accord with the principles of GEAR and with the promise of an open regional economy impossible at this stage. It argues in passing that the response of South Africa should be to contribute to the economic revival and development of the region with a view to making some eventual liberalization of the movement of labour possible.

CDE would contest this approach, on two grounds. First, *while development assistance to countries in the region is to be recommended as a good thing under any circumstances,* the notion that South Africa could make a sufficient contribution, while necessarily pursuing its own more rapid growth, to lead to a meaningful *reduction in disparities* in the foreseeable future, is very optimistic indeed. Unless the countries of southern Africa were to adopt uniformly good economic policies and South Africa bad economic policies, wide disparities in levels of welfare will persist for several decades. Sound policies on cross-border migration cannot be delayed for this length of time.

Second, as CDE points out on the basis of international research, development assistance in the short run tends to increase the propensity of the citizens of the developing country to migrate, firstly because the development raises expectations, and secondly because the citizens have more resources for travelling.

Hence, while development assistance to other countries in southern Africa has to be strongly endorsed, it will most certainly not have effects sufficiently quickly to reduce the relative attractiveness of South Africa within a meaningful time scale. To link migration policy to a long-range regional economic strategy is misplaced.

2.2 Although the draft accepts in principle that migration does not reduce job opportunities in the host country, it fails to carry this principle through to its policy proposals in all respects. The draft states that 'Unregulated access ... could lead to unacceptable competition for jobs' (1.4.7: 16). Leaving aside the issue of political viability which is complex and requires much more analysis than the draft accords it, 'unacceptable competition for jobs' sounds very much like the zero-sum economic argument which the draft explicitly rejects. This lack of logical consistency is not at all helpful in formulating policy.

CDE is able to refer to convincing evidence from the United States, where the disparities between that country and Latin America are just as great as those which exist in southern Africa, to the effect that no convincing proof exists that Mexican or other migrants have taken jobs away from native Americans – in fact, their relatively cheaper labour has stimulated the economy in certain sectors, thereby creating growth in employment for US citizens. The same would apply in South Africa.

At present most of the occupations which the unregistered cross-border migrants take are not the kind of jobs to which unemployed South Africans aspire. Therefore, there is much less competition for employment between migrants and South African citizens than is commonly assumed. If effective competition existed there would in fact be much less of a demand for foreign migrant labour in certain occupations than is manifestly the case. Given that migrants accept work which is unpopular among South Africans, the presence of the migrants is of benefit to the economy in certain sectors and on aggregate serves to add jobs to the South African employment market.

2.3 The draft correctly identifies the inherent discrimination in the present arrangements in terms of which contracts with sending countries are entered into and exemptions granted for annual quotas of *male* migrant contract workers from neighbouring states to work on the mines and in commercial agriculture in certain provinces. It proposes in effect to extend this system to include women and sectors other than mining and agriculture, and to fix general quotas for several Southern African countries.

Extended and rationalized or not, such a system would in essence remain a *migrant contract labour system* in which the initiative would remain with employers to justify requests for cross-border labour. The system would have the same deleterious effects on family life as migrant contract labour at present, and would also amount to bureaucratic control over regional labour allocation. It is also not in keeping with the emphasis given in the document to the need for consistency with provisions of the bill of rights.

The system proposed in the draft Green Paper would ensure the continuation of a segregated or dualistic labour market since the formal contracts would ensure that the work-status of first entry would have to be maintained. This will in fact introduce rigidities into the labour market at the very time that attempts are being made to make the labour market more flexible.

2.4.   In making the proposal that there be fixed and regulated quotas for migrant workers from surrounding states, the draft assures the readers that the intention will be simply to regulate *temporary* migration. Permits are also recommended for temporary cross-border migration for small traders, students and family visits.

One of the motivations in allowing temporary work permits and other means of regulated access on a temporary basis appears to be a trust in the effectiveness of 'safety valves'. The logic would be that in allowing temporary access to migrant contract work, the pressure for illegal migration would be reduced.

CDE accepts that this sounds plausible, but would argue very firmly that the effects will be precisely the opposite. Once in South Africa, the temporary migrant workers or traders establish *social networks* and domestic bases, which in turn become a magnet or a convenient focus for *additional and unregulated migration* by family members and members of home community networks. Illegal migrants the world over seldom travel to places that are completely strange to them — they travel to places where they will be offered shelter, advice and food until they are able to establish some kind of activity on their own. The notion of the 'safety valve' has utility in mechanics but not in the type of social behaviour at issue here.

It is worth recalling that the discredited policy of influx control had its 'safety valves' in the form of Section 10 exemptions, but it was honoured more in the breach than in conformity to the legal prescriptions. The state gradually lost control of infringements, and in the process 'criminalized' millions of determined illegal work-seekers to no good effect at all.

2.5   The draft shows admirable sensitivity in stating that it would not wish to support policies which would 'raid' neighbouring states of their skilled populations. CDE is sympathetic to the sentiments expressed but would argue that in some cases, unless the people involved have opportunities for mobility within the region, they are likely to leave the region or Africa altogether, which would be a loss not only for the country involved but for southern Africa as a whole.

Furthermore, CDE believes migration policy in South Africa should not encourage neighbouring states in their attempts to control the choices of individuals in their labour markets. Productive labour forces are labour forces in which individuals can exercise choices. All of Southern Africa must aim at achieving situations in which skills are retained and attracted on the basis of choice and preference.

2.6   CDE supports the argument made in sections of the draft to the effect that many if not most migrants from the southern African region do not want to migrate permanently. It is regrettable, however, that the evidence on which these arguments are based is not adequately referenced. On pages 22, 24 and 28, readers are referred to SAMP research or to 'research', which seem to cover very vital issues, but no means of gaining access to such vital insights are provided.

As regards the policy implications of such research, CDE finds the conclusions drawn somewhat confusing. If it is true that most cross-border migrants do not want to stay in South Africa on a permanent basis, why is it necessary to have an elaborate system of temporary migrant work quotas to secure it?

2.7   The proposals in the draft relating to skilled migration are less problematic in some respects, but even they fall short of accepting the points of departure on which they are claimed to be based. The draft states a commitment to the macro-economic strategy GEAR, which, *inter alia* includes the goal of achieving optimal *labour market flexibility*.

Yet when it comes to making recommendations as regards the entry of skilled persons, the suggested provisions are for an elaborate system of occupational categorization of the South African labour market to be undertaken by the Department of Labour. A points-based assessment of immigrants will be established based on such a categorization. This hardly sounds like labour market flexibility.

The kind and quality of occupational information on which a valid points-based system could be built will be very difficult and costly to assemble. Even the latest population census, when its full results are eventually available, will not allow the refined differentiation between grades and types of skills that will be sensitive to employer needs. Any system which requires elaborate information will not only be very costly to establish and maintain but will inevitably lead to distortions in the allocation of skills in the labour market. It is most unlikely to function better than a system which simply requires the would-be immigrants to describe their qualifications and skills and provide proof that their skills were useful in an economic and vocational sense in their country of origin.

CDE would also argue, for example, that the craft skills of an Indian goldsmith, the metal casting skills of a West African bronze artist, the acquired skills of a formally untrained computer-graphics expert from Croatia, a Chinese herbalist or of an experienced carpet merchant from Lebanon are unlikely to be adequately identified in a categorization of skilled occupations by any government department. Labour market flexibility requires simplicity of categorization based on the demonstrated value of skills on a case by case basis.

It is very likely that the provisions for bureaucratic prescription of skills required by the economy will discourage recognition of less-formal accomplishments, particularly of abilities in small-scale entrepreneurship. Such skills are not always associated with formally recognized training. South Africa will have to develop new sectors of enterprise, particularly in fields like small-scale production as well as 'cultural' production for tourist markets, and these skills are not the types of skills listed in gradings of occupations. CDE would argue that the would-be immigrants and their occupational track records should speak for themselves!

2.8. *CDE's greatest concern with the proposals lies in the feasibility of their implementation* by the proposed Department of Citizenship and Immigration Services (DCIS). This department, *simultaneously*, will have to transform itself, establish an elaborate categorization of the skills required in the labour market, regulate the migrant worker quotas, sanction employers who employ unregistered cross-border workers, apply a points-based system of skilled immigration, control the informal immigration of non-SADC migrants and, most onerous of all, attempt to curb the entry of large numbers of unregistered SADC migrants whose entry will be facilitated by the new social and home community networks that the expanded migrant labour system will create.

In fairness, it is proposed that the service be strengthened by the addition of a new directorate in charge of a force of migration officers. But where will these people be recruited from, when most of the existing 'inspectorates' in the public sector like health, customs and excise, the revenue service, not to mention the South African Police Service, are all seriously understaffed and find it very difficult to attract recruits with the required skills and aptitudes?

CDE accepts that the system proposed may improve over time, but the initial requirement of recruitment and training, and the establishment of the required information systems will inevitably mean a slow start. Hence in the initial two to three years an accumulation of unregistered persons will occur which will mean that as it gets ready to implement the new policies, the new service will have to surmount a 'hump' of illegality and devote its resources to crisis management. In other words, a situation very akin to that facing the new police service will probably arise. And the proposed expansion of controls and administration will have to occur at a time when the macro-economic strategy, GEAR, requires a *reduction* of public sector personnel. CDE, therefore, cannot see how the proposals could be viable in the short to medium term.

3. Suggested alternatives

On the basis of its examination of the situation, CDE has identified some key requirements that new policies relating to cross-border migration have to fulfil. These requirements and alternative policy proposals are set out in full in the policy document, *People on the Move: A New Approach to Cross-border Migration in South Africa*. Briefly summarized, the requirements are as follows:

Unskilled migration from SADC states

3.1 Any policy has to address the national interest first and foremost. The national interest, however, has to be approached in a broader context than that dictated by any single issue. Hence, CDE believes that one of the issues most critical to the national interest is that the government counter the all too pervasive image that it cannot administer some of its most important policies. *An image of ungovernability is perhaps the most costly penalty that a country seeking to build economic and investor confidence can pay.*

For this reason, one simply cannot risk a situation in which a failure to get to grips with unregistered cross-border migration will strengthen the image already created by the 'grey economy', tax evasion, crime and non-payment of service charges.

3.2 It is also necessary to minimize the costs of controlling and administering cross-border migration, and maximizing the economic benefits which the migrants bring to South Africa. The policies which are adopted should be within the existing capacity of the Department of Home Affairs, with a modest upgrading of its information and control systems.

With these considerations in mind, CDE has proposed an approach to cross-border migration which will actually encourage the SADC migrants to register themselves. It does involve quite considerable liberalization of the controls on these migrants (as opposed to unskilled non-SADC immigrants).

The proposal, very briefly, is that all unskilled SADC citizens be allowed to register as work-seekers and potential immigrants *provided* they pay a small fee and furnish full contact details, which they will be required to update in the case of changes in circumstances. Hence the names and details will be captured on a formal registry and the migrants will be traceable if they default.

In return for this formalization of their status, they will go through two successive periods of 'probation' in which they will have to prove that they can support themselves, pay all taxes and rates due and, in short, demonstrate that they can contribute meaningfully to the South African economy and not become dependent on the state.

The costs of this liberalization will no doubt be a significant increase in the numbers of *legal* immigrants, and these migrants will be perceived (wrongly in our view) to be competing with South Africans for jobs. The proposals allow, however, for only the very minimum access to state services until a period of five years has elapsed when successful migrants will achieve South African citizenship.

Against the costs of this increase in legal immigration, one has to weigh the following:

- It will be in the migrants' interests to play according to the rules of the game and therefore the government will regain control of a substantial proportion of migration. The government will therefore be able to concentrate its scarce resources on a smaller number of unskilled 'illegals', mainly from countries other than the SADC states.
- As the draft Green Paper itself concedes, impact of the cross-border migrants on the job opportunities of South Africans is substantially overestimated, as is the contribution of SADC migrants to crime.
- As the draft Green Paper also acknowledges, by no means all the registered migrants will stay permanently; most will choose to retire to their home countries, and the freedom of economic opportunity while in South Africa will speed up the rate at which they are able to accumulate sufficient resources on which to retire.
- It is clearly evident that most cross-border migrants find some form of occupation, and prominent among the occupations is trading with their home countries. The net effect of the addition of a large number of legal cross-border migrants will be to expand the number of economically active persons in relation to the total population and actually *reduce* the levels of dependency on the state and rate of unemployment as measured against all economically active persons.
- There may be fears among trade unions that the cross-border migrants will undercut the wage rates of local unionized labour. However, the provisions for institutional and central bargaining in the Labour Relations Act seem to reduce this danger quite significantly.

Hence the costs, in CDE's view, are much more modest than is conventionally assumed, and considerably lower than the costs for the country and the economy of a perceived breakdown in the implementation of legislation.

Skilled migration from anywhere in the world

The major reason for encouraging the immigration of skilled people is the economic resources they import in the form of skills, networks and in some cases investment capital. This is fully acknowledged in the draft Green Paper.

As with most economic inputs and factors of production, the market is the best way of allocating resources. For this reason CDE would avoid a points-based system, because, as we have indicated, the current state of occupational and economic information is such that critical distortions in supply and demand are bound to be caused by any system based on available official databases. In particular, as we have said, the field of self-employment and entrepreneurship would be particularly badly served by a points system based on available occupational data.

For this reason CDE is in favour of broadening the definition of skills to make sure that it includes most forms of small-scale entrepreneurship, and allows anyone with the minimum level of defined skills to enter the country.

No doubt there will be an oversupply of some skills as a result, but the whole point about skills is that people who have them are more likely to be able to *create their own work* and stimulate a demand for their skills than is the case among unskilled people. This applies even to the much maligned fields of arts, literature and social science.

The main point, however, is that a policy along these lines will be very simple to administer and as such will be very cost effective, thoroughly in line with the GEAR proposals.

The comparisons between the capacity and other implications of the draft Green Paper proposals and those of CDE are worth contemplating (see Table 18).

Table 18   Green Paper and CDE proposals compared

Draft Green Paper	*CDE*
Skilled migration	
Establishing and maintaining a sophisticated occupational database and keeping it compatible with the country's changing skills requirements	Allow in skilled workers from anywhere in the world
Administering a points-based skilled worker entry control system	Only requirement is proof of skills/experience beyond minimum level (specified in simple schedule)
Setting annual targets and quotas	–
Distinguish between SADC and non-SADC skilled migrants	–
Unskilled migration	
Distinguish between people from SADC and other countries	Distinguish between people from SADC and other countries
Setting annual targets and quotas	Name and address list of all probationary entrants
Domestic employers must demonstrate their need to employ SADC citizens	Policing the entry of far fewer SADC unskilled migrants and non-SADC unskilled and repatriating them
Social partners in South Africa to negotiate industry-specific quotas	Monitoring and granting rights to those registered migrants who meet the progressive requirements
Distinguish between employers who are observing minimum employment standards and employ South Africans and those who do not	Mainly individualized approach to controls inside South Africa of those who fail to comply with simple requirements for residence rights
Establishing and administering an expanded system of labour contracts which at present is privately administered for the mining industry	Feasible within current budgetary constraints
Policing the illegal entry of large numbers of SADC and other cross-border migrants and repatriating them	–
Mass old-style 'pass raids' of nameless, faceless 'illegals'	–
Create a new, professionally trained cadre of immigration officers	–
Immediately requires more money and resources	–

4. A comment on the political leadership required of sound migration policy

At the time of preparing these comments, yet another survey has appeared in which large majorities of South Africans of all races appear to support tougher action to exclude illegal migrants from South Africa. This comes as no surprise to us since we have conducted such surveys ourselves.

These results should be seen in the following light. Unemployment is today perceived to be the greatest single problem facing government in South Africa among all groups. When ordinary people are asked about illegal migration an immediate negative response is triggered by first, its definition as something *illegal* (no one is inclined to support illegality of any kind) and second, its popular association with competition for jobs.

We can, however, point to surveys in which tough action against illegal immigrants is compared with other priorities for government action, and the remarkable finding is that the former does *not* emerge among the highest priorities. Negative responses to illegal immigration are easy to demonstrate simply because it is the most *obvious* type of answer to give if one does not have sufficient information to understand the problem in its context.

CDE acknowledges that, like the GEAR strategy itself, a liberalization of controls on in-migration will not be immediately popular, but if political leaders are prepared to spend some effort in pointing out the complexities of the problem, as we have discussed above, we are convinced that opposition to such liberalization will begin to abate. The government is having to do precisely this with its macro-economic strategy, and there is no reason why it should not do the same in the case of cross-border migration from SADC states.

The penalty for not grasping this nettle will most certainly be a policy high on good intentions but very low on implementability. This will simply deepen the government's problems in facing its stakeholders and constituencies.

CDE's alternative proposals go further than measures to avoid wasting precious fiscal resources on cost-inefficient policies. In an important sense, CDE proposes that South Africa use the skills, economic benefits and labour resources which migrants can bring. Our proposals will encourage migrants to register their status and domiciles. This in turn would facilitate the reestablishment of legitimate control by the government. This, we believe, is the most which can be achieved in pursuit of our national interests.

Note

By February 1998 the South African government had not yet responded to the Green Paper, or responses to it by CDE or any other parties. Doubts were being expressed that any policy movement would take place prior to the country's second inclusive democratic election, scheduled for 1999.

Bibliography

Abadan-Unat, N., Leles, R., Penninx, R., van Renselaar, H., van Vlezen, L. and Yenisey, L. (1976) *Migration and Development: A Study of the Effects of International Labour Migration on Bogaziliyan District*. Ankara: Ajams-Turk Press.

Abowd, J. and Freeman, R.B. (eds) (1991) *Immigration, Trade and the Labour Market*. Chicago: University of Chicago Press for the National Bureau of Economic Research.

Acevedo, D. and Espenshade, T. (1991) 'Implications of a NAFTA for Mexican migration into the United States' *Population and Development Review*, **18**(4), December, pp. 729–44.

Adelman, H. and Sorensen, J. (1994) *African Refugees: Development and Repatriation*. Boulder: CO, Westview Press.

Adler, S. (1981) *A Turkish Conundrum: Emigration, Politics and Development, 1961–1980*. Geneva: ILO.

Africa Group Geneva (1990) Refugees and migration flow in Africa. Paper presented by the African Group in Geneva to the UNHCR Working Group on Protection and Solutions. Geneva: UNHCR.

Akerman, S. (1976) 'Theories and methods of migration research'. In H. Rundblom and H. Norman (eds), *From Sweden to America*. Minneapolis: University of Minnesota Press.

Alarcon, R. (1992) 'Norteización: self-perpetuating migration from a Mexican town'. In J. Bustamante, C. Reynolds and R. Hinojosa-Ojeda (eds), *U.S.–Mexican Relations: Labour Market Interdependence*. Stanford, CA: Stanford University Press.

Alba, F. (1978) 'Mexico's international migration as a manifestation of a development pattern', *International Migration Review*, **12**, Winter, 502–13.

Alba, F. (1992) Migrant labour supply and demand in Mexico and the United States: a global perspective. In J. Bustamante, C. Reynolds and R. Hinojosa-Ojeda (eds), *U.S.–Mexican Relations: Labour Market Interdependence*. Stanford, CA: Stanford University Press.

Angley, J. (1989) 'Australia's new migrant selection system'. Background paper, Legislative Research Service. Canberra: Department of the Parliamentary Library.

Appleyard, R. (1989) 'Migration and development: myths and reality', *International Migration Review*, **23**(3), Fall, 486–99.

(1992) 'Migration and development: a critical relationship', *Asian and Pacific Migration Journal*, **1**(1), 1–12.

Arboleda, E. (1991) 'Refugee definition in Africa and Latin America: The lesson of pragmatism', *International Journal of Refugee Law*, **3**(2), 185–207.

Archdeacon, T. (1983) *Becoming American: An Ethnic History*. New York: Free Press.

Ascencio, F. (1993) *Bringing It Back Home: Remittances to Mexico from Migrant Workers in the United States*. La Jolla, CA: UCSD Centre for U.S.–Mexican Studies.

Asch, B. (ed.) (1994) *Emigration and its Effects on the Sending Country*. Santa Monica, CA: Rand.

Australian Population Council (1977) *Immigration Policies and Australia's Population: A Green Paper*. Australian Government Printing Service.

Azizah, K. (1991) 'Recruitment and employment of Indonesian workers: problems and major policy issues'. Kuala Lumpur: ILO.

Bach, R. and Meissner, D. (1990) *America's Labour Market in the 1990s: What role should immigration play?* Washington: Carnegie.

Banerjee, B. and Kanbur, S.M.R. (1981) 'On the specification and estimation of macro rural-urban migration functions, with an application to Indian data', *Oxford Bulletin of Economics and Statistics*, **43**, February, 7–29.

Bean, F., Edmonston, B. and Passel, J. (eds) (1990) *Undocumented Migration to the United States: IRCA and the experience of the 1980s*. Washington: The Urban Institute Press.

Bean, F., Schmandt, J. and Weintraub, S. (eds) (1989) *Mexican and Central American Population and U.S. Immigration Policy*. Austin: Centre for Mexican American Studies, University of Texas.

Bean, F.D. and Fix, M. (1992). 'The significance of recent immigration policy reforms in the United States'. In G.P. Freeman J. and Jupp (eds), *Nations of Immigrants: Australia, the United States, and International Migration*. Melbourne and New York: Oxford University Press.

Bendix, Reinhard (1978) *Kings or People: Power and the Mandate to Rule*. Berkeley CA: University of California.

Berg, A. (1992) 'The importance of the skill component'. In *Proceedings of the Second National Immigration Outlook Conference*, Sydney, 11–13 November.

Bernstein, A. (1985) 'Influx control in South Africa: an international and empirical view'. In H. Giliomee and L. Schlemmer (eds), *Up Against the Fences*. Cape Town: David Philip.

Birrell, B. (1994a) 'The scale and consequences of professional migration movement to Australia since 1983'. Draft paper presented at a Workshop on Mobility in Australia.

(1994b) 'The 1994–95 Immigration Program', *People and Place*, **2**(2), 40–6.

(1990) *The Chains that Bind: Family Reunion Migration to Australia in the 1980s*. Canberra: Bureau of Immigration Research.

Birrell, B., Healy, E. and Smith, T.F. (1992) 'Migrant selection during the recession'. Background Paper No. 3, Legislative Research Service. Canberra: The Department of the Parliamentary Library.

(1992) 'The impact of recession on the recently arrived migrant workforce'. In *Proceedings of the Second National Immigration Outlook Conference*, Sydney, 11–13 November.

(1993) 'Recent Canadian immigration developments'. *People and Place*, **1**(1), 27–30.

Birrell, R. (1994) 'Immigration Control in Australia', *The Annals of the American Academy of Political and Social Science*, **534**, 106–17.

Blay, Sam, and Andreas Zimmerman. (1994) 'Recent Changes in German Refugee Law', *American Journal of International Law*, **88**(2).

Böhning, W.R. (1972) *The Migration of Workers in the United Kingdom and the European Community*. Oxford: Oxford University Press for the Institute of Race Relations.

(1984) *Studies in International Labour Migration*. London: Macmillan.

Böhning W.R. and M. Schloeter-Paredes (1993) *Economic Haven or Political Refugees: Can Aid Reduce the Need for Migration?* Geneva: Proceedings of a May 1992 ILO-UNHCR Conference.

(eds.) (1994) *Aid in Place of Migration?* Geneva: International Labour Office.

Böhning W.R. and J. Werquin (1990) *Some Economic, Social, and Human Rights Considerations concerning the Future Status of the Third-Country Nationals in the Single European Market*. Geneva: International Labor Office.

Borjas, G. (1988) *International Differences in the Labour Market Performance of Immigrants*. Kalamazoo. MI: W.E. Upjohn Institute.

(1989) 'Economic Theory and International Migration', *International Migration Review*, **23**(3), 457–85.

(1990) *Friends or Strangers: The Impact of Immigration on the U.S. Economy*. New York: Basic Books.

(1994) 'The Economics of Immigration', *Journal of Economic Literature*, **32** (December), 1667–717.

Boudahrain, A. (1985) *Nouvel Ordre Social International et Migrations*. Paris: L'Harmattan.

Briggs V.M. Jr. (1984) *Immigration Policy and the American Labour Force*. Baltimore: Johns Hopkins.

(1992) *Mass Immigration and the National Interest*. New York: M.E. Sharpe.

Burstein, M. (1992) 'Immigration Management Control and Policy Concerns'. Paper presented at a Conference at York University (March).

Bustamante, J., Reynolds, C. and Hinojosa-Ojeda, R. (eds) (1992) *U.S. Mexican Relations: Labour Market Interdependence*. Stanford CA: Stanford University Press.

California Senate (1961) 'California's Farm Labour Problems: Part 1'. Senate Fact Finding Committee on Labour and Welfare.

Callaghy, T.M. (ed.) (1983) *South Africa in Southern Africa: The Intensifying Vortex of Violence*. New York: Praeger.

(1986) 'The State as Lame Leviathan: The Patrimonial Administrative State in Africa' in Zaki Ergas (ed.), *The African State in Transition*. New York: Macmillian.

Callovi, G. (1990) 'Regulating Immigration in the European Community'. Paper presented to the CES Europeanists Conference in Washington DC, March 23–25.

Calva J.L. (1992) *Probables Efectos de un Tratado de Libre Comercio en el Campo México*. Mexico: Fontamara.

Canada. Minister of Employment and Immigration (1992) *Government Proposes Changes to Immigration Program*. Press release, Ottawa, June.

Cassen, R. (1987) *Does Aid Work?* Oxford: Oxford University Press.

Castells, M. (1989) *The Informational City: Information Technology, Economic Restructuring and the Urban-Regional Process.* Oxford: Basil Blackwell.

Castles, S., Iredale, R.R. and Vasta E. (1994) 'Australia's Immigration between Globalization and Recession', *International Migration Review,* **28**(2), 370–83.

Castles, S. and Miller M.J. (1993) *The Age of Migration: International Population Movements in the Modern World.* New York: Guilford Press.

Castles, S., Mitchell, C., Morrissey, M. and Alcorso C. (1989) *The Recognition of Overseas Trade Qualifications.* Canberra: Bureau of Immigration Research.

CEC (Commission of the European Communities) (1994) Communication from the Commission to the Council and the European Parliament. Brussels, COM(94) 23 final.

Centre for Development and Enterprise (1997a) *People on the Move: Lessons from International Migration Policies.* CDE Research no 6, Migration Series. Johannesburg: CDE.

(1997b) *People on the Move: A New Approach to Cross-border Migration in South Africa.* CDE Research no. 7, Migration Series. Johannesburg: CDE.

Centre for Immigration Studies (1994) *Backgrounder: Immigration-Related Statistics – 1994.* Washington DC.

Chapman, B.J. and Iredale, R.R. (1993) 'Immigrant Qualifications: Recognition and Relative Wage Outcomes', *International Migration Review,* **27**(2), 359–87.

Chiswick, B. (ed.) (1982a) *The Gateway: U.S. Immigration Issues and Policies.* Washington DC: American Enterprise Institute.

(1982b) 'The Impact of Immigration on the Level and Distribution of Economic Well-being'. In B.R. Chiswick (ed.) *The Gateway: U.S. Immigration Issues and Policies.* Washington DC: The American Enterprise Institute.

Chretien, J.P. (1985) 'Hutu et Tutsi au Burundi'. In Jean-Loup Amselle and Elikia M'Bokolo (eds), *Au Coeur de l'Ethnie: enthnies, tribalism et e'tat en Afrique.* Paris: La De'couverte. pp. 143–66.

Citizenship and Immigration Canada (1994a) *A Broader Vision: Immigration and Citizenship, Plan 1995–2000.* Annual Report to Parliament. Ottawa: Minister of Supply and Services.

(1994b) *Highlights: Into the 21st Century: A Strategy for Immigration and Citizenship.* Ottawa: Minister of Supply and Services.

(1994c) *Immigration Consultations Report.* Ottawa: Minister of Supply and Services.

(1994d) *Into the 21st Century: A Strategy for Immigration and Citizenship.* Ottawa: Minister of Supply and Services.

(1994e) 'The Relative Performance of Selected Independents and Family Class Immigrants in the Labour Market'. Draft paper. Economic and Demographic Research and Analysis Division, Strategic Research and Analysis Branch. Policy Sector. Ottawa-Hull.

Coale, A. (1978) 'Population Growth and Economic Development: The Case of Mexico', *Foreign Affairs* **56**(2), (Jan), 415–29.

Cohen, Robin (1997) 'Brain-drain migration'. Paper prepared for the international migration Green Paper government task team, as published on the internet: www.polity.org.za/govdocs/green_papers/migration/.

Coleman, Gale S. (1989) 'Overcoming mootness in the H-2A temporary foreign farmworker program' *Georgetown Law Journal,* **78**, 197–238.

Commission on Workforce Quality and Labour Market Efficiency (1989) *Investing in People: A Strategy to Address America's Workforce Crisis*. Washington DC: U.S. Department of Labor.

Commission to Investigate the Development of a Comprehensive Labour Market Policy (1996) *Restructuring the South African Labour Market*, RP 83/1996. Pretoria: Government Printers, June.

Congressional Research Service (1980) 'Temporary worker programs: background and issues'. Prepared for the Senate Committee on the Judiciary (February).

Connell, J., Dasgupta, B., Laishley R., and Lipton M. (1976) *Migration from Rural Areas: The Evidence from Village Studies*. Delhi: Oxford University Press.

Cooper, F. (1981) 'Africa and the World Economy'. In *African Studies Bulletin*, **24**, 2–3.

Cornelius, W. (1992a) 'The politics and economics of reforming the Ejido Sector in Mexico: an overview and research agenda'. LASA Forum. XXIII, **3**, 3–10.
(1992b) 'From sojourners to settlers: the changing profile of Mexican immigration to the United States'. In J. Bustamante, C. Reynolds and R. Hinojosa-Ojeda (eds) *U.S. Mexican Relations: Labor Market Interdependence*. Stanford CA: Stanford University Press.

Cornelius, W.A. and Martin, P.L. (1993) *The Uncertain Connection: Free Trade and Mexico–US Migration*. San Diego: Centre for US–Mexican Studies.

Cornelius, W., Hollifield, J.F. and Martin, P.L. (1994) *Controlling Immigration: A Global Perspective*. Stanford: Stanford University Press.

Craig R.B. (1971) *The Bracero Program: Interest Groups and Foreign Policy*. Austin: University of Texas Press.

Crocker, C.A. (1993) *High Noon in Southern Africa: Making Peace in a Rough Neighborhood*. New York: W.W. Norton.

Cross, G.S. (1983) *Immigrant Workers in Industrial France*. Philadelphia: Temple University Press.

Cross, H. and Sandos, J. (1981) *Across the Border: Rural Development in Mexico and Recent Migration to the United States*. Berkeley. Institute of Governmental Studies, University of California.

Crush, Jonathan (1997) 'Contract migration to South Africa: past, present and future'. Paper prepared for the international migration green paper government task team, as published on the internet: www.polity.org.za/govdocs/green_papers/migration/.

Davis, D.R. 'Bilateral trade in a multilateral world: is Heckscher-Ohlin trade north-south trade?'. Harvard Institute of Economic Research, Discussion Paper No. 1700 November 1994.

Dawkins, P., Forster, W., Lowell, L. and Papademetriou, D.G. (1992) 'The microeconomic effects of immigration in Australia and the United States'. In G.P. Freeman and J. Jupp (eds), *Nations of Immigrants: Australia, the United States, and International Migration*. Melbourne and New York: Oxford University Press.

Deardorff, A.V. (1994) 'Testing trade theories and predicting trade flows'. In R.W. Jones and P.B. Kenen (eds) *Handbook of International Economics. Vol. 1*, Amsterdam: North-Holland.

Deng, F. (1993) *Protecting the Dispossessed*. Washington DC: Brookings Institution.

Department of Employment, Education and Training (1994) *Skilled Vacancy Survey* (November, Monthly). Canberra.

Department of Home Affairs (1997) *Permanent Residence: Republic of South Africa.* Policy document, January.

Dolan, Chris and Nkuna, Vusi (1995) ' "Refugees", "illegal aliens" and the labour market — the case for a rights-based approach to labour movement in South Africa'. Paper presented to the Labour Market Commission, 6.

Drummond, J. H., Paterson, A.N.M, and Tuckey, H. .P (1995) 'Changing academic staff employment patterns at the University of the North West, South Africa'. Paper presented at the annual conference of the Society for Research into Higher Education, 'The changing university', at Heriot-Watt University, Edinburgh, Scotland, 12–14 December.

Durand, J. and Massey, D.S. (1992) 'Mexican Migration to the United States'. *Latin American Research Review,* **27**(2), 3–42.

Eaton, J. (1989) 'Foreign public capital flows'. In H. Chenery and T.N. Srinivasan (eds), *Handbook of Development Economics.* Vol. 2. Amsterdam: North-Holland.

Economic Council of Canada (1991) *Economic and Social Impacts of Immigration.* Ottawa: Minister of Supply and Services.

Economic Planning Unit (1993) 'Mid-term review of the Sixth Malaysia Plan 1991–1995'. Kuala Lumpur.

Einaudi, J.-L. (1991) *La Bataille de Paris.* Paris: Seuil.

Employment and Immigration Canada (EIC) (1990) *Annual Report to Parliament: Immigration Plan for 1991–1995.* Ottawa: Minister of Supply and Services.

(1992) *Managing Immigration: A Framework for the 1990s.* Ottawa. Minister of Supply and Services.

Encarnacion, J. and Wells, T. (1986) 'Evaluating foreign investment'. In T.H. Moran *et al.* (eds) *Investing in Development: New Roles for Private Capital.* Washington: Overseas Development Council.

Engelen-Kefer, Ursula (1990) *Aspekte der Auslanderbeschaftigung. Bericht '90: Zur Situation der auslandischen. Arbeitnehmer und ihrer Familien — Bestandsaufrahme und Perpektiren fur die 90er* Jahre. Bonn.

Ethier, W.J. (1986) 'International Trade and Labour Migration', *Research in Human Capital and Development,* 4.

Eurostat (1994) 'Asylum-Seekers and Refugees. A Statistical Report'. Vol. 1. Luxembourg, Office for Official Publications of the European Communities.

EXCOM (1982) (Executive Committee of the High Commissioner for Refugees) *Executive Committee of the High Commissioners Programme.* A/AC.96/606.

(1992) *Persons covered by the OAU Convention Governing the Specific Aspects of Refugee Problems in Africa and by the Cartagena Declaration on Refugees.* Executive International Protection. EC/1992/SCP/CRP.6.

(1993) *Executive Committee Reports of the High Commissioner's Programme.* A/48/12.

(1994) *Note on International Protection.* A/AC.96/830.

Faini, R. and de Melo, J. (1994) 'Trade liberalization, employment and migration: some simulations for Morocco'. Paper presented to the OECD Workshop on Development Strategy, Employment and Migration. Paris: OECD.

Faini R. and Venturini, A. (1993) 'Trade, aid and migrations', *European Economic Review,* **37**, April, 435–42.

(1994) *Migration and Growth: The Experience of Southern Europe.* Mimeo: University of Brescia.

Fawcett, J.T. (1989) 'Networks, Linkages, and Migration Systems', *International Migration Review*, **23**, 521–44.

Federal Ministry of the Interior, Federal Republic of Germany (1993) *Survey of the Policy and Law Concerning Foreigners in the Federal Republic of Germany.* A1-937 020/15, 80.

Fix, M. (1991) 'The Paper Curtain'. *Employer Sanctions' Implementation, Impact, and Reform.* Washington: Urban Institute Press.

Fix, M. and Hill, P. (1990) *Enforcing Employer Sanctions: Challenges and Strategies.* Washington: Urban Institute Press.

Foley, F. (1989) *Current and Future Demand for Asia-Related Skills in the Australian Workforce.* Asia Studies Council. Canberra: Australian Government Publishing Service.

Freeman, G. (1992) 'Migration policy and politics in the receiving states', *International Migration Review*, **26**(4), (Winter).

(1994) 'Can liberal states control unwanted migration?', *Annals of the American Academy of Political and Social Science*, **534**, (July).

Freeman, G. and Jupp, J. (eds) (1992) *Nations of Immigrants: Australia, the United States, and International Migration.* New York: Oxford University Press.

Fuller, V. (1942) 'The supply of agricultural labour as a factor in the evolution of farm organization in California'. Unpublished Ph.D. dissertation. U.C. Berkeley, 1939. Reprinted in *Violations of Free Speech and the Rights of Labour Education and Labour Committee.* [The LaFollete Committee]. Washington: Senate Education and Labour Committee, 1942. pp. 19778–894.

(1991) *Hired Hands in California's Farm Fields.* Berkeley: Giannini Foundation.

Garcia y Griego, M. (1981) 'The importation of Mexican contract labourers to the United States, 1942–1964: antecedents, operation, and legacy'. Working Paper 11. La Jolla CA: Program in U.S.–Mexican Studies, UCSD.

(1989) 'The Mexican labour supply, 1990–2010'. In W. Cornelius and J.A. Bustamante (eds) *Mexican Migration to the United States: Origins, Consequences and Policy Options.* La Jolla CA: UCSD Centre for US–Mexican Studies.

Garnaut, R. (1990) *Australia and the Northeast Asian Ascendancy. Report to the Prime Minister and the Minister for Foreign Affairs and Trade.* Canberra: Australian Government Publishing Service.

General Accounting Office (1986) 'Illegal aliens: limited research suggests illegal aliens may displace native workers'. PEMD–86–9BR (April).

(1988) 'Illegal aliens: influence on illegal workers on wages and working conditions of legal workers'. PEMD–88–13BR (March).

Geyevu, Samuel Agbeko (1997) 'The socio-economic impact of Ghanaian non-professional illegal aliens on Durban metropolitan area and suggested policy framework'. Master's thesis, University of Durban-Westville.

Goodwin-Gill, G. 1983. *The Refugee in International Law.* Oxford: Clarendon Press.

Goonerate W., Martin, P. and Sazanami, H. (eds) (1994) *Regional Development Impacts of Labour Migration in Asia.* United Nations Centre for Regional Development, Nayoga, Japan. UNCRD Research Report Series No. 2.

Gould, J.D. (1979) 'European inter-continental emigration, 1815–1914: patterns and causes', *Journal of European Economic History*, **8**, 593–679.

Grahl-Madsen, A. (1966) *The Status of Refugees in International Law*. Leyden: Sijthoff.

Gregory, P. (1991) 'The determinants of international migration and policy options for influencing the size of population flows'. In S. Diaz-Briquets and S. Weintraub (eds) *Determinants of Emigration From Mexico, Central America, and the Caribbean*. Vol. 1. Boulder CO: Westview Press.

Grindle, M. (1988) *Searching for Rural Development: Labour Migration and Employment in Mexico*. Ithaca: Cornell University Press.

Grossman, G.M. and Razin, A. (1984) 'International capital movements under uncertainty'. *Journal of Political Economy*, **92**, April, 286–306.

Hailbronner, K. (1993) 'Concept of safe country and expeditious procedure', *International Journal of Refugee Law*, **5**(1).

Handbook of Population and Family Economics. Amsterdam. North-Holland. (forthcoming).

Harris, Nigel (1996) *The New Untouchables: Immigration and the New World Worker*. London: Penguin.

Hathaway, J. (1991) *The Law of Refugee Status*. Toronto: Butterworth.

Hatton, T.J. and Williamson, J.G. (1994) 'What drove the mass migrations from Europe in the late nineteenth century?', *Population and Development Review*, **20**, September, 533–59.

Hawthorne, L. (1994) *Labour Market Barriers for Immigrant Engineers in Australia*. Canberra. Bureau of Immigration and Population Research.

Hayes-Bautista, D., Schink, W. and Chapa, J. (1992) 'The young Latino population in an aging American society: policy issues evoked by the emergence of an age-race stratified society'. In J. Bustamante, C. Reynolds, and R. Hinojosa-Ojeda (eds), *US Mexican Relations: Labour Market Interdependence*. Stanford CA: Stanford University Press.

Healy, E. (1993) '"Specialist" temporary residents: what's happening?', *People and Place*, **1**(1), 13–18.

Heimer, F.W. (1979) *Der Entkoloniserungskonflikt in Angola*. Munich: Weltforum-Verlag.

Helpman, E. and Krugman, P.R. (1985) *Market Structure and Foreign Trade*. Cambridge: MIT Press.

Hiemenz, U. and Schatz, K.W. (1979) *Trade in Place of Migration: An Employment-Oriented Study with Special References to the Federal Republic of the Federal Republic of Germany, Spain and Turkey*. Geneva: International Labour Office.

Higgins, Rosemary (1993) 'The new United Nations and former Yugoslavia', *International Affairs*, **69**(3), 465–83.

Hinojosa-Ojeda, R. and McCleery, R. (1992) 'US—Mexico interdependence, social pacts and policy perspectives: a computable general equilibrium approach'. In Jorge Bustamante, C. Reynolds, and R. Hinojosa-Ojeda (eds) *US Mexican Relations: Labour Market Interdependence*. Stanford CA: Stanford University Press.

Hinojosa-Ojeda, R. and Robinson, S. (1991a) 'Labour issues in a North American Free Trade Area'. In N. Lustig, B. Bosworth and R. Lawrence (eds), *North American Free Trade: Assessing the Impact*. Washington DC: The Brookings Institution.

(1991b) 'Alternative Scenarios of US—Mexico integration: a computable general equilibrium approach'. Working Paper no. 609. Department of Agricultural and Resource Economics. University of California, Berkeley.

Holborn, Louise. (1975). *Refugees. A Problem of Our Time: The Work of the United Nations High Commissioner for Refugees, 1951–1972.* Methuen, NJ: Scarecrow Press.

Hollifield, J. (1992) *Immigrants, Markets, and States: The Political Economy of Immigration in Postwar Europe and the US.* Cambridge: Harvard.

Hönekopp, E. (1992) 'Auswirkungen eines EG-Beitritts der Türkei auf Demographie und Arbeitsmarkt in der Eg und in Deutschland', *Mimeo,* (February).

Hudson Institute (1987) *Workforce 2000: Work and Workers for the 21st Century.* New York.

Hue, Gervaise (1990) 'Legalité, Efficacité et Travail Clandestin'. Unpublished paper.

Huerta, M.M. (1990a) 'The impact of Maquiladoras on migration in Mexico'. Working Paper 51 of the US Commission for the Study of International Migration and Cooperative Economic Development (July).

(1990b) *Maquiladoras y Migración en México.* Puebla. Asesoria y Consultoria Economica.

Hufbauer, G. and Schott, J. (1992) *North American Free Trade: Issues and Recommendations.* Washington: Institute for International Economics.

Human Rights Watch (1994) 'Arming Rwanda: The Arms Trade and Human Right Abuses in the Rwanda War', *Human Rights Watch Arms Project,* **6**(1).

IGC (1993) (Intergovernmental Consultations on Asylum, Refugee and Migration Policies in Europe, North America and Australia). *'Return of rejected asylum-seekers'.* Working paper. Geneva: IGC/RET/030/93.

(1994a) *Summary Descriptions of Asylum Procedures in States in Europe, Not America and Australia.* Geneva.

(1994b) *Answers by Participating States to the Questionnaire on Trafficking of Aliens.* Geneva. IGC/TRAF/7/94.

(1994c) *Working Paper on Reception in the Region of Origin.* Geneva.

Independent Commission on International Humanitarian Issues (1986). *Refugees: Dynamic of Displacement.* London: Zed.

Inglis, C. and Wu, C.-T. (1990) 'The "New" Migration of Asian Skill and Capital to Australia: Implications for Theory and Research'. Draft paper.

International Labour Office (1989) *Informal Consultation Meeting on Migrants from Non-EEC Countries in the Single European Market after 1992.* Geneva (April).

Isnard, J. (1993) 'Rwanda: selon les services de renseignements francais, les rebelles. Beneficieraient du soutien de l'armee ougandaise', *Le Monde,* 17 February.

Jackson, R.H. (1990) *Quasi-states: sovereignty, international relations and the Third World.* Cambridge: Cambridge University Press.

Jacobsen, Karen, with Wilkinson, S. (1993) 'Refugee movements as security threats in Sub-Saharan Africa'. In Myron Weiner (ed.), *International Migration and Security.* Boulder: Westview.

Jay K. and Michalopoulos, C. (1988) 'Donor policies, donor interests and aid effectiveness'. In A.O. Krueger, C. Michalopoulos and V.W. Ruttan (eds), *Aid and Development.* Baltimore: Johns Hopkins University Press.

Johnson W.B. (1987) *Workforce 2000: Work and Workers for the 21st Century.*

Report to the US Department of Labour. Indianapolis IN: Hudson Institute.

Joly, Daniele (1994) 'Harmonization of Asylum in the 90's'. In *International Journal of Refugee Law*, **6**(2).

Jones, F.L. (1988) *The Recent Employment and Unemployment Experiences of First, Second and Later Generations of Immigrants in Australia*. Canberra: Office of Multicultural Affairs.

Joske, S. (1989) 'The Economics of immigration: who benefits?' Background Paper, Legislative Research Service. Canberra: The Department of the Parliamentary Library.

Kane-Berman, John (1990) *The Silent Revolution*. Johannesburg: Southern Books.

Kaplan, H. (ed.) (1983) *Angola: A Country Study*. Washington DC: US Government Printing Office.

Keely, Charles, B. and Stanton Russell, Sharon (1994) 'The future shape of developed countries' asylum policies: national security concerns and regional issues'. Unpublished paper. Washington DC: Georgetown University.

Kindleberger, C.P. (1967) *Europe's Postwar Growth: The Role of Labour Supply*. Cambridge MA: Harvard University Press.

Kiser, G.C. and Woody Kiser, M. (eds) (1979) *Mexican Workers in the United States*. Albuquerque: University of New Mexico Press.

Knight, J.B. and Sabot, R.H. (1983) 'The role of the firm in wage determination: an African case study', *Oxford Economic Papers*, **35**, March, 45–66.

Koener, H. (1990) *Internationale Mobilitaet der Arbeit. Eine Empirische und theoretische Analyse der internationalen Wirtschaftsmigration im 19. und 20. Jahrhundert*. Darmstadt: Wissenschaftliche Buchgesellschaft.

Koslowski, R. (1994) 'Intra-EU migration, citizenship and political union', *Journal of Common Market Studies*, **32**, 3 (September), 369–402.

Kratochwil, Friederich (1993) 'Contract and regimes. Do issue specificity and variations of formality matter?' In Volker Rittberg (ed.), *Regime Theory and International Relations*. Oxford: Clarendon Press.

Krauss, M.B. (1976) 'The economics of the "Guest Worker" problem: a Neo-Heckscher-Ohlin approach', *Scandinavian Journal of Economics*, **78**, 470–76.

Krueger, A.O., Michalopoulos, C. and Ruttan, V.W. (eds) (1988) *Aid and Development*. Baltimore: Johns Hopkins University Press.

Lary, D., Inglis, C. and Wu, C.-T. (1993) 'Hong Kong migration to Australia and Canada: a comparison'. Paper presented at York University, (May).

Lattes, A. and de Lattes, Z.R. (1994) 'International migration in Latin America: patterns, determinants and policies'. In M. Macura and D. Coleman (eds) *International Migration: Regional Processes and Responses*. New York and Geneva. United Nations.

Layard R., Blanchard, O., Dornbusch, R. and Krugman, P. (1992) *East West Migration: The Alternatives*. Cambridge MA: MIT Press.

Lebon, Andre (1994) *Immigration et présence étrangére en France: Le bilan de l'année 1992–1993*. Paris: Nministere des affaires sociales, de la sante et de la ville, March.

Lemarchand, Rene. (1970) *Rwanda and Burundi*. New York: Praeger.

Lemarchand, Rene, and Martin, D. (1974) *Selective Genocide in Burundi*. London: Minority Rights Group.

Levy, S. and Nolan, S. (1991) 'Trade and foreign investment policies under imperfect competition: lessons for developing countries', *Journal of Development Economics*, **37**, November, 31–62.

Levy, S. and van Wijnbergen, S. (1992) 'Mexico and the Free Trade Agreement between Mexico and the United States', *The World Bank Economic Review*, **4**(3), 481– 502.

Lewis, David and Kaplan, David (1997) 'Skills shortgage result of voodoo economics', *Business Day*, 19 February.

Lim, L.L. and Abella, M. (1994) 'The movement of people in Asia: internal, intra-regional and international migration', *Asian and Pacific Migration Journal*, **3**(2–3), 209–50.

Lloyd, P. (1970) 'Immigration policy: the economic case for change'. Cited in Wooden *et al.* 1990.

(1993) 'The Political Economy of Immigration'. In James Jupp and M. Kabala (eds) *The Politics of Australian Immigration*. Canberra: Bureau of Immigration Research.

Loescher, Gil, (1993) *Beyond Charity. International Cooperation and the Global Refugee Problem*. New York: Oxford University Press.

Loescher, Gil and Scanlan, John A. (1986) *Calculated Kindness: Refugees and America's Half-open Door. 1945 to the Present*. New York: Free Press.

Los Angeles County (1992) 'Impact of Undocumented Persons and Other Immigrants on Costs, Revenues and Services in Los Angeles County'. November 6.

Lucas R.E.B. (1975) 'The supply of immigrants function: An econometric analysis', *Journal of Development Economics*, September.

(1985) 'Mines and Migrants in South Africa'. Boston University. African Studies Centre Working Paper 106.

(1987) 'Emigration to South Africa's mines', *American Economic Review*, June.

(1990) 'Why doesn't capital flow from rich to poor countries?', *American Economic Review*, **80**, May, 92–96.

(1993) 'On the determinants of direct foreign investment: evidence from east and southeast Asia', *World Development*, **21**, March, 391–406.

(1997) 'Internal migration in developing countries'. In M. Rosenzweig and O. Stark (eds) *Handbook of Population and Family Economics, Volume IB*. Amsterdam: North Holland.

Lusting, N. (1992) *Mexico: The Remaking of an Economy*. Washington: Brookings Institution.

Lutz, V. (1963) 'Foreign workers and domestic wage levels with an illustration from the Swiss case', *Banco Nazionale del Lauro Quarterly Review*, **16**(64–7), 3–68.

Mann, M. (1984) 'The autonomous power of the state: its origins, mechanisms, and results', *European Journal of Sociology*, **25**, 185–213.

Marie, C.-V. (1994) 'From the campaign against illegal migration to the campaign against illegal work', *The Annals of the American Academy of Political Science*, **534**, 118–32.

(n.d.) 'Evolution de la réglementation en matiere de lutte contre le travail clandestin et les trafics de main d'oeuvre et l'emploi non-declare'. Unpublished paper

Markusen, J.R. (1983) 'Factor trade and commodity trade as complements', *Journal of International Economics*, **14**, May, 341–56.

Martin, P. (1980) *Guestworker Programs: Lessons from Europe*. Washington: Department of Labor, International Labor Affairs Bureau.

(1983) *Labor Displacement and Public Policy*. Lexington MA: Lexington Books.

(1990) 'The Outlook for Agricultural Labour in the 1990s', UC Davis *Law Review*, **23**(3), 499–523 (Spring).

(1991) *The Unfinished Story: Turkish Labour Migration to Western Europe*. Geneva: ILO.

(1993) *Trade and Migration: NAFTA and Agriculture*. Washington DC: Institute for International Economics.

(1994a) 'Collective Bargaining in Agriculture'. In P. Voos (ed.), *Contemporary Collective Bargaining in the Private Sector*. Madison WI: Industrial Relations Research Association.

(1994b) 'Good intentions gone awry: IRCA and US Agriculture', *The Annals of the American Academy of Political Science*, **534**, 44–57.

(1998) *Germany: Reluctant Land of Immigration*. Washington DC: American Institute for Contemporary Germany Studies.

Martin, P., Hönekopp, E., and Ulmann, H. (1990) 'Europe 1992: effects on labour migration', *International Migration Review*, **24**(91), 591–603, (Fall).

Martin, P. and Martin, D. (1993) *The Endless Quest: Helping America's Farmworkers*. Boulder CO: Westview Press.

Martin, P. and Midgley, E. (1994) 'Immigration to the United States: journey to an uncertain destination'. Population Reference Bureau Population Bulletin, **49**(2), (September).

Martin, P. and Olmsted, A. (1985) 'The agricultural mechanization controversy', *Science*, **227**(4687), 601–6 (8 February).

Masalha, N. (1992) *Expulsion of the Palestinians*. Washington DC: Institute for Palestine Studies.

Massey, D.S. (1988) 'Economic development and international migration in comparative perspective', *Population and Development Review*, **14**(3), September.

(1989) 'Social structure, household strategies, and the cumulative causation of migration'. *Population Index*, **56**, 3–26.

Massey, D., Alarcon, D., Durand, J. and Gonzales, H. (1987) *Return to Aztlan: The Social Process of International Migration from Western Mexico*. Berkeley: University of California Press.

Massey, D.S., Arango, J., Hugo, G., Kouaouci, A., Pelligrino, A., and Taylor, Edward J. (1993) 'Theories of international migration: an integration and appraisal', *Population and Development Review*, **19**(3) (September), 431–66.

(1994) 'An evaluation of international migration theory: the North American case', *Population and Development Review*, **20**(4) (December), 699–751.

Massey, D., Donato, K., and Liang, Z. (1990) 'Effects of the immigration reform and control act of 1986: preliminary data from Mexico'. In Bean, Frank, Barry Edmonston and J. Passel (eds), *Undocumented Migration to the United States: IRCA and the Experience of the 1980s*. Washington: The Urban Institute Press, 183–210.

Mehmet, O. (1988) *Development In Malaysia: Poverty, Wealth, and Trusteeship*. Kuala Lumpur: Insan.

Mehrlander, U., Ascheberg, C., Ueltzhueffer, J. (1997) *Situation der auslandischen Arbeitnehmer und ihrer Familienangehoerigen in der Bundesrepublik Deutschland.* Bonn: Bundesministerium fuer Arbeit und Sozialordung Forschungsbericht 265.

Meissner, D. and Papademetriou, D. (n.d.) 'Changing immigrant selection: how understanding Canada can help'. Draft.

Meissner, D., North, D.S. and Papademetriou, D. (1986) *Legalization of Undocumented Aliens: Lessons from Other Countries.* Washington DC: Carnegie Endowment for International Peace.

Mendiluce, Jose-Maria. (1994) 'War and disaster in the former Yugoslavia: the limits of humanitarian action, *World Refugee Survey.* Washington DC: US Committee for Refugees.

Miller, M.J. (1981) *Foreign Workers in Western Europe: An Emerging Political Force.* New York: Praeger.

(1987) *Employer Sanctions in Western Europe.* Staten Island NY: Center for Migration Studies.

(1992) 'Never ending story: the US debate over illegal immigration'. In G.P. Freeman and J. Jupp (eds), *Nations of Immigrants: Australia, the United States, and International Migration.* Melbourne and New York: Melbourne University Press.

(ed.) (1994a) 'Strategies for immigration control: an international comparison', *The Annals of the American Academy of Political and Social Science,* 534, (July).

(1994b) 'Towards understanding state capacity to prevent unwanted migration: employer sanctions enforcement in France, 1975–1990', *West European Politics,* 17(2), (April).

Miller, M. and Martin, P. (1982) *Administering Foreign Worker Programs.* Lexington MA: Lexington Books.

Ministry for Welfare and Population Development (1996) *Draft White Paper for a Proposed Population Policy and Strategies for South Africa.* September.

Minnaar, Anthony, and Hough, Mike (1996) *Who goes there? Perspectives on Clandestine Migration and Illegal Aliens in Southern Africa.* Pretoria: HSRC.

Mitchell, B. (1993) 'The impact of immigration in the trades' labour market'. *People and Place,* 1(2), 23–7.

Mitchell, Christopher (ed.) (1992) *Western Hemisphere Immigration and United States Foreign Policy.* University Park: Pennsylvania University Press.

Mitchell, W. (1992) 'Skilled migration and structural unemployment in Australia', *Proceedings of the Second National Immigration Outlook Conference, 11–13 November.* Sydney.

Morris, B. (1994) *1948 and After.* London: Oxford University Press.

Muller, T. and Espenshade, T. (1995) *The Fourth Wave: California's Newest Immigrants.* Washington: The Urban Institute Press.

Mundell, R.A. (1957) 'International trade and factor mobility', *American Economic Review,* 47, 321–35.

Murphy, J. (1994a) 'Causes of the high unemployment experienced by recently arrived immigrants with bachelor degrees', *People and Place,* 2(3), 28–35.

(1994b) *Change in the Employment Status of Points-tested Immigrants: Results from the Prototype Longitudinal Survey of Immigrants to Australia.* Canberra: Australian Government Publishing Service.

Nagel, J. (1978) *Mexico's Population Policy Turnaround.* Washington DC: Population Reference Bureau.

Nash, A. (1991) 'The Hong Kong brain drain', *Policy Options,* **12**(9), 21–3.

National Centre on Education and the Economy (1990) *America's Choice: High Skills or Low Wages. The Report of the Commission on the Skills of the American Workforce.* Washington DC.

National Council on Employment Policy (1976) 'Illegal aliens: an assessment of the issues: a policy statement and conference report with background papers'. Washington: NCEP.

National Population Inquiry [Borrie Report] (1975) *Population and Australia: A Demographic Analysis and Projection,* 2 vols. Canberra: Australian Government Publishing Service.

Navamukundan, A. (1993) 'Structural changes and policy options for the plantation industry in Malaysia', in *Structural Changes and Policy Options for the Malaysian Plantation Industry.* Report of the ILO–NUPW Seminar, October 27–30, Kuala Lumpur.

Nayagam, J. (1993) 'The impact of structural changes on labour in the plantation industry', *Structural Changes and Policy Options for the Malaysian Plantation Industry.* Report of the ILO–NUPW Seminar, October 27–30. Kuala Lumpur.

Nevile, J.W. (1991) 'Immigration and macroeconomic performance in Australia'. In J.W. Nevile (ed.), *The Costs and Benefits of Immigration Growth,* **39**, 18–34.

The New Europe and International Migration (A special edition of *International Migration Review*) (1992) *International Migration Review,* **26**(2), Summer.

Newbury, M.C. (1983) 'Colonialism, ethnicity, and rural political protest: Rwanda and Zanzibar in comparative perspective' in *Comparative Politics,* **15**(3), 253–80.

North, D. and Houstoun, M. (1976) *The Characteristics and Role of Illegal Aliens in the US Labor Market: An Exploratory Study.* Washington: New Transcentury.

Oloka-Onyango, Joe. (1991) 'Human rights, the OAU convention and the refugee crisis in Africa: forty years after Geneva, *International Journal of Refugee Law,* **3**(3), 453–60.

Organisation for Economic Co-operation and Development (1978) *Migration, Growth and Development.* Paris: OECD.

Paine, S. (1974) *Exporting Workers: The Turkish Case.* Cambridge: Cambridge University Press.

Palfreeman, A.C. (1967) *The Administration of the White Australia Policy.* Melbourne: Melbourne University Press.

Papademetriou, D. (1991) 'International migration in North America: issues, policies and implications'. Paper presented at Informal Expert Group Meeting on International Migration. 16–19 July. Geneva.

Papademetriou, D. and Martin, P. (eds) (1991) *The Unsettled Relationship: Labour Migration and Economic Development.* Westport CT: Greenwood Press.

Papademetriou, D. and Meissner, D. (1988) 'The Canadian immigrant selection system: a technical report'. Draft.

Penninx, R. (1982) 'A critical review of theory and practice: the case of Turkey', *International Migration Review,* **16**, 781–818.

Penninx, R. and Muus, P. (1989) 'No limits for migration after 1992: the lessons of the past and a reconnaissance of the future', *International Migration*, XXVII, **3**, (September).

Picard, J. (ed.) (1979) 'Les Conventions Bilatérales Passées par la France'. *Les Travailleurs Etrangers et le Droit International*. Société Francaise pour le Droit International. Paris. Editions A. Pedone, 107–115.

Pillai, P. (1992) 'People on the move: an overview of recent immigration and emigration in Malaysia'. Institute of Strategic and International Studies. Malaysia ISIS Issue Paper.

Piore, M.J. (1979) *Birds of Passage: Migrant Labour and Industrial Societies*. New York: Cambridge University Press.

Plummer, C. (1992) 'US tomato statistics: 1960–90'. US Department of Agriculture. Economic Research Service, Statistical Bulletin No. 841. Washington: USDA.

Portes, A. and Walton, J. (1981) *Labour, Class, and the International System*. New York: Academic Press.

President's Commission on Migratory Labour (1951) *Migratory Labour in American Agriculture*. Washington. US Government Printing Office.

Prognos (1989) *The Development of the EC Labour Market to 2,000*. Basel: Prognos.

Prunier, G. (1994). 'La crise Rwandaise: structures et deroulement', in *Refugee Survey Quarterly*, **13**(2&3), 13–46.

Przeworski, A. and Teune, H. (1970) *The Logic of Comparative Social Inquiry*. New York: John Wiley and Sons.

Ravenstein, E.G. (1889) 'The laws of migration', *Journal of the Royal Statistical Society*, **52**.

Razin, A. and Sadka, E. (1997) 'International Migration and International Trade. In M. Rozenzweig and O. Stark (eds) *Handbook of Population and Family Economics, Volume IB*. Amsterdam: North Holland.

Reder, M.W. (1963) 'The economic consequences of increased immigration', *Review of Economics and Statistics*, **45**, 221–30.

Reich, R.B. (1983) *The Next American Frontier*. New York: Penguin Books.

Reitzes, Maxine (1995) *Divided on the Demon: Immigration Policy since the Election*. Johannesburg: Centre for Policy Studies. September.

(1997) 'Undocumented migration: dimensions and dilemmas'. Paper prepared for the international migration green paper government task team, as published on the internet: www.polity.org.za/govdocs/green_papers/migration/.

Reitzes, Maxine and Bam, Sivuyile, assisted by Thulare, Paul (1996) 'One foot in, one foot out: immigrants and civil society in the Winterveld'. Research Report no. 51. Johannesburg: Centre for Policy Studies. November.

Reitzes, Maxine and De Villiers, Riaan (eds) (1995) *Southern African Migration: Domestic and Regional Policy Implications*. Johannesburg: Centre for Policy Studies. April.

Reynolds, C. (1992) 'Will free trade agreement lead to wage convergence? Implications for Mexico and the United States'. In J. Bustamante, C. Reynolds and R. Hinojosa-Ojeda (eds), *US–Mexican Relations: Labour Market Interdependence*. Stanford CA: Stanford University Press.

Ricca, S. (1990) *Migrations Internationales en Afrique*. Paris: L'Harmattan.

Richmond, Anthony H. (1993) 'Reactive migration: sociological perspectives on refugee movements', *Journal of Refugee Studies* (1), 7–24.

(1994) Global Apartheid: Refugees, Racism, and the New World Order. Toronto: Oxford University Press.

Rogers, R. (ed.) (1985) Guests Come to Stay: The Effects of European Labour Migration on Sending and Receiving Countries. Boulder CO: Westview Press.

(1992) 'The future of refugee flows and policies', International Migration Review, 26(4), (Winter).

Rothman, E. and Espenshade, T. (1992) 'Fiscal impacts of immigration to the United States', Population Index, 58(3), 381–415, (Fall).

Roxström, Erik (1995). National Refugee Law in Africa. University of Bergen, Institute of Public Law, publication series.

Ruddick, E. and Burstein, M. (1993) 'New directions for the management of the Canadian immigration program', People and Place, 1(4), 24–9.

Russell, S. Stanton (1989) 'Politics and ideology in migration policy formulation: the case of Kuwait', International Migration Review, 23(1) (Spring).

Russell, S. Stanton, Jacobsen, K., and Stanley, W. Deane (1990) International Migration and Development in Sub-Saharan Africa. Washington DC: World Bank.

Russell, S.S. and Teitelbaum, M.S. (1992) International Migration and International Trade. Washington DC: World Bank Discussion Paper No. 160.

Salt, J. (1989) 'A comparative overview of international trends and types, 1950–80'. International Migration Review, 23(3), (Fall), 431–56.

Sanderson, S. (ed.) (1985) The Americas in the New International Division of Labor. New York: Holmes and Meier.

Sassen, S. (1988) The Mobility of Labour and Capital: A Study in International Investment and Labour Flow. Cambridge: Cambridge University Press.

Schiller, G., Drettakis, E. and Boehning, R. (1976) Auslandische Arbeitnehmer, and Arbeitsmarkete. Nurnberg: IAB-BA. Beitr AB7.

Schlemmer, L. and Worthington, K. (1996) 'Better news on unemployment', Fast Facts. Johannesburg: South African Institute of Race Relations, September.

Schlichter, S. (1929) 'The Current Labour Policies of American Industries', Quarterly Journal of Economics, 37(2), 393–435 (May).

Scott, J.C. (1985). Weapons of the Weak: Everyday Forms of Peasant Resistance. New Haven CT: Yale University Press.

Select Commission on Immigration and Refugee Policy (SCIRP) (1981a) US Immigration Policy and the National Interest. Washington DC: United States Government Printing Office.

Select Commission on Immigration and Refugee Policy (1981b) Final Report. Washington: SCIRP.

Sender, J., Standing, G. and Weeks, J. (1996) Restructuring the South African Labour Market: The South African Challenge – An International Labour Organisation Review. United Nations Development Programme, Labour Market Commission and the ILO Regional Office for Africa.

Shimada, H. (1994). Japan's 'Guest Workers': Issues and Public Policies. Tokyo: University of Tokyo Press.

Shami, S. (1994) Population Displacement and Resettlement: Development and Conflict in the Middle East. New York: Centre for Migration Studies.

Sideaway, J.D. and Simon, David (1993) 'Geopolitical transition and state formation: the changing political geographies of Angola, Mozambique and Namibia', Journal of Southern African Studies, 19(1), 6–28.

Simon, J.L. (1989) *The Economic Consequences of Immigration*. New York/Oxford: Basil Blackwell.

Skeldon, R. (1992) 'International migration within and from the East and Southeast Asian Region: a review essay', *Asian and Pacific Migration Journal*, 1(1), 19–63.

Smith, T.F. (1993) 'Is there a brain drain? The case of engineers'. *People and Place*, 1(3), 43–6.

(1994a) 'The movement of engineers in and out of Australia', *People and Place*, 2(1), 25–9.

(1994b) 'The employment situation of migrant professionals holding tertiary qualifications', *People and Place*, 2(2), 13–18.

Solomon, Hussein (1997) *Towards the Free Movement of People in Southern Africa?* Institute for Security Studies Papers 18, March.

Solomon, Hussein and Cilliers, Jakkie (eds) (1996) *People, Poverty and Peace: Human Security in Southern Africa*. Monograph no. 4. Johannesburg: Institute for Defence Policy. May.

Stahl, C.W. (1982) 'Labour emigration and economic development', *International Migration Review*, 16(4), 869–99.

Stalker, P. (1994) *The Work of Strangers: A Survey of International Labour Migration*. Geneva: International Labour Organization.

Stanley, W. (1993) 'Blessing or menace? The security implications of central American migration'. In Myron Weiner (ed.), *International Migration and Security*. Boulder: Westview 229–60.

Stark, O. (1991) *The Migration of Labour*. Cambridge: Basil Blackwell.

Stark, O. and Lucas, R.E.B. (1988) 'Migration, remittances, and the family', *Economic Development and Cultural Change*, 36(3), (April).

Stark, O. and Taylor, J.E. (1991) 'Migration incentives, migration types: the role of relative deprivation', *The Economic Journal*, 101, September, 1163–78.

Stein, Barry (1987). 'ICARA II: burden sharing and durable solutions'. In John R. Rogge (ed.), *Refugees: A Third World Dilemma*. Totowa, NJ: Rowman and Littlefield.

Straubhaar, T. (1987) 'Freedom of movement of labour in a common market'. EFTA Bulletin. 9–12 (April).

(1988) *On the Economics of International Labor Migration*. Bern: Haupt.

(1992a) 'Allocational and distributional aspects of future immigration to Western Europe', *International Migration Review*, 26(2), 462–483, (Summer).

(1992b) *On the Economics of International Labour Migration*. Bern: Haupt, 1988.

Suhrke, Astri (1994a) 'Safeguarding the right to asylum'. Papers of the Expert Group Meeting on Population Distribution and Migration, preparatory to the International Conference on Population and Development, 1994. New York: UN: ESA/P/WP.126.

(1994b) 'Towards a comprehensive refugee policy: conflicts and refugees in the post-Cold War world'. In W.R. Bohning and M.-L. Schloeter-Paredes (eds), *Aid in Place of Migration?* Geneva: ILO.

Summers, Robert and Heston, Alan (1988) 'A new set of international comparisons of real product and price levels: estimates for 130 countries, 1950–85', *Review of Income and Wealth*, March, 1–25.

Taylor, J.E. (1986) 'Differential migration, networks, information and risk'. In O. Stark (ed.), *Research in Human Capital and Development, Migration, Human*

Capital, and Development. Greenwich CT: JAI Press, 147–71.

(1987) 'Undocumented Mexico-U.S. Migration and the returns to households in rural Mexico', *American Journal of Agricultural Economics*, **69**, 626–38.

(1992) 'Remittances and inequality reconsidered: Direct, indirect, and intertemporal effects', *Journal of Policy Modeling*, **14**, 187–208.

Teitelbaum, M. (1985) *Latin Migration North*. New York: Council on Foreign Relations.

Teitelbaum, M. and Stanton Russell, S. (1994) 'International migration, fertility, and development'. In R. Cassen (ed.) *Population and Development: Old Debates, New Conclusions*. Washington DC: Overseas Development Council.

Thomas, B. (1973) *Migration and Economic Growth*. London: Cambridge University Press.

Tilly, C. (1985) 'War making and state making as organized crime'. In P. Evans, D. Rueschmeyer and T. Skockpol (eds), *Bringing the State Back In*. Cambridge: Cambridge University Press, 169–91.

Todaro, M. (1969) 'A model of labour migration and urban unemployment in less developed countries', *American Economic Review*, **59**, 138–48.

Toolo, Hilton and Bethlehem, Lael (1994) 'Migration to South Africa: problems, issues, and possible approaches for organised labour'. National Labour and Economic Development Institute discussion paper. October.

UNHCR. (1992) *A Comprehensive Response to the Humanitarian Crisis in the Former Yugoslavia*. Geneva: IMFY/1992/2.

(1993a) *The State of the World's Refugees*. New York: Penguin.

(1993a) *A Selection of Speeches and Statements by Mrs. Sadako Ogata, United Nations High Commissioner for Refugees*. Vols I–II. Geneva.

(1994) *UNHCR's Operational Experience with Internally Displaced Persons*. Geneva: UNHCR, Division of International Protection. Geneva.

US Agency for International Development (1992) *Latin America and the Caribbean: Selected Economic and Social Data*. Washington DC: USAID.

US Committee for Refugees (1994) *World Refugee Survey*. Washington: DC.

US Commission for the Study of International Migration and Cooperative Economic Development (1990) *Unauthorized Migration: An Economic Development Response*. Washington DC. July.

US Commission on Agricultural Workers (1992) *Final Report*. Washington DC: US Government Printing Office.

US Council of Economic Advisors (1986) 'The economic effects of immigration', *Economic Report of the President*. Washington DC: Council of Economic Advisors, 213–34.

US Department of Labor, International Labor Affairs Bureau (1989) *The Effects of Immigration on the US Economy*. Washington DC, 25, 27.

US Immigration and Naturalization Service. Annual. *Statistical Yearbook of the Immigration and Naturalization Service*. Washington DC.

US Industrial Commission (1901) *Reports*, US Industrial Commission. Vol. XV, Part III. Washington DC. Government Printing Office.

Veugelers, J.W.P. and Klassen, T.R. (1994) 'Continuity and change in Canada's unemployment-immigration linkage (1946–1993)', *Canadian Journal of Sociology*, 19(3), 351–69.

Wallerstein, I. (1974) *The Modern World System, Capitalist Agriculture and the Origins of the European World Economy in the Sixteenth Century*. New York: Academic Press.

Wattenberg, B. (1987) *The Birth Dearth*. New York: Pharos.

Weiner, M. (1975) *Internal Migration Policies: Purposes, Interests, Instruments, Effects*. Cambridge, MA: Centre for International Studies.

(1993) (ed.) *International Migration and Security*. Boulder CO: Westview Press.

(1995) *The Global Migration Crisis: Challenges to States and to Human Rights*. New York: HarperCollins.

Weintraub, S. (1984) *Free Trade between Mexico and the United States*. Washington DC: The Brookings Institution.

(1990) *A Marriage of Convenience: Relations between Mexico and the United States*. New York: Oxford University Press.

(1992) 'North American Free Trade and the European Situation Compared', *International Migration Review*, **26**(2), Summer, 506–24.

Wiarda, H.J. (1993) *Introduction to Comparative Politics*. Belmont CA: Wadsworth.

Widgren, Jonas. (1992) 'The need to improve co-ordination of European asylum and migration policies'. Paper prepared for the Conference on Comparative Law of Asylum and Immigration in Europe, Trier, 12–13 March.

(1994) *The Key to Europe – A Comparative Analysis of Entry and Asylum Policies in Western Countries*. Vienna: ICMPD.

Williams, L.S. (1992) 'Immigrants and the Australian Labour Market: The experience of three recessions'. Proceedings of the Second National Immigration Outlook Conference, 11–13 November. Sydney.

Withers, G. (1988) 'Immigration and Australian economic growth'. In *The Economics of Immigration: Proceedings of a Conference at the Australian National University*, 22–23 April 1987. Canberra: AGPS.

(1991) 'Immigration and Australia's development'. In J. Nevile (ed.), *The Costs and Benefits of Immigration Growth*, **39**, 11–17.

Woldring, K. (1994) 'The concrete ceiling: a sympathetic view of a waste of talent'. Paper presented at ANZAM 1994 Annual Conference, 7–10 December, Victory University. Wellington, New Zealand.

Wooden, M., Holton, R., Hugo, G. and Sloan, J. (1990) *Australian Immigration: A Survey of the Issues*. Canberra: Bureau of Immigration Research.

Working Nation: Policies and Programs (1994) Government White Paper. Canberra: Australian Government Publishing Service.

Zabin, C., Kearney, M., Runsten, D. and Garcia, A. (1993) *A New Cycle of Rural Poverty: Mixtec Migrants in California Agriculture*. Davis CA: California Institute for Rural Studies.

Zolberg, Aristide R. (1985) *Creating Political Order: The Party-States of West Africa*. Chicago: Rand McNally, 1966; reprinted by the University of Chicago Press, 1985.

(1989) 'The Next Waves: Migration Theory for a Changing World'. *International Migration Review*, **23**(3) (Fall), 403–30.

(1990) 'The roots of US refugee policy'. In Robert W. Tucker, Charles B. Keely and Linda Wrigley (eds), *Immigration and US Foreign Policy*. Boulder: Westview.

(1992) 'The spectre of anarchy', *Dissent*, Summer.

(1995) 'From invitation to interdiction: US foreign policy and immigration since 1945'. In Michael Teitelbaum and Myron Weiner (eds), *Threatened Peoples, Threatened Borders: World Migration and US Foreign Policy*. New York: W.W. Norton.

Zolberg, Aristide R., Suhrke, Astri and Aguayo, Sergio (1989) *Escape from Violence: Conflict and the Refugee Crisis in the Developing World*. New York: Oxford University Press.

Zucker, Norman L. and Zucker, N.F. (1987) *The Guarded Gate: the Reality of American Refugee Policy*. San Diego: Harcourt Brace Jovanovich.

Index